THE BOOK OF LISTS FOR KIDS

THE BOOK OF LISTS FOR KIDS

Sandy and Harry Choron

HOUGHTON MIFFLIN COMPANY
BOSTON • NEW YORK

Library of Congress Cataloging-in-Publication Data
Choron, Sandra.
The book of lists for kids / Sandy and Harry Choron.
p. cm.
Includes bibliographical references (p.).
Summary: Presents more than 300 lists about everything from freckles to video games, money to amusement parks, and breakfast cereals to rock music.
ISBN 0-395-70815-X
1. Handbooks, vade-mecums, etc.—Juvenile literature.
[1. Handbooks, manuals, etc.] I. Choron, Harry. II. Title.
AG106.C47 1995
031.02—dc20 95-24385
CIP
AC

For information about this and other Houghton Mifflin trade and reference books and multimedia products, visit The Bookstore at Houghton Mifflin on the World Wide Web at http://www.hmco.com/trade/.

Printed in the United States of America

QUM 10 9 8 7 6 5 4 3 2

For Kristen Ann Carr,
who graduated with high honors

CONTRIBUTORS

Jim Abbate
Barbara Alpert
American Cancer Society
Amnesty International
Ed Asner
Ben and Jerry
Mayim Bialik
Peter Billingsley
Gareth Brainwyn at *Wired*
Bill Bryson
Carol Burnett
Kristen Carr
Sasha Carr
Casey Choron
D.A.R.E.
The Dark Warrior, via CompuServe
The Disney Channel
Mike Donner
Kim Fields
Sandi Gelles-Cole
John Glenn
The Graduate School of Education at Northern Illinois University
Häagen-Dazs
Alexa Hamilton
Hasbro Toy Company
Jim Henson
Ice Skating Institute of America
International Paper Company
Chuck Jones
Jacqueline Kennedy
The Kids on the Block
Carole King
Robin Leach
Lefthander's International
Shari Lewis
John Marr
Dave Marsh
Mattel
Fred Meyer of the International Wizard of Oz Club
National Association of the Deaf
National Association of Fan Clubs
Nickelodeon
North American Association of Ventriloquists
Omni magazine
Bob Oskam
Peace Education Foundation
Pet Haven Cemetery
Public Broadcasting Service
Randi Reisfeld
Ringling Brothers and Barnum & Bailey Circus
Fred Rogers
Roseanne
Ellen Rosenberg
Paul Ruben
Carl Sagan
Ron Schaumburg
William Shatner
The Special Olympics Committee
Peter Stewart
Sally Struthers
Martha Thomases at D.C. Comics
U.S.A. Gymnastics
Chris Warren of the Amusement and Music Operators Association
Ziggy

ACKNOWLEDGMENTS

Special thanks to Marnie Patterson, our editor, for being behind us all the way. Also, a hug to Ellen Rosenberg, a wonderful writer whose book, *Growing Up Feeling Good,* provided a lot of inspiration for our book.

CONTENTS

1. MAKING IT IN A KIDS' WORLD
9

2. GETTING IT TOGETHER WITH OTHER KIDS
83

3. TOYS, GAMES, AND HOBBIES
123

4. FOOD
169

5. BOOKS, MAGAZINES, THE COMICS, AND CYBERFUN
193

6. TV, MOVIES, AND MUSIC
265

7. IT'S A FACT
329

8. JUST FOR FUN
373

INDEX
395

BIBLIOGRAPHY
407

CHAPTER ONE

MAKING IT IN A KIDS' WORLD

CARL SAGAN LISTS 12 THINGS HE WISHES THEY TAUGHT AT SCHOOL

We're flattered that Dr. Sagan has agreed to let us share this important list with our readers. Professor of astronomy and space sciences at Cornell University, Dr. Sagan has played a leading role in the *Mariner, Viking,* and *Voyager* expeditions to the planets. His scientific research has enhanced our understanding of the greenhouse effect on Venus, dust storms on Mars, the origin of life, and the search for life elsewhere. He is president of the Planetary Society, the largest space-interest group in the world. His book *The Dragons of Eden* won the Pulitzer Prize, and his award-winning TV series *Cosmos* was the most widely watched series in the history of American public television. His accompanying book, also called *Cosmos,* is the best-selling science book ever published in the English language.

1. Baloney detection. A baloney detector helps tell us when we're being lied to. If you're after the truth, it's usually a good thing to separate out the baloney first. Fallacies (baloney) are everywhere—in schools, in the mass media, and in government. Sometimes the error is unintentional, sometimes it's not. High school algebra and geometry, by the way, are subjects that teach you how to separate the baloney from everything else.

2. Pick a difficult thing and learn it well. This is one of the greatest of human joys. While you learn a little about many subjects, make sure you learn a great deal about one or two. It hardly matters what the subject is, as long as it deeply interests you, and you place it in its broader human context. After you teach yourself one subject, you become more confident about your ability to teach yourself another. You gradually find you've acquired a key skill. The world is changing so rapidly that you must continue to teach yourself throughout your life. But don't get trapped by the first subject that interests you, or the first thing you find yourself good at. The world is full of wonders, and some of them we don't discover until we're all grown up. Most of them, sadly, we never discover.

3. Don't be afraid to ask "dumb" questions. Many simple questions—such as why grass is green, why the sun is round, or why we need 55,000 nuclear weapons in the world—are, in reality, profound questions. It is important to know the answers, and asking questions is the way. The answers can be a gateway to real insights. To ask "dumb" questions requires courage on the part of the asker and knowledge and patience on the part of the answerer. And don't confine your learning to schoolwork. Discuss ideas in depth with friends.

In 1983 Samantha Smith, who was 10 years old, wrote a letter to the leader of the Soviet Union, Yuri Andropov, expressing her fear that the Soviet Union and the United States might have a war. Mr. Andropov responded to her letter and invited Samantha to visit the Soviet Union and meet with him. She made the trip, met with Mr. Andropov, and learned that the Russian people, like Americans, wanted peace. Upon her return to the United States, she traveled throughout the country informing people of her experience. She became a symbol for peace across the world.

4. Listen carefully. Many conversations are a kind of competition that rarely leads to discovery on either side.

When people are talking, don't spend the time thinking about what you're going to say next. Instead, try to understand what they're saying and what you can learn from or about them. Older people have grown up in a world very different from yours, one you may not know very well. They, and people from other parts of the country and from other nations, have important ideas that can enrich your life.

5. Everybody makes mistakes. Everybody's understanding is incomplete. Be open to correction, and learn to correct your own mistakes. The only embarrassment is in not learning from your mistakes. (Governments almost never admit mistakes. What can we learn from this fact?)

6. Know your planet. It's the only one we have. Learn how it works. We're changing the atmosphere, the surface, the waters of the earth, often for some short-term advantage when the long-term consequences are unknown. Especially in a democracy, the citizens should have at least something to say about the direction in which we're going. If we don't understand the issues, we abandon the future.

7. Science and technology. You can't know your planet unless you know something about science and technology. School science courses, I remember, concentrated on the trivia of science but left out many important ideas. The great discoveries in modern science are also great discoveries of the human spirit. For example, Copernicus showed that—far from the earth being the center of the universe—the earth is just one of many small worlds. This may make us "earthlings" feel less important, but it opens us up to our view of how vast and awesome our universe really is.

8. Nuclear war. This is the most immediate and most dangerous threat to our species and our world. Learn enough about nuclear weapons to be able to understand the threat they pose and how to help resolve the growing crisis. If you can make a contribution to this subject, you will have done something for all generations that are and ever will be.

9. Don't spend your life watching TV. You know what I'm talking about.

10. Culture. Gain some exposure to the great works of literature, art, and music. If such a work is hundreds or thousands of years old and is still admired, there is probably something to it. Like all deep experiences, it may take a little work on your part to discover what all the fuss is about. But once you make the effort, your life has changed; you've acquired a source of enjoyment and excitement for the rest of your days. In a world as tightly connected as ours is, don't limit your attention to American or Western culture. Learn how and what people elsewhere think. Learn something of their history, their religions, their viewpoints.

11. Politics. A basic part of American democracy, and one of the principles on which the nation was founded, is the protection and encouragement of unpopular beliefs. (Think again about Copernicus.) No nation, sect, or political party speaks the *whole* truth. So consider unpopular ideas and see if any of them make sense to you. Why, exactly, are they unpopular? Learn something about practical politics. Involve yourself in a local political campaign. Understand how political power is used. There are many evils—slavery, say, or smallpox—that were overcome worldwide, through the combination of new insights and political power. Understanding these advances can help us to deal with other evils in our time.

12. Compassion. Many people believe that we live in a very selfish time. But there is a loneliness that comes from living only for yourself. Humans are capable of great compassion, love, and tenderness. These feelings, however, need encouragement to grow.

Look at the delight a 1- or 2-year-old takes in learning, and you see how powerful is the human will to learn. Our passion to understand the universe and our compassion for others jointly provide the chief hope of the human species.

MAYIM BIALIK'S LIST OF MISCONCEPTIONS KIDS HAVE

You know her best as TV's "Blossom," but we liked her best as the young Bette Midler in the movie *Beaches*.

1. Our parents "don't understand"; they never will.
2. Old people tell boring stories.
3. If everyone else is doing it, why shouldn't I?
4. Reading is for nerds.
5. Vegetables are yucky.
6. TV is better than real life.
7. All celebrities are completely happy and have no problems.
8. The faster I grow up, the happier I'll be.

15 EARLY WARNING SIGNS OF MATURITY

You are on a sinking ship. The captain calls out to the crew, "Save the women and children first!" and no one comes to your rescue. Here are some other signs that you are reaching maturity.

1. Your parents stop sounding stupid.

2. You start remembering to do your chores without being reminded.

3. You've stopped bullying your little brother or sister.

4. All your homework gets done, all the time.

5. You read a book and it made you think.

6. You've made friends with a geek.

7. You can sit through one hour of educational television without falling asleep or wanting to.

8. You've asked for a raise in your allowance, explained why, and your parents agreed.

9. Your body starts changing so fast that your best friend doesn't recognize you. In fact, *you* don't recognize you!

10. You realize that your dad's 1989 Ford station wagon can take you anywhere your neighbor's new Corvette can.

11. Someone calls you "mister" or "miss," "sir" or "ms."

12. You'd rather read *Jurassic Park* than watch the movie.

13. You can sip through a straw without being tempted to blow bubbles out the other end.

14. You discover that when you eat candy before dinner, it really does spoil your appetite.

15. You've walked away from a fight because the argument was stupid.

HOW TO PROTECT YOURSELF WHEN YOU'RE OUT IN PUBLIC

1. Stay alert! Always be aware of where you are and the people around you.

2. Watch where you're going and appear confident.

3. Stay on busy streets where there are people. Stay out of dark alleys, woods, and other shortcuts. Avoid being alone.

4. Keep your valuables in pockets or in fanny packs.

5. If you have something valuable, keep it out of sight and don't talk about it. Resist the temptation to show off.

6. Don't play in deserted areas where you wouldn't be able to get help if you needed it.

7. Don't hang around public bathrooms.

8. If you have a locker at school, don't tell anyone the combination to the lock.

9. If you must stay in the school building after classes have let out, stay only in the area that is under supervision. If you need to go to another part of the building for any reason, get someone else, preferably an adult, to go with you.

10. If other kids tell you that you must give them money or they will beat you up, tell your parents and make sure they call the police and the school. *Your parents can do this without giving your name.* Gangs of kids who demand "protection money" exist in all parts of the country. You can't stop them, but the police and the school system can.

11. Don't talk to strangers. That may sound like something you've been hearing since you were a baby, but it's good advice. Don't give any information about yourself to people you don't know. Even telling something simple like where your mother works can lead to trouble.

12. Don't get on or off an elevator with a stranger if you are alone.

13. If someone or something scares you, look for bright lights and people and run for help, screaming along the way.

14. Say no—loudly—to anyone who bothers you.

15. Do not agree to keep a secret from your parents.

16. If someone threatens to attack you unless you give them your money, give them the money. In most cases, muggers are after money, not you. Since you probably won't be able to overpower these people, and since your life is more important than your money, give them what they want and then get away as soon as possible. Immediately report what happened to the police.

17. Never hitchhike! Getting into a car with a stranger is asking for trouble. If you must do this because you are stranded somewhere or need help, don't accept a ride from a car that has been circling the area, and try to remember as many details about the car and the person who gives you the ride as you can: the model, color, and license plate of the car; the color of the person's hair and eyes; what they were wearing; and any other distinct characteristics.

18. If a stranger asks you for help with a problem, such as finding a lost dog or assisting them with packages, suggest that they find another adult to help them. If these people have good intentions, they will understand your refusal to help.

19. If someone approaches you wearing a uniform and tells you to cooperate with them, ask to see some identification. Make sure they're really who they say they are!

20. When you take jobs at other people's homes or go out on job interviews, even if you're just over at a friend's house, be sure to let your parents know exactly where you are and when you plan to come home.

21. If you witness a crime, call 911 and calmly, clearly tell what you saw. You do not have to give your name.

HOME ALONE!

How to Stay Safe

1. Always make sure that the doors and windows are locked.

2. Don't open the door for anyone you don't know well. If the person who knocks on the door has real business in the house—for example, if they've come to repair something—they can come back another time. If they claim they need help, tell them you won't open the door but that you will call the police for them.

3. Make up a password that only you and your parents know. That way, if someone really has to get into your house when you are alone and claims to have been sent by your parents, you can ask them for the password.

4. If someone bothers you at the door and won't go away, make them think that you are not really alone. Tell them your father is sleeping but that you're going to wake him up. In the meantime, call the police.

5. If you get an annoying phone call from a stranger who asks you personal questions or says weird things to you, hang up the phone immediately, no matter how tempted you are to tell that person off. If you get a few of these calls, see that your parents report them to the police and to the telephone company.

6. Be careful what you say to other people about your plans. Your friends obviously are not interested in harming you, but they could repeat things in the presence of strangers. Avoid discussing things like your family's plans to go on a vacation, the times at which you are home alone, where you're planning to babysit, where your family hides valuables, where your family hides an extra house key.

14 THINGS EVERY BABYSITTER SHOULD KNOW

The list of things you should know if you're going to be responsible for the care of a child may seem like a long one, but babysitting is serious business, and you really do need to know a lot more than just what you'll be doing with the child while you're together. You also need to know what to do in case of an emergency, what to do if someone calls, and how to handle any unexpected circumstance. It might be a good idea for you to make copies of this list and to keep the information in a notebook so that if you babysit for the same people more than once, you won't have to ask them about all the details each time.

When babysitting, always remember to keep the doors locked at all times, to check on the children every half-hour or so once they're in bed, and to stay awake until the parents return.

1. The name of the family and the child's name

2. The address and phone number (which you should leave at your own home)

3. Whom to call in case of emergency

4. Where the parents can be reached

5. The family doctor's name and phone number

6. When the parents will return

7. Instructions for handling phone calls and visitors

8. The location of

clothing, bed linens, food, and first-aid supplies

9. Where you can find a house key in case you have to leave with the child in an emergency

10. What games the child may play and TV programs he or she may watch

11. The child's bedtime and eating habits (and if there are any allergies or illnesses you should be aware of)

12. Everything the child must do at bedtime, such as brushing teeth, taking medicines, and cleaning up

13. How to handle any pets that may be present

14. Instructions for operating the burglar alarm if they have one

6 WAYS TO TELL IF YOU SHOULD REPORT A STRANGER TO THE POLICE

The police department recommends that you call them if you come in contact with anyone who seems suspicious to you. Here are some things to watch out for.

1. Any stranger who asks you weird questions, like where you live, who your parents are, or anything about your friends

2. Any adult who tries to join you while you are playing

3. Any stranger who asks you to go with him or her

4. Anyone who tries to have a conversation with you in the movies

5. Anyone who tries to touch you

6. Anyone who tries to get you to disobey the rules of safety that you have learned

10 DOOR-TO-DOOR SAFETY TIPS

Whether you are raising money for charity, getting a petition signed, trick-or-treating, or selling candy, always be extra careful when you approach the homes of strangers. And be sure you understand these rules before you start out.

1. Never go alone. Always bring a friend.

2. Always let your parents or another adult know the area you will be in and what time they should expect you home.

3. Don't leave this area without letting someone know your plans have changed.

4. If you feel uncomfortable going to an unfamiliar area, don't go there.

5. Never enter anyone's home under any circumstances. Don't accept their food or beverages.

6. If you need to use a bathroom or make a telephone call, go to a well-lighted public area or a local store.

7. Always carry some change for an emergency phone call.

8. Be aware of what is going on around you.

9. If you are collecting money and expect to handle cash try to have someone with you.

10. Trick-or-treaters: Don't sample any of your goodies until you've gotten home and let an adult examine what you have collected.

7 THINGS TO DO IF YOU OR A FRIEND IS BEING ABUSED

More than 1.5 million children are abused by an adult each year. Kids who are abused are either physically or emotionally hurt by an adult. This adult can be a parent, stepparent, aunt or uncle, grandparent, teacher, or neighbor, or even another kid. Many kids who are abused feel that they somehow deserve the punishment they receive and that the abuser has a right to treat them any way they want.If you are being abused, you don't deserve it! If you or a friend are being abused you must seek help. The only person responsible for child abuse is the person committing the abuse, not you and not your friend. Try your best to get help from someone who can really help you. Your friends may be sympathetic, but they may not know all the options available to you. There is help out there. Here are some ways of getting help.

1. Talk to an adult member of your family that you love and trust.

2. Talk to a teacher or your guidance counselor even if you don't have a close relationship with him or her.

3. Talk to a religious leader.

4. Call the police.

5. Talk to your family doctor or go to any hospital emergency room.

6. Get the phone number of a child abuse, family services, or mental health agency from your telephone book and call them.

7. Get in touch with the National Council on Child Abuse and Family Violence: 1-800-222-2000. This call won't cost you any money.

5 PUNISHMENTS THAT ARE NOT CONSIDERED ABUSE

You may not want to be punished or disciplined by your parents, but it is their responsibility to do so when they feel it is necessary or appropriate. The following are examples of nonabusive punishments.

1. Being grounded for being irresponsible, for example, for not doing your homework

2. Being sent to your room without dinner

3. Having a privilege like watching television taken away

4. Having your allowance taken away

5. Being scolded in a nonviolent manner

11 REASONS KIDS TAKE DRUGS

We all know that drug abuse and addiction are very serious problems. Even as a kid you may be exposed to drugs, and as you get older the pressure to take drugs will increase. Drugs such as tobacco, alcohol, and marijuana are the most commonly used. Although not everyone who tries one of these drugs becomes addicted to them, most drug addicts started off their drug usage with one of them. D.A.R.E. (Drug Abuse Resistance Education) is a program, run primarily through schools, that educates kids about the dangers that are out there. Here are the reasons they give for why kids take drugs in the first place.

1. Curiosity. The desire to try a new experience.

2. Peer group pressure. Wanting to do what your friends are doing and being accepted because of it.

3. Insecurity. The desire for respect, a sense of identity with your friends, and even the desire for affection.

4. Boredom. Kids who lack excitement or challenges in their lives may see drugs as their answer.

5. Escape. If you are lonely, have problems, or feel like a loser, drugs can seem like a solution.

6. Defiance of authority. This can be directed against your parents, school, friends, or society in general.

7. Values. Not understanding the importance of staying healthy and being safe.

8. Ignorance. Not understanding the dangers of drug and alcohol abuse.

9. Physical and emotional problems. Sometimes people take drugs to overcome some sort of pain or stress.

10. Stimulation. To get instant physical or mental energy.

11. Modeling. This means imitating what your parents do. If your parents take drugs, they are setting an example for you.

8 WAYS TO BE *REALLY* DARING

The Drug Abuse Resistance Education program, better known as D.A.R.E., unites kids with local police departments in an effort to prevent drug abuse. Here are D.A.R.E.'s recommendations for dealing with someone offering you drugs:

1. Say "No thanks."

2. Give an excuse or a reason.

3. Be a broken record. Repeat your reason as many times as necessary.

4. Walk away.

5. Change the subject.

6. Avoid the situation. The best way to avoid drugs is to not be around people who are taking drugs.

7. Give them the cold shoulder. Let the person who is offering you drugs know that you are offended by just ignoring him.

8. There's strength in numbers. If you are with other kids who are also not interested in drugs, refusing an offer will be much easier.

6 HOTLINES FOR KIDS WHO HAVE RUN AWAY FROM HOME

These people help kids find shelter in a place where they can work out their problems *safely* and *sanely.* They also provide a service that lets runaways get messages to their families back home without revealing the whereabouts of the child or teen. These services are *confidential* and *free.* The call is free, too.

1. 1-800-231-6946
2. 1-800-392-3352
3. 1-800-621-4000
4. 1-800-THE-LOST
5. 1-800-448-3000
6. 1-800-551-1300

6 THINGS BRUCE SPRINGSTEEN REMEMBERS ABOUT GROWING UP

1. When I was growing up, there were two things that were unpopular in my house. One was me, and the other was my guitar.

2. In the third grade a nun stuffed me in a garbage can under her desk because she said that's where I belonged. I also had the distinction of being the only altar boy knocked down by a priest during Mass.

3. The student body at college tried to get me expelled because I was just too weird for them, I guess.

4. I didn't even make it to class clown. I had nowhere near that amount of notoriety. I didn't have the flair to be a complete jerk. It was like I didn't exist.

5. I never got into being discouraged because I never got to hoping. . . . I got used to failing.

6. My first guitar was one of the most beautiful sights I'd ever seen in my life. It was a magic scene. There it is. The Guitar. It was real and it stood for something. "Now you're real." I had found a way to do everything I wanted to do.

MICHAEL JORDAN'S WORST CHILDHOOD MEMORIES

One of the all-time stars of basketball had problems when he was a kid, too.

1. Michael was not popular in grade school.

2. He usually felt awkward.

3. He thought he was so ugly that he would never be able to get married. In fact, he was so convinced of this that he had his mother teach him how to cook, do laundry, and clean house so he would always be able to take care of himself living alone.

4. Kids in school made fun of him.

5. In high school he rarely dated.

8 THINGS YOU CAN DO IF YOU'RE AFRAID OF THE DARK

First of all, don't let anyone fool you into thinking that only babies are afraid of the dark; lots of adults are, too. But here are some ways for you to deal with the fear.

1. Use your imagination to create nice, pleasant things from the shapes you see in the shadows. It's just like pretending that clouds are real objects. For instance, if that huge ball of darkness on your ceiling looks like a monster at first, turn it into a big fluffy kitten or a circus balloon.

2. Sing. Noise helps to scare away fear. Sing out loud. Practice your very favorite songs.

3. Keep a flashlight by the bed. If something scares you, shine the light directly on it. You'll see there's nothing there.

4. Keep a notepad next to your bed. If something scares you, write it down on the paper and then rip the paper—and the fear—into shreds.

5. Try to put yourself into a trance that will help you fall asleep. Here's a technique you can use: First think about the scary shapes in the room that are bothering you. Introduce yourself to these "monsters" out loud. Once you've made friends with them, ask them to leave. As they start to go out the door, concentrate on your own breathing. Count slowly. Before you reach 100, chances are you'll be asleep.

6. If you see shadows that scare you, try to find out what's *really* creating them. Maybe the "monster" you're imagining is really the shadow of your favorite tree.

7. Read a book, listen to music, or write a letter to a friend to take your mind off your fears.

8. Ask someone to check your room for you to make sure nothing is there. Say, "This might seem silly, but I'll get to sleep a lot faster if you do this for me."

WHEN A PET DIES

1. Take the time to think about your emotions. You may find yourself feeling angry (at whatever caused your pet to die), sad (because you have lost a friend), guilty (if the pet died because of something you did), or even jealous of other kids who still have their pets. Or you may be feeling a combination of all of these. All of these feelings are normal.

2. Share your feelings with others. If you have a brother or sister you don't get along with, this is a time when you may get closer. Even if you think you have nothing in common with your sibling, the fact is that you both knew the pet, and you both miss him. So you *do* have something to talk about! Remember that people who have never had pets might not understand what you're going through. Don't get mad at them.

3. Have a ceremony to say goodbye to your pet, whether it's a burial or just a time that you take to think about your pet. Invite others who loved your pet to be part of this. This is a good time to decide what you want to do with your pet's belongings.

4. Keep a remembrance of your pet. Even though you are sad now, the pet was your friend. Maybe you can hang up a picture of the pet in your room. You can write a poem that others might enjoy reading, or you can plant something—like a tree—as a memorial.

5. Continue your normal activities. Some things may have changed but not all of them.

6. Be extra nice to your other pets—they may be sad, too.

7. Think about other pets that might need your care. You may not want to adopt another one right away, but keep in mind that you can sometimes make yourself feel better by being nice to others. There are plenty of people and pets out there who need your love.

8. Say thank you to people who were nice to your pet. Let them know that their caring made a difference in the life of your pet.

9. Say a prayer. Albert Schweitzer, the great philosopher, wrote this, probably at some point in his life when his own pet died:

Hear our humble prayer,
O God,
For our friends the animals,
Especially for animals who are suffering;
For any that are hunted or lost
Or deserted or frightened or hungry;
For all that must be put to sleep.
We entreat for them all
Thy mercy and pity,
And for those who deal with them
We ask a heart of compassion
And gentle hands and kindly words.
Make us be true friends to animals
And so to share
The blessings of the merciful.

12 RUDE THINGS THAT PARENTS DO

Parents can be so rude! Parents who are otherwise polite and conscious of the rules of etiquette sometimes violate these rules when it comes to their own kids. If your parents do one of the following things, talk to them and tell them how their actions make you feel.

1. They criticize you in front of your friends.

2. They tell your private secrets to other members of the family.

3. They open your mail.

4. They ask you to "perform" for company.

5. They invite your friends over to dinner without checking with you first.

6. They ask you to be friends with certain kids just because they're friends with the kid's parents.

7. They invite their friends to your birthday party.

8. They hang around when your friends come over.

9. They ignore you when their friends come over.

10. They forget your friends' names and call them by the wrong names.

11. They invade your privacy by entering your room without knocking.

12. They ask your friends rude questions, like what their parents do for a living.

PEOPLE YOU CAN TALK WITH IF YOU CAN'T TALK TO YOUR PARENTS

1. An older brother, sister, or friend

2. An aunt, uncle, grandparent, or other relative

3. A teacher whom you trust

4. The school guidance counselor

5. A friend's parent

6. The family doctor

7. A religious leader

8. A school social worker

9. The school nurse

10. The school principal or assistant principal

11. Your godparent

12. A public health or social worker. You can locate such a person by checking the yellow pages under any of these listings: Social Service Organizations; Social Workers; Mental Health Services; Clinics; or Human Service Organizations.

13. A social leader, such as the leader of your Boy Scout or Girl Scout troop.

14. A member of the Alanon/Alateen organization, which helps families whose members have alcohol problems. Look in the yellow pages under Alcoholism Information and Treatment Centers to locate one of these. (See also "43 Organizations That Work with and for Kids," page 87.)

15. A youth service organization, which helps families whose members have alcohol problems. Look in the yellow pages under Alcoholism Information and Treatment Centers.

16. Any of the volunteers listed in "6 Hotlines for Kids," page 25.

11 LIES PARENTS TELL

There's no doubt about it—parents do tell lies every now and then. And although we're not saying that it's ever okay to tell lies, parents sometimes have an understandable reason for the ones they come up with. For instance, if they tell you that your aunt is going to be alright when it's plain that she's probably going to die, chances are they're doing that to protect you from a lot of worry. And when your mom tells you that you're the most gorgeous kid in the world even though you know you wouldn't stand a chance in a beauty contest, that's usually because to her you really are the most beautiful kid. The point here is that parents sometimes don't think they're lying when they are. If you think you're old enough to be told the real truth about something before they realize you are, sit down and talk about your feelings with your parents. Sometimes it's just hard for them to understand how fast you're growing up.

ROSEANNE'S LIST OF "THINGS I DON'T DO ANYMORE"

Would TV's funniest mom lie to you?

1. Lie
2. Steal
3. Brag
4. Yell
5. Be rude
6. Swear
7. Smoke
8. Eat too much
9. Spend too much
10. Go to the bathroom

1. Money—how much they have or if they're having financial problems

2. If someone close to you is ill

3. When they're not getting along
4. If you are adopted
5. Death
6. Sex
7. That you're good-looking
8. That they're worried about something
9. Their age
10. What they do with their friends
11. What they were really like when they were your age

7 STATISTICS ABOUT STUTTERING

You can get help with a stuttering problem by contacting the National Center for Stuttering, 200 East 33 Street, New York, N.Y. 10016.

1. Two and a half million Americans stutter.

2. Five times as many men stutter as women.

3. The I.Q. of the average stutterer is 14 points higher than that of the general population.

4. While stuttering begins in childhood, 75 percent can expect to shed the problem by adolescence.

5. Stuttering usually begins between the ages of 2 and 7 years.

6. Stuttering has physical causes (a spasm of the vocal cords).

7. New techniques for the treatment of stuttering have yielded extremely high success rates.

4 THINGS YOU CAN DO ABOUT A NOSEBLEED

Use the following suggestions for a simple nosebleed only. If your nose is bleeding and the blood is going down the back of your throat, you should see a doctor as soon as you can.

1. Stuff a piece of wet cotton or gauze into the side of the nose that is bleeding. Wetting the cotton with white vinegar is a good idea.

2. Pinch the side of your nose that is bleeding for about 6 minutes. If this doesn't stop the bleeding right away, place fresh cotton or gauze back in and apply pressure for another 6 minutes. Sit up while you are doing this. Never tilt your head backwards, and don't lie down.

3. Place an ice pack on your nose.

4. Never pick at your nose after the bleeding has stopped. This can start the bleeding all over again.

HOW TO AVOID MOTION SICKNESS

On a boat it's called seasickness, on land it's car sickness, and on a plane it's airsickness. Whatever it's called, motion sickness is no fun. Here are a few tips to get you through:

1. If you think you are going to throw up, you probably will. Try to think about feeling well instead.

2. If you are with other people who are feeling sick, try to avoid them. We know this doesn't sound considerate, but if you try to help them you may only wind up feeling sick yourself.

3. Avoid unpleasant odors and get some fresh air as soon as possible.

4. If you travel at night you are less likely to get sick because you can't see motion as well.

When Richard Byrd was only 13 years old, his parents, understanding his adventurous spirit, gave him permission to travel around the world by himself. As an adult, Byrd became the first man to fly over both the North and South Poles.

5. Being well rested before a trip can help prevent motion sickness. You will be stronger and more resistant to motion sickness.

6. In a car, sit in the front seat and face front.

7. On a boat, keep your eyes fixed on an object that is not moving. Keeping your eyes on the horizon is a good idea.

8. Do not read on a plane if it is a bumpy flight. Reading during a car or boat ride can also make you sick.

9. Drinking a carbonated cola drink can help settle your stomach if you feel nauseous.

10. Eating soda crackers can help your stomach to feel better.

10 WAYS TO STOP THE HICCUPS

Charles Osborne of Anthon, Iowa, got the hiccups in 1922 and didn't stop hiccupping for the next 22 years, hiccuping just over 400 million times. That's the worst case of the hiccups ever. Most doctors will tell you that hiccups will usually go away by themselves after a few minutes even if you don't do anything. But if you want faster results:

1. Swallow a teaspoon of dry sugar.

2. Chew and swallow a piece of dried bread.

3. Pull your knees up to your chest.

4. Rinse your mouth with salt water.

5. Suck on crushed ice.

6. Suck on a lemon.

7. Hold your breath, then swallow when you feel a hiccup coming on.

8. Ask someone to tickle you or surprise you.

9. Breath rapidly into a brown paper bag about ten times.

10. Drink a glass of water while you are upside down. Be careful: this one is tricky. Save it as a last resort.

7 THINGS YOU CAN DO ABOUT FRECKLES

If you have freckles and don't like them, remember that people who don't have them often wish they did. Some people even consider freckles a sign of good luck. If you're determined to do something about them, you should know that you won't be able to rid yourself of freckles entirely. Whatever you do, check with your doctor before you try anything, since skin can be very sensitive to anything you put on it, and blotches caused by an irritation will certainly look a lot worse than freckles ever could! Here are some things you can do to reduce your freckles:

1. Once a day, apply plain yogurt to your freckles. Leave it on for one minute, then rinse your face with cold water.

2. Apply fresh lemon juice to your freckles. Rinse with cool water, then apply a light coat of vegetable oil. If your skin becomes irritated, stop the treatment immediately.

We heard this freckle reduction recipe recently and just had to include it, but don't even think about trying it: Mix buttermilk with some lemon juice, and then apply this to your freckles *using a live frog!* Then set the frog free.

3. Rub the juice of fresh cranberries on your freckles. Rinse with cool water and apply a light coat of vegetable oil, just as in the instructions above. Again, if your skin becomes irritated, discontinue the treatment.

4. An old folk remedy suggests rubbing your freckles with a penny and then throwing the penny away. Whoever finds the penny gets your freckles!

5. This one is based entirely on superstition: Squeeze some lemon juice into a cup of rainwater and add ten raisins. Stir the mixture every day for nine days and then wash your freckles with it on the tenth day.

6. In the nineteenth century, it was believed that you could get rid of freckles by applying a mixture of dried wild cucumber roots, dried narcissus roots, and brandy.

7. Learn to love them.

HOW TO WIN THE BATTLE WITH ZITS

Acne is not caused by eating too much chocolate or having dirty hair or skin. Acne is genetic—it's a condition you inherit from your parents. Here are some facts and hints about acne and pimples (zits) that can help you.

1. Never squeeze a pimple. This can lead to an infection and will make things worse.

2. Never squeeze a whitehead. This can cause the fluid inside to spread, and this can cause pimples.

3. Blackheads can be squeezed. This will not cause a pimple.

4. Medications and creams can be helpful. It is important to ask for a doctor's advice.

5. When you use any type of acne medicine, stay out of the sun. Remember to always clean your skin extremely well.

6. Never use more than one kind of medicine at a time, especially if one of them is a drug prescribed by your doctor.

7. Acne can be a serious condition; sometimes a doctor's care is required. If you feel you have a serious problem, ask your parents for their help.

10 TIPS FOR LOOKING GOOD IN YOUR SCHOOL PICTURE

1. Wear clothing that you are comfortable in. (A battle with one of your parents might be necessary here. Explain that you'll look better if you're relaxed. Promise to smile; that usually works.)

2. Wear a solid color.

3. Don't wear white.

4. Don't wear jewelry or things in your hair unless you do normally.

5. Stand (or sit up) straight.

6. Don't fidget.

7. If you wear braces, practice your smile.

8. Be yourself.

9. Avoid blinking during the flash by relaxing and not looking directly at the camera.

10. If you get a zit, don't panic and don't try to cover it up—it just winds up looking like you have a zit you're trying to cover up. A big smile will overpower any zit. If you're determined to cover up one, get someone who's experienced with makeup to help you. (And don't use anyone's makeup without their permission.)

FRED ROGERS LISTS 8 THINGS THAT WILL MAKE STARTING A NEW SCHOOL EASIER

Can you say "ter-ri-fy-ing"? That's how the first day at a new school may seem. Here are some things that might help.

1. Try to get together with kids in the neighborhood who will be going to your school.

2. Visit the building before the first day of school to get an idea of what it's like.

3. Try to find someone to walk with to and from school (or the bus, if you take one).

4. Try to have a calm morning routine before you leave for school.

5. Take a small object from home to school with you so it won't seem like home is so far away.

6. Keep a photograph of your old school friends in your notebook to look at when you feel lonely.

7. Remember that the other kids are not all staring at you. Even if they are curious about you, you can take that as a compliment.

8. Think of this as a new beginning.

Eight-year-old Linda Carol Brown, of Topeka, Kansas, was the first African-American child to be enrolled in a white school. This took place in 1954, when the U.S. Supreme Court ruled that segregation in schools was illegal.

9 WAYS TO IMPROVE YOUR MEMORY

These suggestions will help you to remember names, important dates, chores you're supposed to do, find that missing toy you've been looking for, and may even help you on test scores.

1. When you meet someone and have to remember their name, find one feature about that person and connect it to their name. For example, if the person's name is Armstrong, you may want to visualize that person with big muscles.

2. If you have an important errand to do and you don't want to forget to do it, put a rubber band around your wrist as a reminder.

3. If you have a list of things to remember, make up a story about them. For instance, if you are going to the store for your mom and she wants you to pick up some milk, eggs, bread, and a newspaper, your story can be about a *cow* that is eating an *egg* sandwich on white *bread* while reading a *newspaper.*

4. If you are trying to remember the name of an explorer during a history exam and can't think of it, try to remember the name of the country he came from, which may help you to remember the language spoken, which may help you to remember his name.

5. If you have difficulty remembering words, it's because you are not using the words often enough. Whenever you learn a new word, you should try to you use that word in a sentence during normal conversation. Reading frequently is also a good way to learn and remember words.

6. If you have lost something, a good way to find it is to close your eyes and mentally retrace the steps you took before you used that item last. So that you don't lose something in the first place, make a mental photograph of that object exactly as you place it, just like you are taking a picture.

7. Sometimes making a mental picture is not enough. If you talk to yourself and say, "I'm leaving this toy under my bed," this will help you later. Don't be embarrassed about talking to yourself. This method will really help you.

8. Relax. It is much easier to remember something when you are relaxed. If you panic it will be much harder, if not impossible, to remember what you want.

9. The only way to really learn how to spell properly is to use the words in your everyday vocabulary, unless the word is something like antidisestablishmentarianism.

7 THINGS YOU CAN DO IF YOU THINK YOUR TEACHER DOESN'T LIKE YOU

1. Stop talking, fidgeting, throwing spitballs, or passing notes in class. (Behave!)

2. Ask to speak with your teacher privately and tell them you get the feeling they don't like you that much. Let them know how badly you feel and ask if you did something to make them mad. If you did, apologize and ask for another chance.

3. Write a note and tell your teacher how you feel.

4. Talk to your parents and let them know how frustrated you are. Perhaps you and your parents can speak with the teacher about these feelings.

5. Say hello to your teacher if you see him or her in the halls. Try to start a conversation. See what kind of response you get.

6. Remember that teachers are there to teach, not to be your friends or pay extra attention to you. Some teachers just aren't that friendly. If they are really being fair and teaching you what you need to know, that's all you can expect.

7. If you tried talking with the teacher and it didn't help, you can talk to the guidance counselor, school principal, or assistant principal and ask them what they think you should do.

JOHN GLENN LISTS 3 THINGS HE WISHES KIDS WOULD THINK ABOUT

On February 20, 1962, John Glenn became the first American and the third man in history to be put into orbital space flight. But Glenn is notable for being more than an astronaut. Back on earth, he became involved in politics and was elected United States senator from Ohio in 1974.

When we asked Mr. Glenn to share some of his thoughts about growing up, he supplied us with many useful and thoughtful comments, including some excellent advice for kids about school: "While you have the chance, go to school, study and learn as much as you can, use that knowledge to help yourself today and tomorrow," he wrote. "While I can't promise you that this task will be an easy one, I can guarantee you that it will be challenging, rewarding, and well worth it."

1. Realize that school isn't just a chore. It's also the key that will open the door to your future. I know it often means spending time doing tough homework problems and not watching part of that favorite TV show. It means studying history and geography and practicing your multiplication, when playing outside on your bike or rollerblades would be more fun. It means giving just a little bit more time to solving that word problem or writing that report before going over to a friend's house. But it's worth it. Keep your mind open to learning.

2. Remember that through school you have the chance to shine. Here's your chance to use your talents and gifts, to be somebody. Always try—try to work just a little harder and study a little more to understand, not just because you have to or because somebody said to, but because you want to.

When Harvey Friedman of Highland Park, Illinois, was 7, he started studying mathematics. By the age of 16 he entered the Massachusetts Institute of Technology without a high school diploma. One year later he earned a doctoral degree that would normally take at least eight years to achieve.

3. Realize that education goes on forever. This may be the hardest thing of all. You will always be learning new skills and developing new ideas. We are always "in school." Throughout your life you must never close the door—for it is only through learning that you will continue to grow.

THE 10 WORST THINGS ABOUT SKIPPING A GRADE

Thanks for this one to Alexa Hamilton, who's been there!

1. The older kids in the new grade think you are "cute" because you're smaller than they are. So they pinch your cheeks and treat you like a baby.

2. You don't get to see your friends in the grade below.

3. Your old friends all still have the same experiences together, so when you see them, you don't have as much in common with them anymore.

4. You don't get invited to all the parties that your old friends go to.

5. Teachers forget that even though you're smart enough to be in an advanced grade, you're still not as mature as everyone else, and they expect too much of you.

6. You leave the school a whole year before your friends, and then you never get to see them.

At the age of 11, William James Sidis became the youngest person accepted to Harvard University.

7. Some people treat you like you're stuck up, even though skipping wasn't even your idea.

8. You get scared that maybe you won't be able to do the work and then they'll put you back in the old grade and you'll be embarrassed.

9. Since everyone in your class is older than you, they get privileges—like going out at night and dating—before you do, so you feel left out.

10. You get more homework!

TONY RANDALL LISTS 4 WAYS TO IMPROVE YOUR VOCABULARY

Tony Randall loves words almost as much as he loves acting, so when the International Paper Company asked him to tell how he acquired his enormous vocabulary, they got some great tips as a reply. "The better command you have of words," says Mr. Randall, "the better chance you have of saying exactly what you mean, of understanding what others mean—and of getting what you want in the world." Here are some ways in which to achieve all that.

The International Paper Company believes that today the printed word is more important than ever and that there is a need for all of us to learn to read better, write better, communicate better. For this reason they asked a number of famous people to talk about how people can improve their word skills, and they used the replies in a series of advertisements called "Power of the Printed Word." If you would like copies of any of the ads or the entire series, send your request to: Power of the Printed Word, International Paper Company, Dept. KL, P. O. Box 954, Madison Square Station, New York, N.Y. 10010.

1. Try to guess the meaning of a word from the way it's used. You can often get at least part of a word's meaning just from how it's used in a sentence. And a good way to get better at this guessing game is to read different kinds of things—magazines, books, and newspapers. Of course, to find out exactly what a word means, you need to consult a dictionary.

2. Learn about root words and their meanings. The root is the basic part of a word—its heritage, its origin. Most roots come from Latin or Greek words. For instance, the root word of *manacle* is *manus,* which is Latin for *hand.* Other words using the same root word are *manual,* which means to do something by hand; *manage,* which means to handle something; and *manufacture,* which means to make something. (Originally all things were made by hand!) Learning these roots will help you to remember words better, to understand the meanings of more words, and to learn the meanings of groups of words all at once. Think of the root as a clue to what the word means.

3. Learn prefixes and their meanings—these give you further clues to the meanings of words. A prefix is a word part that attaches at the front of a word and affects its meaning. Prefixes are usually Greek and have meanings all their own. For instance, the prefix *con,* which means with, is found in the word *conform,* meaning to form with. And the prefix *contra,* meaning against, is used in the word *contradict,* which means to say something against. Since there are about one hundred important prefixes in the English language, it shouldn't take all that long to familiarize yourself with them and thereby learn the meanings of many more words than you already know.

4. Use the new words you learn right away. This is really the best way to remember them. Say them out loud; write them in sentences—you'll impress your friends and expand your vocabulary at the same time!

JAMES MICHENER EXPLAINS HOW TO USE A LIBRARY

The International Paper Company asked Pulitzer Prize-winning novelist James A. Michener, author of *Hawaii*, *Chesapeake*, and many other books, to tell how you can benefit from one of the most helpful services in your community, the library, and Michener responded with these tips. It's no wonder that Michener is such a great fan of libraries. His books, which are counted among the great fiction of our time, required lots of research, in addition to his writing talents. (He's also married to a librarian!)

"It's hard for me to imagine what I would be doing today if I had not fallen in love, at the ripe old age of seven, with the Melinda Cox Library in my hometown of Doylestown, Pennsylvania," says Mr. Michener. "At our house, we just could not afford books. The books in that free library would change my life dramatically. Who knows what your library can open up for you?

"My first suggestion for making the most of your library is to do what I did: read and read and read. For pleasure—and for understanding." Here are the other tips Mr. Michener offers.

1. First, kick the TV habit. Here's how: "Take home from the library a stack of books that might look interesting. Pile them on the TV set. Next time you are tempted to turn on a program you really don't want to see, reach for a book instead."

2. Learn to use the card catalog in the library. The card catalog lists every book in the library by author, title, and subject. If you're unfamiliar with the setup, get the librarian to explain it to you. Always have a pencil and paper when you use the card catalog. That way, you can jot down the numbers of the books you want to find and you can have them ready when you search through the shelves.

3. Learn to use the "stacks"—or shelves. Browse through and find out which books are located in certain areas. Feel free to explore and to pick up books on subjects you're unfamiliar with. You never know what's going to grab your attention. "A learned mind is the end product of browsing," says Mr. Michener, and he offers this note as well: "If you take a book from the stacks, do not try to return it to its proper place. That's work for the experts. If you replace it incorrectly, the next seeker won't be able to find it."

4. Get to know the reference librarian. "Introduce yourself. State your problem. You'll be amazed at how much help you will receive." But Mr. Michener cautions: "Don't waste the librarian's time by asking silly questions you ought to solve yourself. Save the reference librarian for the really big ones."

5. Learn to use the *Reader's Guide to Periodical Literature.* This reference book, organized by subject, enables you to find magazine and newspaper articles on the subject you're researching and thus "provides a guide to the very latest expert information on any subject that interests you. When you use this wonderful tool effectively, you show the mark of a real scholar."

6. "Take notes when you use magazine articles, since you usually can't take these home. Or find out if your library has a photocopy machine and copy the pages you might have to

refer to later."

7. "If you are working on a project that will require repeated library visits, keep a small notebook in which you record the numbers of the books you will be using frequently. This will save you valuable time, because you won't have to consult the card catalog or search aimlessly through the stacks each time."

8. "Practice using the library by taking up projects that can be both fun and rewarding. For instance, try tracing your roots. Find out who your ancestors are by consulting books on genealogy. Or use the local history books in your library to find out if George Washington ever spent time in your neighborhood. Or plan a Polynesian feast using the cookbooks you find. You name it—your library has it all!"

JOHN IRVING'S TIPS FOR BECOMING A BETTER SPELLER

John Irving is the author of *The World According to Garp* and *The Hotel New Hampshire,* among other books. He may be considered one of the best American contemporary novelists but admits that he was a hopelessly bad speller—until he began using some special tricks. The International Paper Company asked Mr. Irving to list these, and here is how he responded.

1. Obviously, if you don't know how to spell a word, looking it up in a dictionary is going to be one likely solution. But Mr. Irving says that each time he looks up a word, he makes a mark next to that word in the dictionary. If you find yourself looking up the same word lots of times, stop and think about that word and take extra time to learn it.

2. When does a word end with *ery* as opposed to *ary?* Here's an easy way to remember: There are only six words in the English language that end in *ery*. These are:

cemetery	*monastery*
millinery	*confectionery*
distillery	*stationery* (*the paper kind*)

All the other *ery/ary* words end in *ary*.

3. As for word ending in *efy* or *ify,* all you need to do is memorize the four words that end in *efy* and use *ify* for all the rest. The four words ending in *efy* are:

stupefy *putrefy* *liquefy* *rarefy*

4. If you don't even know how a word starts and therefore can't look it up in the dictionary, look up another word that has the same meaning. Chances are you'll find the spelling of the word you really need to look up under the definition of the synonym.

5. When do you add *able* or *ible* to the end of a word? There's a rule: You add *able* to the end of a full word, as in *adaptable* or *workable*. You also add *able* to words that end in *e*—as long as you drop the *e,* as in *lovable*. But if the word ends in two *ee*'s, you keep them both and add *able* to the whole word, as in *agreeable*.

You add *ible* if the base word is not a full word that can stand on its own, as in *credible, horrible, terrible*. You also add *ible* if the root word ends in a soft *c* (but drop the final *e*), as in *forcible*. Those rules may not be all that simple to remember, but you'll finally get them if you use them often enough.

19 TIPS FOR GETTING GOOD GRADES ON TESTS

Even when you're out of school, there are tests to take, whether they're driving tests, tests for getting jobs, or tests to get into other schools. So it's best to develop good studying and test-taking skills early. Here are a some tips from experts.

1. When studying, read all the material straight through first. Then go back and underline the important points.

2. Never wait until the last minute to study for a test; it will make you panic. The best time to study is two days before a test. The night before should be used for reviewing the most important points.

3. Have all your reference materials right in front of you when studying so you don't have to go hunting for anything. Keep a dictionary, encyclopedia, and any other things you need close by.

4. Two heads are better than one! Studying with a friend is a good idea as long as you really study. Give each other quizzes. Tutor your friend in the parts you understand well and let him or her do the same for you.

5. Rehearse for your test. Have someone give you a practice test. This does more than help you learn the answer; it also helps you get used to the test, so you're less nervous.

6. Keep old tests. Review the earlier tests, even those you didn't do well on. Most teachers have certain kinds of questions that they ask, and you'll be ahead of the game if you come to know what to expect. If you have a friend or older sibling who had the same teacher, see if they have tests you can look at.

7. A good way really to get to learn something is to talk about it out loud. Pretend you're teaching it to someone else (the mirror?), or try discussing the material with your family at the dinner table.

8. Get a good night's sleep before a test. You'll be able to relax better if you're well rested.

9. The night before the test, right before you fall asleep, picture the important material in your mind. This is the time when your brain is most open to learning. You'll be surprised how much memorizing you can do this way.

10. Your brain needs proper food before a test. Make sure to eat a good breakfast if the test is in the morning. If the test is in the afternoon, don't eat too much sugar or junk food for lunch. Scientists have proved that this kind of food clouds your mind and makes it harder for you to think.

11. Bring all the things you'll need to the test—sharp pencils with erasers, working pens, ruler, etc.

12. Wear comfortable clothes on the day of the test. You'll have an easier time concentrating if you don't feel restricted in any way.

13. Before arriving in the classroom, find a quiet corner and review the important material right before the test. If you've got it written down, this is your last chance to go over it.

14. If you can, get to the classroom a few minutes early and get seated so you'll definitely be ready when the test begins.

15. When taking the test, always make sure you give yourself enough time to understand the material fully, especially the specific question that is being asked. If you have trouble with the instructions, get the teacher to help you.

16. Take your time; use all the time allotted for the test. Don't try to rush, or you're likely to forget the material and may even miss some of the questions.

17. Don't panic. If you can't answer a question, skip it and go on to the next. After you've done the last question, if you still have time, go back and see if you can get some of those you missed.

18. During test-taking time, listen carefully to your teacher's instructions. *This is extremely important!*

19. Remember to do the best you can and that the world won't come to an end no matter what grade you get (although your parents might not want you to know this). Relax during an exam and you will think more clearly.

16 ALTERNATIVES TO "THE DOG ATE MY HOMEWORK"

Over the years, we have heard a lot of funny alternatives to the age-old excuse "The dog ate my homework." Here are some of the best ones:

1. "I left it in my pocket and then my mom put my shirt in the washing machine and it got ruined."

2. "I did the homework but I used invisible ink by mistake."

3. "It flew out the car window on the way to school."

4. "My father took it to work by mistake."

5. "I didn't know you were going to collect it."

6. "The cat had kittens on it and it's still wet."

7. "I thought it was optional."

8. "You said you don't give homework on weekends." (If problem occurs on a Monday.)

9. "I got mixed up with the homework from two nights ago that I forgot to do, so I did the wrong assignment."

10. "I had to babysit until really late last night and there weren't any pencils."

11. "We went to the car wash on the way to school this morning and my mother, genius that she is, left the windows open, so all my homework dissolved."

12. "The maid threw it out."

13. "Don't you remember? I came in early this morning to give it to you, but you were busy. You told me to leave it on your desk."

14. "It's in my locker, but someone jammed the locker up with bubble gum, and so I can't open it."

15. "You already *gave* us that assignment."

16. "Whoops!"

19 EXERCISES FOR YOUR BRAIN

Try doing three of these exercises (pick different ones each day) to keep your brain in gear. It's like calisthenics for your head.

Before you do any of these, take a moment to relax so that you can really concentrate on what you're doing and get the most out of the exercise.

1. Picture your room where you sleep. Create a mental map of the room and of where everything is. Now imagine rearranging the furniture. Make sure that each piece of furniture changes position.

2. Read a newspaper and memorize ten facts.

3. Recite three tongue twisters (see page 379).

4. Think of an important event in history. Now think of how history would have been different if one part of that event changed. For instance, "What if...the telephone had not been invented?"

5. While you are traveling, make a mental map of the route you are taking.

6. Write down a word that has more than 12 letters and see how many smaller words you can make from it.

7. Doodle.

8. Play a video game. Just one.

9. Stare at a cloud and try to imagine that it's different objects. Look for faces in the clouds.

10. Do a crossword puzzle as fast as you can.

11. Read ten pages of a novel.

12. Play Scrabble or another word game.

13. Think about something you really believe is true. Now try to prove that you're wrong.

14. Think about being in *the perfect place.* Look at everything around you and make a list of 20 things you see in your perfect place.

15. Do a jigsaw puzzle.

16. Memorize a list of the first ten objects you see when you wake up in the morning.

17. Think about how many windows there are in your house. How many doors? How many chairs? Closets?

18. Imagine that you are the main character in a book you have read. What would you have done differently?

19. Use your instruction manual to learn to do something new on your computer.

ROBIN LEACH TELLS KIDS HOW TO BECOME RICH AND FAMOUS

For more than ten years, Robin Leach has been taking us into the homes of the world's most rich and famous people through his TV program *Lifestyles of the Rich and Famous.* Follow his tips and someday he might do a show about you!

1. Stay in school.

2. Keep setting and achieving targets and goals.

3. Be dedicated to everything you do.

4. Do *extra* homework.

5. Read *extra* books (others than the ones you have to read for school).

6. Learn about how the stock market works and make believe you have investments. Follow their progress by checking their performance in the newspaper.

7. Instead of accepting a weekly allowance, work for the money.

8. Open a savings account at a bank and deposit all gifts of money into it.

9. Learn everything you can about the profession you have chosen for yourself.

10. Offer to work for free at any job that is related to your chosen profession.

At the age of 3, little Ruth Slenczynska was forced to practice the piano for nine hours a day. The hours paid off, however, and at the age of 4, in 1929, she was playing in public for a fee of $1,000 per performance. That was enough to support her family, who moved to Europe and lived comfortably on Ruth's salary. She retired at the age of 15!

HOW TO MAKE SURE YOU GET TREATED WELL WHEN YOU GO SHOPPING

Some kids complain that they have problems when they go shopping. They say they feel they are being watched closely for shoplifting, even if they would never dream of doing such a thing. They also say that salespeople often ignore them, and that they are sometimes cheated out of the right amount of change. Here are some things you can do when you go shopping to make sure you get the respect you deserve.

1. If you act like an adult, you'll have a better chance of being treated like one. When you enter a store, be polite at all times and don't go around the store picking up items you have no intention of buying. Tell the salesperson exactly what you are looking for so they can help you find it.

2. Don't be afraid to speak up if you are mistreated, but do it in a polite way. If someone tries to get ahead of you in line, if someone gives you the wrong amount of change, or if you have any other complaints, ask to speak to a manager.

3. Shop with an adult for really expensive items or for things that are complicated to buy, like clothing that needs to be tried on. If you're buying something for a parent and you want it to be a surprise, ask someone older to go with you.

4. Keep all the receipts for the things you buy in case you need to return them. But if you need to return something and you *don't* have the receipt, ask to speak to a store manager and politely tell him or her your problem. If you speak confidently, most managers will help you.

7 THINGS YOU CAN DO IF YOU GET RIPPED OFF

If the toy you got for your birthday doesn't work the way it's supposed to, or if something you bought doesn't do what the advertisement for it said it would, or if something breaks after you've only used it a few times and you're sure it's because the item was badly made (and not because your little brother ran over it with his Power Rangers Big Wheels), you don't have to just throw the thing out and chalk it up to experience. Here are some ways to get your money back.

1. Bring the item back to the store (even if you don't have the receipt) and politely explain the problem. Small neighborhood stores and even some large chains are likely to be helpful, since they do generally value you as a customer. Always ask to speak to the manager. It's a good idea to bring an adult with you if you think you'll have trouble explaining your problem.

2. Call your state or local consumer protection agency. These organizations exist to help people with consumer problems and to act against people who run unfair businesses. To find out if your state has one of these, call the state capital (listed in your phone book under Government). If you have trouble doing this, ask a librarian or a telephone operator to help you.

3. Complain to the manufacturer. You can always find the manufacturer's name on the packaging the item came in. Or you can call the store where the item was purchased and ask them for the proper address.

4. Call the Better Business Bureau. The directory assistance operator will help you locate the office nearest you.

(There's usually one in the state capital, if not in your area.) The Better Business Bureau helps people with consumer complaints. It also gives information on how reliable certain companies are and keeps tabs on advertising to make sure that products live up to the promises that are made about them. Sometimes the Bureau will help you settle your problem; sometimes it will send you to a different agency.

5. If the problem you have concerns the safety of an item and you feel that someone's health or well-being is being endangered, you should get in touch with the U.S. Consumer Products Safety Commission, which has the power to ban products or to regulate their sale to reduce the risk of injury. To locate the office nearest you, dial the national toll-free number: (800) 638-2772.

6. If you feel that your gripe is really aimed at an industry rather than at a specific product, you can file a complaint with the trade association that represents the industry. Ask the reference librarian at your local library for help in locating the appropriate address. To complain about practices in the toy industry, write to the Toy Manufacturers of America; they keep an eye on the toy people. Their address is: 200 Fifth Avenue, New York, N.Y. 10010.

7. Go to court. If you've tried everything else and you're still not satisfied—and you're in the mood for a fight—you can sue the company or store that's cheated you by getting in touch with the small-claims court in your state. You won't need a lawyer, but you'll probably need an adult to help you fill out some forms. You'll get a court date at which the person you're suing will be told to appear and answer your charge. You will be asked to explain your case, produce receipts and any letters you have written or received on the case, and show evidence why the court should decide in your favor. If you call any local courthouse, they will tell you how to get in touch with the proper small-claims court in your area.

HOW TO BUY SCHOOL SUPPLIES THAT LAST

Neatness counts! One way to make sure that your school supplies and materials always look like you take care of them is to buy top-quality stuff in the first place. (As in the case of toys or anything you buy, it makes sense to shop around for the best prices.) Here are some basic things to look for when considering quality.

1. When the metal spirals on notebooks unwind, they can get caught in your clothing and even cause injuries. To avoid the problem, get notebooks that have double rather than single spirals. (Double spirals stay wound better.) If the ends of the wires still look as if they may unwind at some point, try using a pair of pliers to turn the ends upward. Plastic spirals will not solve the problem; they don't unwind, but they do tend to break.

2. Look for notebooks with heavyweight covers that will last longer. There are lots of great looking notebooks in the stores with colorful pictures of TV and film stars on the covers, but most of these are printed on cardboard that's likely to rip after just a few weeks of school.

3. Try to stay away from plastic-covered ring binders. The trouble with these is that if the plastic winds up in a very hot or very cold place, it gets brittle and starts to tear. Those blue canvas binders that have been around forever are really your best buy, which is why they've been around forever. They're also the cheapest.

4. When buying ring binders, open and close the rings to test them before you make the purchase. They should open and close easily (but not too easily), and the two halves of the ring should come together evenly.

5. Stay away from erasable pens. Kids like them for the obvious reason—you can get rid of your mistakes faster than you can say "whoops"—but these pens don't necessarily write as smoothly as the regular kind. They tend to skip, and because the ink isn't all that permanent, you can smear your writing if you touch the page.

PETER PIPER PICKED A PACK

10 Things to Look For When You Buy a Backpack

1. It should be made of woven nylon. Nylon is strong and weighs very little.

2. The straps should be adjustable and should have foam pads so they don't cut into your shoulders.

3. There should be plenty of small compartments for special items, like keys and money, but not so many that you have to stand there and open seven different zippers just to find a pencil.

4. Make sure all the zippers, snaps, and clasps open and close easily.

5. All stitching should be reinforced, especially where the straps are sewn to the bag. All the seams should be double-sewn.

6. The fabric inside the bag should be sewn back from the zipper so the zipper doesn't get stuck.

7. Make sure that when the bag is closed, rain can't get in through any openings. (You may not always get credit for wet homework!)

8. Try the bag on to see how it feels.

9. It should be roomy enough to carry *all* your stuff. Sometimes the cheaper backpacks are made a bit smaller, and you don't realize it until you can't fit all your stuff in it.

10. It should be machine washable, so you don't have to throw it out if your lunch leaks.

6 WAYS TO TAKE CONTROL OF YOUR MONEY

Bill Daniels got the idea for a bank for kids when he read an article about some fifth-graders who were laughed at when they went into a bank and asked for a loan. Today the Young Americans Bank is the first bank set up especially for young people—under 22. They specialize in small savings accounts, loans, investments, and credit cards and checking accounts for kids over 12. To find out more, write to the bank at 311 Steele Street, Denver, CO 80206; (303) 321-2265. We are grateful to the Young Americans Bank for taking kids seriously and for the two lists that follow here.

1. Open your own bank account.

2. Ask your parents to let you be responsible for part of the family budget.

3. Design a personal budget—and stick to it!

4. Talk to financially successful people to find out how *they* did it.

5. Find out if there are any programs or classes in your community to help you learn about money.

6. Get a job or find a way to make extra money to help buy the things you want.

HOW TO MAKE MONEY GROW

You can't. But here are some things you can do to make sure you put some of it away for special stuff.

1. Keep your money in a piggy bank that has a key. Give the key to your parents and tell them not to return it to you until you've saved enough money to buy the thing you want.

2. When you get your allowance, make up a list of the things you need to spend it on. Be sure to set aside a portion for savings. This is called budgeting yourself.

3. Decide that you're going to save only pennies or nickels. Each time you get these coins as change from a purchase, put them aside in a special jar or bank.

4. Ask your parents if they will help you with a "matching fund." That means that your parents will give you, say, a dollar for every five dollars you save. Your parents are more likely to do this for you if you agree what the money will eventually be spent on.

5. Make a chart that allows you to mark off a box for every dollar you save. At the top of the chart, paste a photograph of the thing you are saving for. There should be one box for each dollar it will take to buy your "prize."

6. Charge yourself a small fine every time a certain thing happens. For instance, each time you don't get a satisfactory grade on a test, add fifty cents to your savings. Or you can "reward" yourself by putting away a dollar each time you get an "A." Be creative with the rules you make up. You can set aside money every time you finish reading a book or make a phone call or bite your nails. Ask your parents for more suggestions. (If they know you're serious about saving up for something, they may help you.)

7. Ask your parents to hold on to part of your allowance and put it aside for you toward a special fund.

8. When you go shopping, don't bring *all* your money with you, just take as much as you need for planned purchases.

5 THINGS YOU AND YOUR PARENTS SHOULD CONSIDER ABOUT YOUR ALLOWANCE

Your allowance is something *you're* going to spend, but your *parents* are going to have to supply it. That makes it a good subject for you all to talk about together. Don't get discouraged if your parents don't see things your way right off. Perhaps by acting responsibly and living up to whatever bargain you make, they will start looking at things differently. Here are some of the things you should talk about.

1. How much allowance you get. Probably the best way to decide on the right amount is to keep an account of the money you spend—and how much you really need—for a few weeks. Then show your list to your parents and decide together which purchases make sense.

2. Decide when you will get your allowance. Once a week is best, and it should always be on the same day. If you need more money before that day comes around, you're going to have to wait until that day comes around. Or set up a rule so that you can get some money sooner if you can prove that you need it for something really important.

3. Keep track of how much money you spend. When you eventually ask for a raise, you'll be able to show where your money has gone and why you now need more. For instance, if you've been paying for your school lunches and the price has gone up, you'll be able to prove it's time for a raise.

4. Agree on what items your allowance is supposed to cover. If the money you receive is supposed to cover the cost of school supplies, you need to know that so you can plan in advance. Also, will you be allowed to spend money on whatever you choose, or will you still need permission to buy certain things?

5. Try to get your parents to agree that your allowance will never be held back as a punishment. Even if you've been terrible, you still have to live!

THINGS YOU SHOULD KNOW IF YOU WANT TO START YOUR OWN BUSINESS

Having an allowance and getting gifts of money is great, but you can't always depend on this money to help you buy the things you want or to save for the future. You may be too young to get a job, but you are not too young to start your own business. If you want to begin your own business, you should first speak with your parents, to get their permission and advice. Your parents may even lend you the money you need to get your business started.

Here are some important things to consider before you start your own business:

1. There are moneymaking opportunities all around you. You must look for them. Use your imagination! If you have a specific talent or interest, try to find jobs that are related to it.

2. List all your hobbies, sports activities, special talents, and any work experience you may have already had. This may give you some job ideas.

3. Consider whether you want to work indoors or outdoors, provide a service or go into retail, and whether you want to work at something you may desire as a career when you are an adult.

4. Keep a list of all your job ideas. Your jobs may change from month to month, depending on the seasons. Be ready for any changes in job opportunities.

5. Any job you select for yourself should be right for your age, appropriate for the time of year, and should be something you know you can handle. You also should consider how much money you need to get this business started.

6. You will only succeed in a business that you are excited about.

7. You MUST write out a plan of action. Name your business, state what it is your business does, when you plan to work, how to get customers and who those customers will be, what you need to get started.

8. It is extremely important to have *goals* planned. Decide how much money you want to earn each week, how many hours you think you will have to work, and how much money you plan on saving. Write these goals down. Always keep your goals in mind when making business decisions.

9. Getting customers for your business will involve your becoming a salesman: You must advertise and sell your product or services.

10. Make a list of customers you already know and people you think may want your services (neighbors, relatives, store owners, senior citizens, etc.).

William Richard Morris is best known as the British industrialist who founded the Morris Motors, Inc., car company. In 1880, when he was only 15, he had supported his family as a bicycle repairman.

11. Write down what you will say to a customer about your business. When you speak to a potential customer, always have a positive attitude about your business; be friendly and courteous; explain to the customer why they need your service and why they should buy that service or product now.

12. There are three inexpensive tools you can use to help you advertise. You can use signs and posters, flyers, and business cards. You can even put your message on a T-shirt and become a walking advertisement for your business.

13. Keep records of all the money you collect, including the name of the customer and the date you were paid. Keep records of all your expenses, including supplies, advertising costs, phone bills, and transportation costs.

8 WAYS TO KEEP A JOB ONCE YOU'VE FOUND ONE

To make sure you have the best chance of keeping your job or of getting a raise when you ask for one, follow these tips.

1. Get to work early and start right away.

2. Ask questions to avoid making mistakes.

3. Make a list of your daily duties so you don't neglect anything. Make this list at home, not at work.

4. Look and ask for extra work. Try to do more than what you have been asked to do.

5. At the end of the day, try not to leave a project unfinished. Even if it involves staying a little later, finish your work before going home.

6. Be loyal to your boss and your job.

7. Be friendly to your co-workers and other work associates you meet.

8. Do your job as if you were the boss.

FRED SAVAGE'S ADVICE TO YOUNG ACTORS

Born on July 9, 1976, Fred Savage has been acting since he was 5. Although he's appeared in more than 70 TV commercials, you probably know him best as Kevin on *The Wonder Years.*

1. Always be yourself.

2. Don't be pressured.

3. Stay out of trouble.

4. Never let 'em see you sweat!

HOW TO CHANGE THE WORLD

1. Define the problem you want to solve. Homelessness, drug abuse, sex education, dangerous traffic situations, and child abuse are all different problems worth working to solve. Pick one and try to aim all your efforts in this one direction.

2. Learn all you can about the problem. Go to the library or use your on-line resources. Talk to people in your neighborhood and at school. Find out what others have already done to try to solve the problem. Learn from their mistakes.

3. Consider different solutions. Encourage people around you to contribute their ideas, and don't be afraid to consider even the "craziest" proposals. Sometimes you have to listen to lots of bad ideas before you can find the one that will really work.

At age 13, Alison Steiglitz of Miami, Florida, decided she wanted to feed the hungry on Thanksgiving Day, so she used money given to her as bat mitzvah gifts to distribute 15 Thanksgiving dinners to elderly homebound people. Today the organization that Alison helped create serves breakfast and lunches to more than 250 people every Sunday!

4. Find out who opposes your ideas. Meet with these people and try to win them over. Find out why they feel the way they do and see if you can find a solution to the problem that takes their views into account. Remember that nobody wins unless everybody wins!

5. Spread the word. Call your local TV and radio stations and ask to speak to a reporter. Tell them what you're doing. (See "How to Contact the Media by Telephone," page 75.) Invite them to come visit you and your friends to film your activities. And be a bigmouth—tell everyone about your activities. You never know who will be able to help.

6. Develop a network. No matter how much you care, you can't change the world all by yourself. Do everything you can (through school, local media, and using on-line forums) to find others who feel the same way you do about your issues and combine forces. Important: Even if you find yourself working with people you don't like, learn to get along with them for the purpose of accomplishing your goal.

7. Choose a plan and make it happen. You can solve big problems by breaking them up into groups of smaller problems. Make a list of these and tackle them one by one.

8. Hang in there! Don't give up if things don't go your way. If your solution fails, find out why and use what you've learned to develop a new solution. Maybe you'll need more people to help you the second time around. Maybe you didn't tell enough people. Maybe you should try to raise money to advertise and get the word out. Whatever the problem was, try to correct it. Remember that sometimes the process of *trying* to accomplish something may be almost as helpful as getting to your goal. You learn so much along the way!

Get a copy of the book *The Kid's Guide to Social Action,* by Barbara Lewis, published by Free Spirit Publishing, 400 First Ave. North, Minneapolis, MN 55401; (612) 338-2068. It offers a wealth of information, from how to raise money for your cause to giving a speech to getting laws changed. You'll find other useful books at the library.

19 GOVERNMENT OFFICES YOU CAN WRITE TO

If you have questions about your government, get the answers. Here are some of the addresses you'll need:

1. The President of the United States
White House Office
1600 Pennsylvania Ave.
Washington, D.C. 20500
(202) 456-1414
The "chief"

2. Vice President of the United States
Old Executive Office Bldg.
Washington, D.C. 20501
(202) 456-2326
Second in line to the chief

3. Office of Management and Budget
Executive Office Bldg.
Washington, D.C. 20503
(202) 395-3080
They help decide how government money will be spent.

4. Council of Economic Advisers
Old Executive Office Bldg.
Washington, D.C. 20500
(202) 395-3000
Analyzes the national economy and reports back to the president.

5. National Security Council
Old Executive Office Bldg.
Washington, D.C. 20506
(202) 395-4974
Military and national security

6. Office of Policy Development
1600 Pennsylvania Ave., NW
Washington, D.C. 20500
(202) 456-1414
Advises the president on foreign and domestic issues

7. Office of the United States Trade Representative

600 Seventeenth Street, NW
Washington, D.C. 20506
(202) 395-3230
Addresses ways in which the U.S. will deal with other countries

8. Council on Environmental Quality
722 Jackson Place, NW
Washington, D.C. 20503
(202) 395-5750
Advises the president on environmental issues

9. Office of National Drug Control Policy
Executive Office of the President
Washington, D.C. 20500
(202) 727-9472
Advises the president on how to control illegal drugs

10. Office of Administration
Old Executive Office Bldg.
Washington, D.C. 20500
(202) 456-7052
Helps the president get things done and handles all his mail

11. Office of Science and Technology Policy
New Executive Office Bldg.
Washington, D.C. 20506
(202) 456-7116
Advises the president on science and technology issues

12. Department of Defense
The Pentagon
Washington, D.C. 20301

13. Department of Education
400 Maryland Ave. SW
Washington, D.C. 20202

14. Department of Energy
1000 Independence Ave. SW
Washington, D.C. 20585

15. Department of Health and Human Services
200 Independence Ave. SW
Washington, D.C. 20201

16. Department of Housing and Urban Development
451 7th St., SW
Washington, D.C. 20410

17. Department of Labor
200 Constitution Ave. NW
Washington, D.C. 20210

18. Department of Transportation
400 7th St. SW
Washington, D.C. 20590

19. Department of Treasury
1500 Pennsylvania Ave. NW
Washington, D.C. 20220

HOW TO CONTACT THE MEDIA BY TELEPHONE

1. Check the telephone directory for the phone numbers of the local TV and radio stations. Your local library will have this information.

2. Before you call, write down what you want to tell them so that if you get nervous you won't forget something important. If you are inviting them to an event, be sure to give them *all* the information they'll need.

3. When your call is answered, state your name and give the person a *short* explanation of why you're calling: "Hello, my name is William Clinton and I'm working with a group of kids to clean up the garbage on Seventh Street." Then ask to speak with "the city desk" or "a reporter who covers social issues."

4. If you get an answering machine, leave your name, phone number, a short version of why you're calling, and the time of day that your call should be returned (after school, evenings, etc.). If your call is not returned, keep trying at different times of day.

5. If a *human* asks you to leave a message, give them the same information but also ask when would be a good time for you to call back. Keep trying if your call is not returned.

6. Never be rude, even if you are treated badly. Let's face it: A lot of adults do not take kids seriously. Convince them that they should by keeping your cool and then following up with a letter that makes your point.

7. When you finally get through to someone, be sure to write down everything they tell you. If you don't understand what they are telling you, *say so* and ask them to say it slower. If there are words you don't understand, don't pretend you do. Ask them to spell names for you so that you are sure to get them right.

8. *Always* thank the person for taking the time to listen to you, even if they have turned down your request. This makes it easier for the next kid who will try to call that reporter.

THE GIRLS' BILL OF RIGHTS

All people, regardless of sex, age, race, or nationality, should be entitled to these rights. Girls Incorporated helps more than a quarter of a million girls between the ages of 6 and 18 by promoting education, awareness, communications, sportsmanship, and pregnancy prevention. You can write to this organization at 30 E. 33rd St., New York, N.Y. 10016-5394.

1. Girls have a right to be themselves—people first and females second—and to resist pressure to behave in sex-stereotyped ways.

2. Girls have a right to express themselves with originality and enthusiasm.

3. Girls have a right to take risks, to strive freely, and to take pride in success.

4. Girls have a right to accept and enjoy the bodies they were born with and not to feel pressured to compromise their health in order to satisfy the dictates of an "ideal" physical image.

5. Girls have a right to be free of vulnerability and self-doubt and to develop as mentally and emotionally sound individuals.

6. Girls have a right to prepare for interesting work and economic independence.

11 WAYS TO FIGHT RACISM

Racism refers to any action or idea, whether carried out on purpose or unconsciously, that puts down anyone because of their skin color or race. Ending racism does not mean pretending that we're all the same. It means learning to live together peacefully *because* of our differences and even to celebrate those differences. *Many* colors make up a rainbow.

1. Learn about each of the cultures in your community. Get to know people of other backgrounds at school and on-line.

2. Participate in discussions about racism with your friends and on computer forums.

3. When someone makes a racist remark, let them know you are offended.

4. If you see something on TV that's racist, write to the station and object.

5. If you have certain racist impressions—if there's a group of people you find yourself disliking for no real reason—think about how you came to feel this way. When did you first see a person of that group? What did you think? Why?

6. If your parents have racist attitudes, talk to them about it. Tell them how you feel.

7. When you celebrate your own cultural holidays, include members of other groups so that they can learn more about you.

8. Attend someone else's religious or cultural celebration.

9. If someone tells a racist joke, don't laugh.

10. Tell *anti*racist jokes: Why are all racist jokes so short? So racists will understand them!

11. Join Amnesty International, a worldwide organization that fights to help people obtain certain basic human rights. You can find out which of their programs involve kids by writing to Amnesty International USA, 322 8th Ave., New York, N.Y. 10001; (212) 807-8400.

15 THINGS KIDS CAN DO TO END HUNGER

Each night, *600 million* people go to bed hungry. Each day, 40,000 children die of hunger. We *can* end hunger, but it's going to take awareness, commitment, and hard work. Here are some things that kids can do.

1. Publicize your efforts. If you are involved in an activity to end hunger, contact newspapers, radio, and TV stations (see "How to Contact the Media," page 75), and on-line services to let everyone know what you're doing. Maybe you'll inspire others to help.

2. Instead of giving gifts for birthdays and holidays, donate the money you were going to spend to a hunger project. Then make a decorative card to give that reads:

> *"Because you are so special, we are*
> *celebrating your special day in a special way.*
> *A donation has been made in your name*
> *to* (name of organization) *so that your spirit*
> *will help end hunger in the world."*

Don't *ever* send a card like this without sending a donation. You do not have to tell your friend how much money you have donated.

3. Enlist the interest of others. Write to politicians, religious leaders in your community, and celebrities and tell them how you feel about the hunger problem. Ask them what they are doing to help.

4. Find out what local efforts are being made in your community to feed the hungry and volunteer to work for these groups. Maybe you'll wind up handing out flyers, or maybe you'll help cook food to be given out at local homeless shelters. To find out which groups exist in your area, call United Way (their local number is listed in the white pages of your phone book.)

5. Feed someone who is hungry. If you're aware of hungry people in your neighborhood, get your parents' permission to share your food with them. Think of those people when you leave a restaurant with a "doggy bag" of leftovers.

6. Talk to managers in the restaurants your family goes to and make sure they have arranged to donate their leftovers to homeless people in the neighborhood.

7. Support World Food Day, October 16. Groups all over the country do something special on this day each year to make people aware of the hunger problem. Contact: U. S. National Committee for World Food Day, 1001 22nd St. NW, Suite 300, Washington, D.C. 20437.

8. Skip a meal and feed the hungry! Each year, on the Thursday before Thanksgiving, many people skip a meal or fast for the whole day and then donate the money they would have spent

on food to Oxfam America, 115 Broadway, Boston, MA 02116. Write to them for more information.

9. Trick or treat for UNICEF on Halloween. You can do this on your own or you can organize a group—and *no one* is too old for this one! For information and collection boxes contact: U. S. Committee for UNICEF, 333 E. 38th St., New York, N.Y. 10016; (212) 686-5522.

10. Organize a supermarket food drive. Get your local market to urge shoppers to always buy one or two extra items to be donated to local shelters. Talk to the store manager and offer to help by making signs explaining the program. Get your parents to help transport the donated food.

11. Start your own chapter of Youth Ending Hunger (YEH). Write to this group at 1388 Sutter Street, San Francisco, CA 94109 to get a starter kit, which will tell you how to organize the kids in your area.

12. Hold a Crop Walk. This is a national effort in which people walk for ten miles (or more or less) and they get people to donate money for each mile they walk. People of all ages can participate. To find out more about organizing one of these, contact Church World Service, 475 Riverside Drive, New York, N.Y. 10115; (212) 870-2257.

13. Support Africare. This group tries to feed people in more than twenty African countries. For ten dollars, you and your friends can provide 100 pounds of fertilizer for crops, feed two people for a month, or buy enough seeds to plant an entire field. Contact: Africare, 440 R Street NW, Washington, D.C. 20001; (202) 462-3614.

Adopt a foster child in another country. Here are two groups that organize such activities:

Children's Aid International
P. O. Box 480155
Los Angeles, CA 90048
(213) 936-8917

Save the Children
54 Wilton Rd.
Westport, CT 06880
(203) 697-0264, or (213) 226-7271

14. Support the American Jewish World Service. This foundation organizes health and agricultural projects for people of all religions in Africa, Asia, and Latin America. Contact: 1290 Ave. of the Americas, New York, N.Y. 10104; (212) 468-7380.

15. Help hungry people start projects to end their own hunger. You can locate such efforts by contacting IDEX (International Development Exchange), 827 Valencia Street, San Francisco, CA 94110; (415) 824-8384.

CAPTAIN PLANET'S TOP 10 ECO-TIPS

Captain Planet and the people at Turner Broadcasting System want to hear what you are doing to help protect the environment. Write to: Captain Planet Division, 1 CNN Center, Atlanta, GA 30303. In the meantime, make sure you and your family adopt the following eco-habits.

1. Start a carpool. To counterattack the smog and acid rain caused by our cars' exhaust, use a carpool or mass transit. Fewer cars on the road means less exhaust. And it's more fun to ride with a friend!

2. Get involved. It's up to us to save our planet, so get involved in an environmental organization. Check with your local zoo, chamber of commerce, or an environmental publication to find one that's right for you.

3. Be an environmentally conscious consumer. You can cast your vote to save the environment each time you open your wallet. Buy products that use recycled materials and less packaging. Buy products in bulk.

4. Check your bulbs. Don't waste energy by using a light bulb that has higher wattage than needed. You can save energy and money by using more efficient, compact fluorescent bulbs. Turn them off when you're not in the room.

5. Get rid of hazardous waste safely. Batteries, antifreeze, pesticides, paint, paint thinners, drain cleaners, mothballs, and many other household products are considered hazardous waste, so don't pour them down the drain or throw them in the trash. Contact your municipal waste facility or local government information center to find out how to dispose of hazardous substances properly.

6. Recycle, recycle, recycle. From newspapers to egg cartons to organic materials such as leaves and yard clippings, lots of things can be recycled. Even coffee grounds can be used as fertilizer for some plants. So don't throw away what you can use again!

7. Save water by checking the location of your sprinklers! Make sure sprinklers are properly located and are turned to a moderate level.

8. Avoid single-serving and multipack food items. Buy food in bulk and store it in resealable containers. Bring your own reusable bag to carry home your groceries.

9. Camp safely. When you go camping or hiking, pay attention to how you clean up. Try washing with soapless hot water and sand—even the mildest soap puts a strain on the environment. If you do use soap, use a biodegradable one. And be sure to dig your latrine as far as possible from water sources to avoid contamination.

10. Use nontoxic cleaners to unclog drains. Instead of using a commercial drain cleaner, which is highly toxic, you can use a solution of baking soda and vinegar to take care of a drain clog. Simply pour a handful of baking soda down the drain followed by a half a cup of vinegar. Cover the drain with a heavy pot or stopper, as this will force the pressure down and clear the clog instead of allowing the mixture to fizz up out of the drain.

CHAPTER TWO

GETTING IT TOGETHER WITH OTHER KIDS

34 GOOD DEEDS

1. Write a letter to an old person.

2. Teach someone younger than you how to do something.

3. Call someone who's sick.

4. Apologize to someone for something wrong you may have done.

5. Look through your closet and drawers for three pieces of nice clothing you don't wear anymore. Get permission to donate these to a local clothing drive.

6. Tell someone you love that you *really* love them.

7. Talk to the shyest person in your school.

8. Read a story to someone who can't read.

9. Let someone get ahead of you in line.

10. Forgive someone you're mad at.

11. Fix something for someone.

12. Let someone win an argument, even if they're wrong.

13. Tell your favorite teacher how you feel about him or her.

14. Collect three toys you don't play with anymore and give them to a younger child.

15. Do something nice for someone and don't let them know it was you who did it.

16. Donate a whole week's allowance to a charity.

17. Smile at someone.

18. Read a story to a small child.

19. Take out a videotape from the library and arrange a showing of it at a local home for the elderly.

20. Stick up for someone.

21. If you're going trick or treating, do it for UNICEF or a local homeless shelter or some other needy cause.

22. Teach a little kid how to do something.

23. In the autumn, plant one red tulip where no one would expect to find it. (Someone will be *very* surprised in the spring.)

24. Offer to copy the homework assignment for someone who's absent from school.

25. Donate blood.

26. Volunteer your time to a community event.

27. Write a letter to a newspaper editor about an issue that is important to you.

28. Write a letter to someone's boss telling them what a good job the employee did.

29. Encourage other people to do good deeds.

30. Make breakfast for someone.

31. Make someone laugh.

32. Fix a broken toy for a small child.

33. Offer to go on an outing with an older person who can't go alone.

34. Don't get mad the next time you have a right to get mad.

10 WAYS TO GET A PEN PAL

Writing to kids in other countries is a great way to find out about life in faraway places and, more than anything else, to learn from the differences. The following organizations help kids find pen pals all over the world.

1. Friends Around the World (FAW)
   P.O. Box 10266
   Merrillville, IN 46411-0266
   (219) 884-9327
   For anyone interested in an international pen pal, FAW matches correspondents on the basis of general interests, age, and sex.
2. Gifted Children's Pen Pal International
   ℅ Dr. Debby Sue van de Vender
   166 E. 61st St.
   New York, N.Y. 10021
   (212) 355-2469
   This service is for gifted children ranging in age from four to eighteen. The child must be certified as gifted or entered in a gifted program.
3. International Pen Friends (IPF)
   P.O. Box 290065
   Brooklyn, N.Y. 11229
   (718) 769-1785
   IPF offer programs for youth organizations and schools. Pen pals are matched by common interests, age, and gender, and can correspond in English, French, German, Portuguese, or Spanish. Cassette-tape exchanges are available for the blind and handicapped.
4. League of Friendship
   P.O. Box 509
   Mt. Vernon, OH 43050
   (614) 392-3166
   Through its foreign pen pal program, the League fosters international understanding and friendship. It supplies matched correspondents for youth aged 12 through 25.
5. Science Fiction Pen Pal Club

P.O. Box 2522
Renton, WA 98056
This club matches correspondents having an interest in science fiction.

6. Student Letter Exchange
215 5th Ave., S.E.
Waseca, MN 56093
(507) 835-3691
Facilitates correspondence for youth ages 10 to 19 within the United States and 50 foreign countries.
7. World Pen Pals (WPP)
1694 Como Ave.
St. Paul, MN 55108
(612) 647-0191
Through its pen pal program, WPP serves nearly 50,000 students between the ages of 12 and 20 living in the United States and in 150 other countries.
8. International Pen Friends
Box 290065
Brooklyn, N.Y. 11229-0001
Connects kids all over the world.
9. Friends Forever PenPals
P.O. Box 20103
Park West Post Office
New York, N.Y. 10025
Send a SASE for information.
10. Creative Kids
P.O. Box 8813
Waco, TX 76714-8813
If you send in your name, address, birthday, and hobbies, they will list this information for more than 50,000 readers. So you may get lots of responses. Talk to your parents before you send the information to find out if they think it is a good idea.

43 ORGANIZATIONS THAT WORK WITH AND FOR KIDS

1. ABA Center on Children and the Law
1800 M St. N.W.
Washington, D.C. 20036
Finds lawyers for kids
2. Al-Anon/Alkateen
Family Groups
P.O. Box 182
Madison Square Station
New York, N.Y. 10159-0182
Help for family and friends of alcoholics

3. Alpha Club
Optimist International
4494 Lindell Blvd.
St. Louis, MO 63108
(314) 371-6000
This organization for elementary school kids stresses self-discovery, service to the community, and spiritual values.

4. American Anorexic/Bulimia Association (AABA)
418 East 76 St.
New York, N.Y. 10021
(212) 734-1114
Helps kids with eating disorders.

5. American Student Council Association
National Association of Elementary School Principals
1516 Duke St.
Alexandria, VA 22314-3483
(703) 684-3345
Helps elementary and middle schools set up student councils in their schools.

6. Amnesty International Children's Special Edition/Urgent Action
P.O. Box 1270
Nederland, CO 80466
(303) 440-0913
Organizes kids in the fourth through eighth grades to write letters to political leaders around the world asking for fair and humane treatment for all human beings.

7. Big Brothers/Big Sisters of America
230 North 13th St.
Philadelphia, PA 19108
(215) 567-7000
This program hooks up kids who are underprivileged in some way with an adult who can help them. They have other programs, too.

8. Boys Clubs of America
771 1st Ave.
New York, N.Y. 10017
(212) 351-5900
For kids from 7 to 18, offers organized recreational, athletic, and social activities.

9. Boy Scouts of America
1325 Walnut Hill Lane
Irving, TX 75015-2079
(214) 580-2000
Activities, character development, and citizenship for boys.

10. Camp Fire, Inc.
4601 Madison Ave.
Kansas City, MO 64112-1278
(816) 756-1950
Camping skills, responsible citizenship, and self-reliance for boys and girls.

11. Child Find of America
P.O. Box 277
New Paltz, N.Y. 12561
Brings missing children home.

12. Child Help USA, Inc.
6463 Independence Ave.
Woodland Hills, CA 91370
Research, prevention, and treatment of child abuse

13. Children's Campaign for Nuclear Disarmament
14 Eviret St.
New Haven, CT 06511
(203) 226-3694
Kids working together to halt the arms race

14. The Coalition to Stop Gun Violence
100 Maryland Ave., N.E.
Washington, D.C. 20002
(202) 544-7190
Focuses on and gives information about gun control

15. 4-H Youth Development
U.S. Department of Agriculture
Washington, D.C. 20250
(202) 447-5853
Agricultural, technological, and interpersonal skills for kids aged 9 to 19. Camping and international exchange programs.

16. Girls Clubs of America
30 E. 33rd St.
New York, N.Y. 10016
(212) 689-3700
Athletic activities and health and education programs for girls, including AIDS awareness and substance abuse prevention

17. Girl Scouts of the USA
830 3rd Ave.
New York, N.Y. 10022
(212) 940-7500
Activities, character development, and citizenship for girls. International programs, too.

18. Hug-A-Tree and Survive
℅ Jaqueline Hunt
6465 Lance Way
San Diego, CA 92120
Teaches kids what to do when they're lost.

19. International Association for the Child's Right to Play
℅ Mr. Robin Moore
Box 7701, NCSU
Raleigh, N.C. 27695
Believes in kids' right to have fun!

20. Jack & Jill of America, Inc.
1065 Gordon, S.W.
Atlanta, GA 30310
(404) 753-8471
Helps mothers and their children develop community social, recreational, and cultural programs.

21. Junior Guardian Angels

5891 S. Military Trail,
Suite 5A
Lake Worth, FL 33463
Local programs of this organization encourage kids to aid the elderly and others who need their help.

22. Let's Play to Grow
8610 Contree Rd.
Laurel, MD 20708
(202) 673-7166;
(301) 776-8054
Organizes playgroups around the country for kids of all ages with mental and physical disabilities.

23. National Association of Anorexia Nervosa and Associated Disorders (ANAD)
P.O. Box 7
Highland Park, IL 60035
(708) 831-3438
Offers help for kids with eating disorders.

24. National Association of Youth Clubs
5808 16th St., N.W.
Washington, D.C. 20011
(202) 726-2044
Community-based clubs with activities sponsored by the National Association of Colored Women's Clubs

25. National Beta Club
151 W. Lee St.
P.O. Box 730
Spartanburg, S.C. 29304
(803) 583-4553
This club is for kids in the fifth through twelfth grades who have outstanding leadership and academic abilities.

26. National Coalition Against Domestic Violence
1000 Sixteenth St., N.W.
Washington, D.C. 20036
Hotline: (800) 333-7233
This group gives free information about organizations that help victims of violence.

27. National Council on Child Abuse and Family Violence
1165 Connecticut Ave., N.W.
Washington, D.C. 20036
Hotline: (800) 222-2000
Helps people find agencies near them that offer family counseling.

28. National Crime Prevention Council
733 15th St., N.W.
Suite 540
Washington, D.C. 20005
(202) 393-7141
Gives information about starting crime watch programs in your community to prevent vandalism, robberies, drug dealing, and other crimes.

29. National Information Center for Children and Youth with Disabilities
P.O. Box 1492
Washington, D.C. 20013-1492
(800) 999-5599;
(703) 893-6061
Provides information on support groups, individual disabilities, laws that affect kids with special needs, and helpful state agencies.

30. National Jewish Council for the Disabled
333 Seventh Ave.
New York, N.Y. 10001
(212) 563-4000 ext. 229
Provides recreational and informal educational programming for kids with disabilities.

31. The National School Safety Center
Pepperdine University
16830 Ventura Blvd., Suite 200
Encino, CA 91436
Helps school groups form violence prevention programs.

32. Reading Is Fundamental
600 Maryland Ave., S.W.
Washington, D.C. 20560
(202) 287-3220
Encourages kids to read by setting up programs in schools.

33. SADD
Box 800
Marlboro, MA 01752
(508) 481-3568
With chapters in thousands of schools, SADD is devoted to spreading the idea that "friends do not let friends drive drunk."

34. Star Serve
P.O. Box 34567
Washington, D.C. 20043
(800) 888-8232
Founded by Mike Love, of the band The Beach Boys, this organization supplies kids with planning materials to start community service projects in their own neighborhoods.

35. Students & Youth Against Racism
P.O. Box 1819
Madison Square Station
New York, N.Y. 10159
(212) 741-0633
Young people work to end racism, homophobia, and sexism.

36. Winners on Wheels (WOW)
2842 Business Park Ave.
Fresno, CA 93727-1328
(209) 292-2171
A national learning and social program, similar to

scouting, for children in wheelchairs.

37. Workshop on Nonviolence
The Martin Luther King, Jr., Center for Nonviolent Social Change
449 Auburn Ave., N.E.
Atlanta, GA 30312
(404) 524-1956
A program that promotes nonviolent solutions to problems, mostly through school programs.

38. World Federalist Association
P.O. Box 15250
Washington, D.C. 20003
(800) HATE-WAR
(800) 428-3927
Promotes a strong, fair-minded United Nations as the means to world peace.

39. YMCA of the United States
101 N. Wacker Drive
Chicago, IL 60606
(312) 977-0031
(800) USA-YMCA
(800) 872-9622
Local Y's offer a variety of athletic programs, summer camp, and childcare facilities. There are national programs, too.

40. YMCA Leaders Clubs
40 W. Long St.
Columbus, OH 43215
(614) 224-2225
Kids participate in community service, social events, and volunteer activities within the Y. Kids 12 and up are trained to be leaders of YMCA community groups.

41. YWCA of the United States
726 Broadway
New York, N.Y. 10003
(212) 614-2700
Offers many programs to foster self-awareness and health for girls and women.

42. Youth Against War & Fascism
46 W. 21st St.
New York, N.Y. 10010
(212) 355-0352
Opposes war, racism, and other forms of discrimination.

43. Zenith Clubs International Training in Communication
2519 Woodland Drive
Anaheim, CA 92801
(714) 995-3660
These clubs offer educational programs for junior high and high school students that encourage communication skills, public speaking, and leadership development.

4 ADDRESSES TO WRITE TO IF YOU WANT TO BE OR HOST A FOREIGN EXCHANGE STUDENT

Getting to know someone from a foreign country can be like visiting that country yourself, and being lucky enough to travel or study far away from home can be one of the most exciting experiences ever. These groups all sponsor exchange programs.

1. American Intercultural Student Exchange
   7720 Herschel Ave.
   La Jolla, CA 92037
   (619) 459-9761
2. Council on Standards for International Educational Travel
   3 Loudoun St. SE
   Leesburg, VA 22075
   (703) 771-2040
3. Open Door Student Exchange
   839 Steward Ave.
   Suite D
   Garden City, N.Y. 11538
   (800) 366-6736
4. U.S. Summer Abroad; The Experiment in International Living; World Learning, Inc.
   Kipling Rd.
   P.O. Box 676
   Brattleboro, VT 05302-0676
   (800) 345-2929

9 ORGANIZATIONS THAT WORK TO GRANT THE WISHES OF CHILDREN WHO ARE VERY SICK OR DYING

1. Brass Ring Society
   7029 N.W. 12th St.
   Oklahoma City, OK 73127
2. Dream Factory
   315 Guthrie Green
   Louisville, KY 40202
3. Famous Fone Friends
   9101 Sawyer St.
   Los Angeles, CA 90035
4. Give Kids the World
   210 S. Bass Rd.
   Kissimmee, FL 34746
5. Mail for Tots
   25 New Chardon St.
   P.O. Box 8699
   Boston, MA 02114
6. Make-A-Wish Foundation of America
   2600 N. Central Ave., #936
   Phoenix, AZ 85004
7. Starlight Foundation
   12233 W. Olympic Blvd.
   Los Angeles, CA 90064
8. Sunshine Foundation
   2001 Bridge St.
   Philadelphia, PA 19124
9. A Wish With Wings
   P.O. Box 3457
   Arlington, TX 76010

8 WAYS YOU *CAN'T* GET AIDS

1. Touching
2. Ordinary kissing
3. Being sneezed on
4. Sitting on a toilet seat
5. Coming in contact with an AIDS victim's sweat
6. Holding hands
7. Hugging
8. Loving

19 THINGS KIDS FEEL PEER PRESSURE ABOUT

Peer pressure can be tough to deal with. But it will help you to remember that you do have choices. No one has the right to force you to do something you don't feel is right, especially if it's dangerous. If someone stops being your friend because you don't join them or won't wear the same clothes or get the same grades or don't want to play the same games, maybe it's time to look for new friends. True friends will respect your right to decide for yourself what is right. Even best friends can have different feelings and values. Each person is, after all, different. Here are some of the situations in which you may encounter peer pressure.

1. Your friends are smoking, drinking, or using drugs and tell you they won't be your friends anymore if you don't do the same.

2. Someone tries to cheat at school by copying your paper or homework and tells you you're not really a friend if you don't let them do so.

3. Your friends want to trespass on someone's private property, and you know you shouldn't.

4. Other kids are wearing certain kinds of clothing that you're not allowed to wear or don't want to wear.

5. Most of the other kids have a girlfriend or boyfriend and you don't.

6. Other kids in the locker room are more or less developed than you are.

7. You're asked to get into a car with a bunch of kids and you know that the driver has been drinking.

8. Everyone else is teasing someone or being mean to them, and you don't want to go along with the "joke."

9. Everyone wants to go see a certain movie and you don't want to see it—or if you've chosen one that no one else is interested in.

10. Everyone else likes a certain kind of music that you don't care for.

11. Kids come over to your house when your parents aren't home and you're not allowed to have them in, but they want to come in anyway. Or they try to break rules around your house when your parents aren't home.

12. An unpopular person asks to spend time with you and you really want to but you know that all the other kids will make fun of you.

13. Friends dare you to do something you know is wrong (like stealing or saying something rotten to someone), and you think they'll think you're a baby if you don't do it.

14. You don't have as much money to spend on things as everyone else does.

15. Someone wants to get involved in kissing or petting, and you just don't feel you're ready.

16. You really want to be nice to a sister or brother, but everyone expects you to be mean to them.

17. Everyone wants to goof off the day before a test, but you really want to study for a good grade.

18. Friends expect you to misbehave in class and throw spitballs or pass notes, but you don't want to.

19. You want to join a club or school team that everyone thinks isn't cool.

KIDS' MOST EMBARRASSING MOMENTS

1. When ice cream falls off your cone onto the street

2. Not having enough money for the pizza you just ordered

3. Finding your friend in town with other friends after he or she told you they had to go to a dentist's appointment

4. Not being able to stay out as late as your friends or having your parents pick you up early when everyone is allowed to stay

5. Opening a sandwich in the lunchroom and having everyone around you yell, "Phew! Gross!"

6. Receiving an award at an assembly and having the person who's presenting it to you get your name all wrong

7. Having to repeat a grade and hearing everyone say you've been "left back"

8. Having to dress up when everyone else is wearing jeans

9. When your parents won't let you go out with your friends

10. When your parent scolds you in front of friends

11. When your parent is drunk in front of your friends

12. When your parent dresses differently than all of your friends' parents

13. Singing an extra word in a chorus concert when everyone else is silent

14. When your teacher catches you sending a note in class and reads it aloud to everyone

15. Being teased about being smaller, taller, or more or less developed than the other kids

16. Listening to a joke, having everyone around you laugh hysterically, and not understanding what they're laughing about

17. If your parents catch you and your girlfriend or boyfriend kissing

18. Being caught in a lie

19. When your mother walks in when you and your friends are trying on her bras and stuffing them with socks!

20. When your sister or brother listens in on your private conversation with your friend and then spreads your secret around the school

21. When your teacher reads the test grades aloud to the class and you failed the test or got one of the lowest marks

22. Getting sick and having to throw up in public

23. Waking up in the morning and finding out you had an accident during the night and wet the bed

24. Kids telling you your haircut looks awful

25. Having the school nerd fall in love with you

26. When you're at a birthday party and the host is opening his or her presents and you realize yours isn't as nice as the others

27. When somebody gives you a Christmas present and you didn't think to get anything for them

28. If a parent or grandparent kisses you and calls you by a pet name in front of your friends

29. When you're "just touching" something at someone's house and it accidentally breaks

30. When you show up at a party wearing jeans and everyone else got dressed up, or vice versa

31. When someone does something gross in front of you

32. When your friends come to visit and your parents are walking around in their underwear or if they look *really bad*

33. When your brother or sister tells your friends something private, like that you sleep with your teddy bear

34. When your parents yell at your friends

7 WAYS TO HANDLE EMBARRASSING MOMENTS

Embarrassment can be a painful experience. It is important for you to remember that everyone at one time or another does something embarrassing, not just you. That includes your friends, teachers, and even your parents.

1. Make a joke out of it.

2. Quietly ask the person who is embarrassing you to stop.

3. Get angry—privately.

4. Leave the room.

5. If someone is teasing you, tease them back in a friendly way.

6. Write down your feelings.

7. Talk to your parents or a friend for support.

12 WAYS TO LET SOMEONE KNOW YOU WANT TO BE THEIR FRIEND

1. Smile and act friendly toward them.

2. Say something nice about how they look or something they did or said.

3. Ask them questions to show that you're interested in them.

4. If you notice they're troubled, you might tell them you're concerned and want them to know that you care enough to listen if they want to talk to you about anything.

5. Walk up to them, introduce yourself, and ask if you can walk to school together or have lunch at the same table.

6. If you need help with a school subject, ask if you could study with them. Or offer to help with something that you know a lot about.

7. Find out if you have any of the same interests (like video games or a favorite rock group) and suggest that the two of you get together.

8. Invite them over to do homework at your house after school.

9. Invite them over on a weekend or to a small party.

10. Call them on the phone if you didn't see them in school and tell them you just wanted to check and see if everything is okay. Offer to get their books and homework for them if the person is out of school because they're sick.

11. Talk about yourself—but don't overdo it. That doesn't mean bragging, it just means letting someone know something about yourself that might interest them.

12. If someone is embarrassed by something, let them know that you're laughing *with* them, not *at* them.

HOW TO TELL SOMEONE YOU DON'T WANT TO BE THEIR FRIEND ANYMORE WITHOUT HURTING THEIR FEELINGS

You can't! The best you can do is to try to be as kind and as caring as possible. Say what you have to say in person, speak softly, and don't put the blame on anyone. Say what you have to say honestly but be sensitive about their feelings, which will hopefully ease the hurt. But remember that there's no way to take away the hurt altogether. Here are some ways to open the conversation.

1. "I really don't want to hurt you, but I think we should be completely honest with each other."

2. "I know you're not going to be happy hearing this, and I feel awful saying it, but I care about you too much not to be honest."

3. "I care about you a lot, but I feel that we spend too much time together. Why don't we give each other some room and then see how we feel about things?"

4. "I like being with you, but I have a lot of other interests and need to have more time to be with other friends."

5. "I think we disagree about too many things to be really close all the time."

HOW TO FIGHT FAIR

1. Stick to solving a particular problem. Don't try to change the whole world—or even one person—in one argument.

2. Listen to the other side with an open mind. Don't interrupt.

3. Think about how the other guy is feeling.

4. Take responsibility for your actions.

5. Tell the truth.

6. Don't try to bully or scare someone into accepting your point of view.

7. No physical violence.

8. No name-calling.

9. Don't make threats.

10. Don't make excuses.

11. If you feel too angry to fight fair, take a cooling off break, then get back to the fight.

12. When the fight is settled, live up to your part of the agreement.

11 WAYS TO HANDLE BULLIES

Bullies are people who want control and are willing to hurt other people in order to get it. Bullies are tough on the outside, but inside they're scared and feel that they're not as good as everyone else. You can learn a lot more about handling bullies by reading an excellent book called *Why Is Everybody Always Picking on Me?,* by Terrence Webster-Doyle (Atrium Society, P.O. Box 816, Middlebury, VT 05753). Here are some ways to handle bullies.

1. Walk away from the fight. This can be hard to do, especially when you know that you are right and that what the bully is doing is wrong. But getting involved in a fight is not going to settle anything.

2. Make friends with the bully. Offer friendship and try to find something the two of you may have in common, like an interest in music or a particular sport.

3. Use humor, but make sure to laugh at yourself and not the bully. If someone is threatening you physically you might say, "Well, it looks like I'm going to be roadkill in about three minutes!"

4. Trick the bully into thinking your parents are about to arrive, you have a serious illness, or that one of your brothers is on the police force.

5. Show that you're not afraid. Stand up to the bully and say, "I'm not afraid of you!" Bullies will sometimes back down if you show you're not afraid.

6. Agree with the bully. If a bully calls you a wimp, say, "You're right, I'm a wimp. Now leave me alone!"

7. Try reasoning. If you're good at arguing, try talking about the situation.

8. Distract the bully. You can do this by raising a subject that will surprise the bully ("Did you know that your father and my father are going fishing together next weekend?"). Or divert his or her attention elsewhere ("Hey, what are all those police cars doing in the parking lot?"). Then RUN!

9. Get someone with authority to help you, such as a teacher, a parent, or an older friend. You may feel this is a cowardly way out, but if you've tried other methods, it may be your only solution. Remember that a bully has no right to hurt you. If *they're* going to change the rules, then so can you.

10. Ignore the bully. This can mean turning your back and walking away, but it can also mean acting like you don't even know that the bully is bullying you. Act stupid! Then the bully may think that you are too crazy to pick on.

11. Practice confidence. Use language, body movements, and facial expressions to let bullies know that you think highly of yourself and that you're not going to let anyone push you around.

THE MANUAL ALPHABET

The following sign language alphabet was kindly supplied to us by the National Association for the Deaf. If you have any questions about deafness or would like to know what other materials they have available, write to them at: 814 Thayer Ave., Silver Spring, MD 20910.

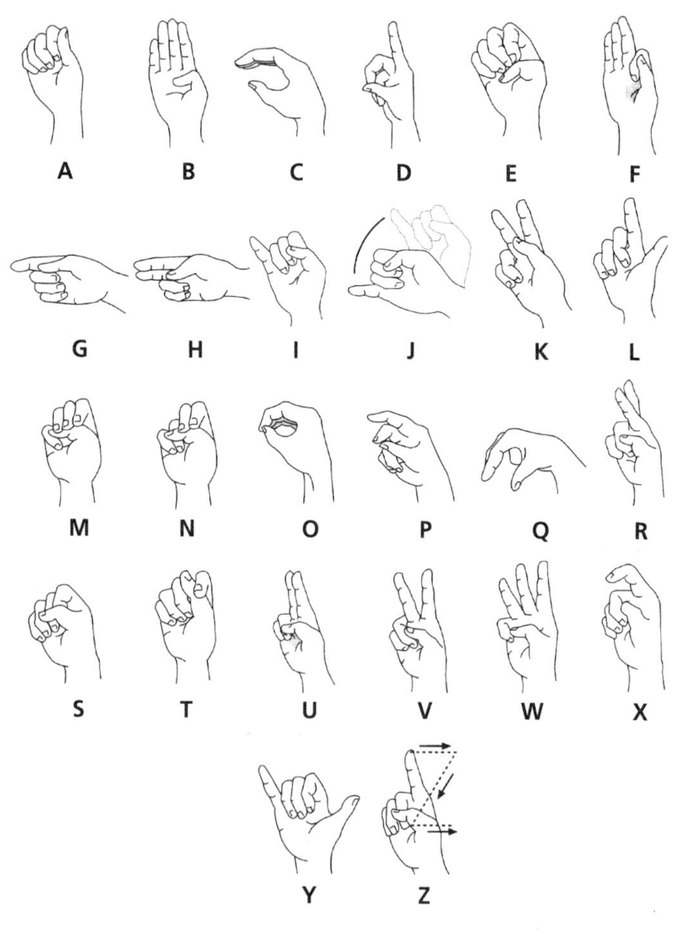

WHEN SOMEONE IN YOUR FAMILY HAS CANCER

Cancer is a serious disease, and if it isn't treated, it can cause death. When someone has cancer, everyone in the family is affected. If this is your situation, be sure to find someone you can talk to about what *you* are going through. Here are some feelings brothers and sisters may have.

1. You worry about your brother or sister. It's hard to watch someone you love when they're in pain. You may feel strange about feeling good about yourself when your brother or sister is stuck at home or in a hospital.

2. You feel incredibly sad. You may feel like crying all the time, and you just don't feel like doing much of anything.

3. You feel guilty and wonder if you did something to cause your brother or sister to get cancer. (That's impossible!)

4. You feel jealous and left out. *This is normal!* Your sibling is probably getting lots of attention, staying out of school, and getting lots of presents. That can look like a pretty good deal. It's okay to feel the way you do.

5. You feel angry. One minute everything seems fine, and the next minute, everything's a mess. You feel angry because you never know what to expect. Illness disrupts the family; plans change constantly.

6. You worry about the kinds of treatments your brother or sister has to go through. Some of them sound scary and painful. Be sure to ask questions and maybe even go along on some treatment visits to learn how chemotherapy and radiation are given.

7. You worry that you or your parents will get it next. You might even feel a little sick yourself, just because you're so scared. You have to remember that you can't catch cancer from other people or animals.

8. You miss your parents, because they always seem to be busy taking care of your brother or sister.

9. You worry about what this is doing to your parents. Talk to them. They need you and your love right now just as much as you need theirs.

12 WAYS TO BE COMFORTABLE WITH A DISABLED FRIEND

Unfortunately, when most people meet a disabled person, they tend to think about the disability first and the person second. But it doesn't have to be this way. For instance, you can try to understand that people have feelings no matter how they talk or walk. Here are some ways that will ease the path for you and a disabled friend.

1. Try to learn more about the disability so that it isn't a mystery between the two of you. Ask questions if you think your friend won't be self-conscious about answering them (and keep in mind that your friend doesn't *have* to answer), or try to get information from the library or from your own parents. Remember that disabilities are not "catching."

2. Try not to let their disability fool you into thinking that they can't be a good friend. Remember that if someone can't walk or talk or even see or hear the way you can, they can still feel just as much as any other human being.

3. Say what you want to say and talk about whatever you

would normally talk about, even if your disabled friend can't do the same things. For instance, if you want to talk about how much fun your soccer game was, go ahead and do so. Your friend will probably be happy to hear about it.

4. Don't act as if the person is not disabled. Disability is not a secret that you have to pretend doesn't exist. If you and your friend can talk about the disability honestly, it will probably bring you closer together.

5. Try not to protect your friend too much. You'd be surprised at what disabled people can do, even if they do it a little differently from you. Let them do as much for themselves as they want to. If you're not sure what to do, wait until you are asked for your help.

6. If you find yourself uncomfortable, talk about your feelings with your friend. For instance, it's okay to say, "It's really strange to see your legs when you take your braces off; it makes me uncomfortable." Or, "Sometimes it's hard for me to talk to you because I don't know if it's okay to say certain things." It's perfectly okay to use words like *see, walk,* and *run* around people who can't do those things.

7. When you're talking to someone who's in a wheelchair, sit down near them so they won't have to stretch their necks to look up at you.

8. It's okay to ask someone with a speech problem to repeat what they said if you didn't understand them the first time.

9. Don't talk loudly to blind people. They can hear.

10. Never pet or play with Seeing Eye dogs. They should never be distracted from their jobs.

11. Remember that the disability is not the person's fault. Your friend may have been born with the condition or been involved in an accident that caused it. If you're really curious about it, wait until you know the person well and then ask how they got that way.

12. Treat a person with a disability exactly the way you would like to be treated.

SOME THINGS YOU FEEL WHEN A FRIEND DIES

The death of a close friend is an experience that will be part of your life for a very long time, and yes, it will hurt. But things will look differently in time, and you can speed up this process by finding someone to talk to about your feelings. You should also try to get a copy of an excellent book called *When a Friend Dies,* by Marilyn E. Gootman. Free Spirit, which publishes the book, also has some other good books on the tougher parts of being a kid. You can write to them for a free catalog: Free Spirit Publishing, 400 First Avenue North, Minneapolis, MN 55401; (612) 338-2068.

1. It's hard to believe that it really happened. You feel pain, but then you keep expecting your friend to walk through the door. Try to remember that you're not always going to feel this way.

2. You feel like the world ended and you no longer have the right to ever enjoy yourself again. You feel guilty if you are having a good time. It is very important for you to continue living your life.

3. You don't know how to act. Sometimes it's hard to know when it's appropriate to smile or cry or which emotion to show. It's important to remember that everyone is entitled to express their feelings in their own way.

4. You keep thinking of things you should have said or done before your friend died. Even if you and your friend had a big fight, that was part of your friendship, too. You can't change anything that already happened, and your friend didn't die because of your fight.

5. You feel angry because you think that someone (doctors, friends, maybe even God) *let* your friend die. You want to blame it on someone. Maybe you're even angry at your friend for dying. Others around you are probably feeling the same way. If you share your emotions, maybe you can all turn your feelings of rage into healthy grief.

6. You miss your friend. You're lonely. You feel like you have been left behind, and you don't think anyone can ever replace the friendship that has been lost. You are right. But each of your relationships is unique, and there are many possible friends out there. You will find new ones when the time is right.

7. You feel frustrated because you have so many feelings you can't express. You just don't have the right words. Maybe you don't need them. Maybe this is a good time to try expressing yourself in some creative way, such as through music or painting.

8. You have weird thoughts or dreams; you feel like you're going crazy. You may want to talk to a professional therapist. If you have your parents' cooperation, you can get a good referral by talking to the guidance counselor at your school or from your family doctor. If your parents are against the idea, talk to the guidance counselor to find out what can be done.

27 THINGS THAT ARE HARD TO TELL YOUR PARENTS

Ellen Rosenberg, author of the excellent book *Growing Up, Feeling Good,* spends most of her time touring schools in the United States and talking to kids about the things that bother them. Special thanks to Ellen for helping us compile this list as well as some of the other lists in this chapter.

1. You got a low grade on a test.

2. You or your friend is drinking or taking drugs.

3. They embarrass you.

4. They treat you like a baby and you want more privileges.

5. You're afraid they're thinking about getting a divorce.

7. You don't like your mom or dad's cooking.

8. You got your period or have started to have wet dreams.

9. They don't spend enough time with you.

10. You don't think they love you as much as they do your brother or sister.

11. You wish they wouldn't compare you to a brother or sister or friend.

12. Anything about sex.

14. You can't stand it when they chew with their mouth open or talk with food in their mouths.

15. You don't like the present they got you.

16. You don't like the clothes they pick out for you and you'd like to start dressing the way *you* want.

17. You're scared they're ill or might die soon.

18. You disagree with some of their religious beliefs.

19. You're embarrassed because you don't like the way your house looks.

20. You'd like to be friends with someone they might not approve of.

21. You need more allowance.

22. You lied about something or did something dishonest.

23. You are embarrassed at the fact that they don't speak English.

24. You did something that goes against your religion.

25. You are afraid of them.

26. You are involved in something violent.

27. You don't want to be something they want you to be.

PROBLEMS THAT COME UP WHEN YOU HAVE TO SHARE A ROOM WITH SOMEONE

(*And What You Can Do about Them*)

1. One person wants to do homework and the other wants to sleep. Set up the room so that the light is facing away from your brother or sister's bed.

2. Both of you want to entertain friends in your room at the same time. Sisters and brothers can agree on which days during the week each gets to have the room privately. If you want to switch days, you can. But set up a schedule that both of you think is fair. Then you'll know which days are yours, and you can respect each other's privacy.

3. One of you wants to listen to the radio or watch TV and the other doesn't. Again, work out a fair schedule.

Remember that every once in a while you're going to have to compromise and give in to the other's wishes. Also, you can agree on certain "quiet hours," when no music or TV will be allowed unless both agree. Those are the times when homework or reading get done in silence.

4. One person needs privacy to talk to a friend on the phone. In a polite way, you can ask if the other person would please leave the room for a while. After all, it's a two-way bargain, and if you cooperate at such times, your brother or sister will, too, when it's their turn. If this doesn't work out, take the call in another room.

5. One person wants to get up earlier than the other but the other person doesn't want to be disturbed. The one who wants to get up earlier can agree to be *verrrry* quiet. He or she can put out their clothes the night before so they don't make a lot of noise when getting dressed. He or she can also keep some books or games near the bed so they have something quiet to do until the other gets up.

6. Both feel they don't have enough room for their things. First, you have to make sure you're really dividing the available space equally. If it's still crowded, ask a parent to help create more room by adding shelves to closets, hanging more hooks for clothes, and getting some storage boxes that can be hidden underneath beds. You can also ask other members of the family if they will let you use some of their drawers or closet space. As a last resort, you can always get rid of some junk.

7. The two of you wind up arguing because one keeps using the other's things. Set down some rules, such as each one having to ask permission for certain items while other things become "common property." Post the rules in the room on a sign. Anyone who breaks a rule has to put a quarter into a special envelope. After a while the money gets used to buy something nice for the room, like a poster, a plant, or a new game that must be shared.

10 THINGS YOU CAN DO WHEN YOUR PARENTS FIGHT

When parents fight, it doesn't mean they don't love each other. There are many reasons why parents argue. They may be pressured or upset about money or work and could be taking out their frustrations on each other. If you are seriously worried about their relationship, wait until the battle is over and talk to them honestly about your concern. Here are some things you can do to avoid the fight; it's rarely a good idea to get involved.

1. Take a walk.

2. Go outside and do something physical (like running or playing ball) to relieve some of your own anger and frustration.

3. Go into your room, shut your door, and turn up the TV, stereo, or radio so you can't hear the noise.

4. Call someone on the telephone and talk to them to take your mind off the fighting.

5. Take a shower.

6. Get involved in a really good book.

7. Go visit someone.

8. Spend the time with a brother or sister who may need your help at this time just as much as you need theirs.

9. Give the dog a bath.

10. Write down on a piece of paper how the fighting is making you feel. Either keep your notes private or share them with your parents later on. After they've read your notes, you can talk with them about your feelings.

KIDS' REACTIONS TO FINDING OUT THAT THEIR PARENTS ARE GETTING SEPARATED OR DIVORCED

If your parents are splitting up, or already have, it may help you to know that other kids have felt the same way you do. Or if a friend's parents are separating, this list will help you understand what your friend might be going through. If the separation is happening in your family, it's very important to talk about your feelings with your parents. If you can't speak to them for any reason, see the list "People You Can Talk with If You Can't Talk to Your Parents" on page 32. They may be able to listen and advise you. Talking can help you understand your feelings better. It can be a comfort just to know someone cares enough to listen. And since it really can hurt to keep all those bad feelings inside, it's often a great relief to get the feelings out.

1. Anger that a parent has already left before you knew they were leaving, with no time for saying goodbye or for getting used to the idea first.

2. Anger that your parents are splitting up when you want so badly for them to stay together.

3. Frustration at not being able to change the situation.

4. Being confused as to how your life will change, whom you will live with, and so on.

5. Confusion, anger, hurt, and sadness at being put in the middle—for instance, when either parent tries to make you think the other is horrible.

6. Not knowing what to do when they compete to win you

over to their side—like if one buys you a lot of things or gives you extra freedom but you know they're only doing it so you'll be on their side.

7. Fear about having your whole life change.

8. Being scared that you won't see one parent that much anymore and that they won't love you as much as they have.

9. Feeling stupid because the whole thing came to you as a surprise and no one even hinted that it was going to happen.

10. Great relief! For many kids, fighting between parents is horrible to hear, and the sadness, strain, and frustration felt when living with parents you know are not happy together are very hard to deal with. Many kids have said they couldn't wait for their parents to separate so they could have a peaceful home again.

11. Confusion over finding yourself behaving in ways you don't understand. For instance, some kids take out their frustration by misbehaving in school or being rude to friends they really like.

11 DIFFERENT KINDS OF FAMILIES

Family life in the United States has changed in recent years, and the term "normal family" has taken on new meanings. There are now many different kinds of families that are considered typical or normal.

1. Dad works and Mom stays at home and takes care of the kids and household.

2. Mom and Dad both work and children have babysitter or go to a day care center.

3. Mom and Dad are divorced. The children live with one

parent and visit the other or take turns living with each parent.

4. Mom works and Dad stays home and takes care of the kids and the household. Ever see the movie *Mr. Mom*?

5. One parent raises the children because the other parent is unable to be there.

6. Two men or two women raise children together.

7. Children live with foster parents or parents that have adopted them.

8. Children live with one natural parent and one stepparent.

9. Children live with relatives.

10. Children live with parents sometimes and other relatives other times.

11. An older person such as a grandparent lives with the family.

9 TIPS FOR KIDS WHO LIVE IN STEPFAMILIES

Today, more than half the kids in the United States live with only one of their real parents. Becoming part of a new family when a single parent remarries can be a great adventure. You sometimes get new siblings, new grandparents, and a new place to live. But leaving the old arrangement behind can hurt, too. Here are some ideas that can help.

1. Try to be happy for the parent who is getting married, even if you are sad for yourself. Chances are they were lonely, just as you would be if you didn't have friends your own age.

2. Talk about how you feel. If you're afraid that your parent doesn't love you the way they used to, tell them, and give them a chance to make things right if they have been ignoring you. Listen to what they have to say.

3. If you have new brothers or sisters, consider yourself lucky: fewer chores for you!

4. You may feel funny about getting along with the new stepparent. You may think that you are not being loyal to another parent if you are nice to this one. But that's not how love works. You can be friendly with your stepparent and still let your absent parent know that you love them and that they are not being replaced.

5. Take the time to get to know your stepfamily. Maybe they know things you want to learn about. Maybe they would like to learn to do something that you know how to do. Look at this time as an opportunity to make your world of knowledge a little larger.

6. Be patient. Friendships don't happen overnight. It is going to take time for your new family to adjust to all the changes, especially the new living arrangements.

7. If you've had to move away from your old neighborhood, try to arrange for an old friend to come visit.

8. If you've tried everything and there's still a lot of fighting going on, call a truce. Sit down with the other family members and say, "We're never going to feel the same way about this issue. Let's just come to some sort of agreement so we can stop arguing all the time."

9. Ask yourself this one important question and answer it honestly: "What's it like to live with me?"

THE 6 WORST THINGS ABOUT BEING PART OF A LARGE FAMILY

Note that the last item on this list also appears on our list of "The 9 Best Things About Being Part of a Large Family."

1. It's hard to have privacy.

2. You usually have to wait to get into the bathroom.

3. Each kid may have less private time with his or her own parents.

4. You have to share your things with more people.

5. You may have more responsibilities (such as having to babysit for a younger brother or sister), which gives you less time to be with friends.

6. You have to wear a lot of hand-me-downs.

THE 9 BEST THINGS ABOUT BEING PART OF A LARGE FAMILY

1. You're hardly ever lonely because there's usually someone around to be with.

2. You can get great hand-me-downs and have lots of extra clothes.

3. You usually have someone around to help you with your homework.

4. There's usually someone there to give you advice when you need it.

5. There's lots of activity in a large family, which makes it fun, and you're rarely bored.

6. You get to meet and have relationships with your sister's or brother's friends.

7. Holiday and birthday celebrations are even more festive with lots of people around.

8. If you get into trouble with your parents, a brother or sister is likely to stick up for you.

9. If something really awful happens, like a family crisis, there are lots of people around to share the feelings with.

THE 10 WORST THINGS ABOUT HAVING A YOUNGER BROTHER OR SISTER

1. They get in the way when your friends are around.

2. You have to babysit for them when you'd rather go out with your friends (or babysit for someone else and get paid for it).

3. They get into your drawers, invade your privacy, or use something of yours.

4. Your parents make a big fuss about them every time they do something "cute," and you feel you don't get as much attention.

5. Sometimes they get the same privileges as you even though you're older.

6. Parents expect you to teach them how to behave, so if they get into trouble, you wind up getting part of the blame.

7. They may embarrass you in front of your friends.

8. They may want to play with your things before they really know how to care for them properly.

9. They can be very noisy when you'd prefer quiet times.

10. They ask a lot of questions.

THE 8 BEST THINGS ABOUT BEING AN ONLY CHILD

1. You always have your parents' complete attention—you're the star!

2. You don't have to share your things with a sister or brother.

3. You get to have your own room.

4. You always have the privacy you need.

5. You don't have to deal with parents always comparing you to a brother or sister.

6. You don't ever have to babysit for a sibling.

7. Parents are more likely to take you on vacation with them, since there's only one to pay for.

8. All your clothes and things are brought especially for you.

THE 7 WORST THINGS ABOUT BEING AN ONLY CHILD

1. Being by yourself can be boring and lonely.

2. There's no one around to introduce you to new friends.

3. There's no older child to give you advice.

4. If you get into trouble with your parents, you have no one to defend you.

5. You don't have a sister or brother with whom to share feelings about your parents or other relatives.

6. Parents tend to be overprotective when they only have one child.

7. There's no one around to borrow things from.

10 PROBLEMS TWINS HAVE

If you're a twin, you know that most of your problems stem from the world expecting you both to be the same. But like any other kid on this planet, you're an original, even if you look exactly like a sister or brother. Be patient if you can; the world will catch on eventually. But here are some of the problems you're likely to encounter in the meantime.

1. Friends sometimes can't tell twins apart.

2. Sometimes people expect twins to always like the same things.

3. One twin gets better grades than the other.

4. One twin gets a girlfriend or boyfriend first.

5. One twin is more popular.

6. One twin has a special talent that the other doesn't have.

7. One twin starts to develop earlier than the other.

8. Everyone expects twins to be close and hang out together, but sometimes twins don't get along.

9. Dealing with kids who are friendly with one twin but not the other.

10. One twin might want to dress the same while the other wants to dress differently.

HOW MARY KATE OLSEN & ASHLEY OLSEN DIFFER

TV's famous twins are not *identical.*

Ashley	*Mary Kate*
Sings	Dances
Righty	Lefty
Wants to be a ballerina	Wants to be a cowgirl
Enjoys reading books	Would rather play Nintendo

CHAPTER THREE

TOYS, GAMES, AND HOBBIES

9 CONTESTS YOU MIGHT WANT TO ENTER

1. National Children's Whistling Championship
Franklin County Arts Council
P.O. Box 758
Louisburg, N.C. 27549

Each year Louisburg, North Carolina, becomes the world's whistling capital. Performances are judged for inventiveness, artistry, and originality. The first-place winner gets a cash prize, a trophy, and a ribbon.

2. All-American Soap Box Derby
P.O. Box 7233
Derby Downs
Akron, OH 44306

Soap Box Derby cars—"cars" that kids build out of crates—have been popular for most of this century, probably because anyone can build them and they're so much fun. This contest is pretty serious, though, and you can only enter if you've won a local Soap Box race first.

3. American Double Dutch League Competitions
P.O. Box 776
Bronx, N.Y. 10451

If jumping rope is your thing, you might want to find out how to start a double dutch contest in your neighborhood. (By the way, for a great example of double dutch rope-jumping, see Whoopi Goldberg do it in the movie *Sister Act.*)

4. National Rotten Sneaker Championship
Montpelier Recreation Dept.

55 Barre St.
Montpelier, VT 05602

If your sneakers look (and smell) like they've been through a world war, this one is for you, and you can enter even if you don't live anywhere near Vermont. To find a local event, write to:

Julie Bohl
Rotten Sneaker Coordinator
Odor-Eaters Insoles
P.O. Box 328 RSM
White Plains, N.Y. 10602

Your smelly old sneakers could win you the grand prize of a $500 U. S. savings bond, plus a lot of other goodies, including a new pair of sneakers!

5. Invent America Contest
U. S. Patent Model Foundation
510 King St.
Suite 420
Alexandria, VA 22314

Robert Patch is the youngest inventor ever. In 1962, when he was only 5, he designed a toy truck that could be taken apart and put back together.

You can only enter this contest through your school, but if you're the kind of kid who's always dreaming up great ideas, here's a chance to cash in on one of them. Many prizes are offered, including a $1,000 U.S. savings bond.

6. Odyssey of the Mind Competitions
Odyssey of the Mind Association, Inc.
P.O. Box 27
Glassboro, N.J. 08028

More than 600 teams of kids work on finding creative solutions to problems. For instance, in one year's contest, kids were asked to use mousetraps to start chain reactions. Another team had to construct a vehicle that would fit into two suitcases. Kids from all over the world compete in these events.

7. Jumping Frog Jubilee
Calaveras County Fair
P.O. Box 96
Angels Camp, CA 95222

Probably one of the oldest frog-jumping contests. You can even read about this one in Mark Twain's famous story "The Celebrated Jumping Frog of Calaveras County." Any frog that sets a new world's record gets a $1,500 prize. The current record is held by Rosie the Ribiter, who jumped a little over 21 feet in one leap.

8. Junior Manure Pitch-Off
Main Organic Farmers and Gardeners Association
P.O. Box 2176
Augusta, ME 04330

This contest stinks! We can't imagine why, but each September at the Main Common Ground County Fair, kids 14 and under get together to find out who can spread the most manure the fastest.

9. National Fence Painting Contest
Hannibal Jaycees
P.O. Box 230
Hannibal, MO 63401

This contest is part of National Tom Sawyer Day, in which boys get dressed up like Mark Twain's famous character and paint fences to see who can do it best and fastest (girls cannot participate in this contest). Other contests at this celebration include bubble gum blowing and watermelon seed spitting (girls can participate in these contests). All sorts of prizes are donated by local merchants.

TIPS FOR EASIER TOY ASSEMBLY

Before you buy any toy, find out, by reading the package, how much assembly is required. If it's clearly something you can't put together yourself, make sure you have help lined up before you spend your money. *Always keep the sales receipts and warranties.* Fill out and send in the warranty registration card if the toy came with one. Then you can begin.

1. Make sure you have a well-lit, clear space to work in.

2. Open the box carefully, so that if the toy has to be returned, it can be replaced just the way you got it. Don't throw anything away!

3. Read through the instructions before you start assembling, just to get an overall idea of what's involved. If anything seems beyond you, get help.

4. The instructions should include a list of parts. Make sure you have all the parts before you begin. If anything is missing, call the store where you bought the toy and ask them how to go about getting a replacement.

5. Have all the tools you'll need ready at hand.

6. Keep things organized while you work. Put all small parts together so they don't get lost. Use small dishes or paper cups to sort the pieces.

7. Work slowly and keep reading the instructions as you do each step. Do one step at a time, even if you think you know exactly what comes next. Be patient.

8. Save spare parts. Store them in a plastic bag together with the instructions and the warranty.

9. Read the instructions for *using* the toy once you're ready to play with it, even if you think you know exactly what to do.

HOW TO AVOID GETTING RIPPED OFF AT 8 CARNIVAL GAMES

Winning a prize at a carnival can be an expensive experience. There are some games that are easier to win at than others and there are some games that seem very easy but are nearly impossible to win. Stay away from any game that has complicated rules or rules that seem to change. Follow these tips and save yourself some money.

1. Wheel of Fortune. You are probably better off staying at home and watching the TV show. The best way to increase your chance of winning is to increase the number of your bets. This will increase your chances of winning. But it will also increase the amount of money you can lose.

2. Basketball. Basketball players beware! The ball you're using could be too large for the hoop. But if you feel like going for the prize anyway, shoot directly at the hoop and not the backboard. Be sure that the ceiling clearance is high enough for this kind of shot. If it isn't, move on to the next game.

3. Ring a Bottle. Throwing a ring around the neck of a bottle is nearly impossible. Some booth operators will themselves place rings around some bottles to mislead you into thinking they have been thrown on. They will also sometimes give you rings that are not wide enough to fit the neck of the bottle.

4. Guess Your Weight. The prize you win if you can fool the person guessing your weight may cost less than what you are paying to play the game. If you want to try your luck anyway, puff up your cheeks, stick out your stomach, and think fat. Good luck!

5. Swinger. This one is impossible to win. A pin or metal bottle is placed directly under a ball that is supposed to swing on a string and knock the pin down. If you miss the pin on the first swing it will never hit the bottle. The game operator will fool you by setting up a pin and knocking it down, only he won't place the pin directly under the ball but slightly off to the side.

6. Plate Pitch. The idea here is to toss a coin onto a plate and have it land on the plate. This is very difficult but not impossible. Aim for the back of the plate and hope it bounces back. If the plate doesn't have a rim, don't play. You'll just be throwing your money away.

7. Baseball and basket. Throwing a baseball into a wooden fruit basket and keeping it from bouncing out is not easy. The bottom of the basket is very springy and will send the ball sailing out. Aim for the side of the rim, even if you have to step off to the side a little. Or throw the ball gently so that it just makes it over the bottom rim.

8. Water Balloon Race. This game only requires a steady hand, good eyes, and a little luck. There is always a winner at this one, and it could be you.

TOY TRIVIA

1. The teddy bear, which first appeared in 1902, was named after President Theodore Roosevelt.

2. The Raggedy Ann doll was named after the comic strip character Little Orphan Annie.

3. Roller skates, which were patented in 1863 by James Plimpton, first became a fad in the 1860s.

4. Silly Putty was first created by the General Electric Company as a substitute for rubber, but it was found to have no industrial uses, so it was marketed as a toy instead.

5. The Frisbee flying disc was named after the Frisbee Company of Bridgeport, Connecticut, which manufactured pie plates. (The flying disc got its start as a toy when someone noticed that college kids liked tossing the plates to one another for fun.)

6. The Hula Hoop is known to be the greatest fad in toy history. When it was first made in the 1950s, it sold 20 million in the first year.

7. The yo-yo got its start as a weapon used by the Philippine Island warriors in the sixteenth century. Theirs was a four-pound sphere with a 20-foot cord. The first toy version appeared in the United States in 1929, developed by Louis Marx, the famous toy manufacturer.

8. Dominoes were created by French monks. They named the game after the first line of Psalm 110 from the Bible, which reads in Latin, "Dixit Dominus meo" ("The Lord said to my Lord").

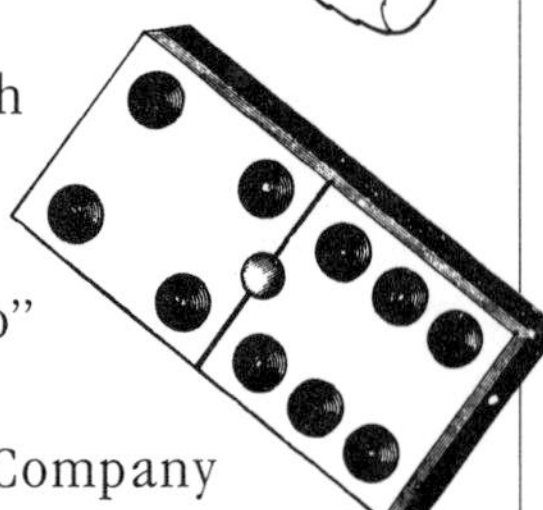

9. Each year the Parker Brothers Company prints more play money than the U.S. Mint prints real money.

HOW TO JUDGE A TOY

If you follow these tips when you go toy shopping, you'll probably wind up with toys that last longer and hold your interest. It really doesn't make sense to spend a lot of money on something that will only last a short time, especially since toy prices have risen so high. (See "5 Tips for Toy Shoppers," which follows this list.)

1. Toys should be creative. This means that you're better off with a toy that does a lot of different things, as opposed to a toy that does the same thing every time you play with it. For instance, Lego and Construx, two building sets that come in different "editions," let you build things a variety of ways, and the different kinds of pieces included challenge your imagination and allow you to make more complicated things as you "grow" with the toy.

2. Toys should be convenient. You probably already know that toys that take a long time to set up get played with far less than toys that are ready when you are. A lot of the racing car sets for sale today look like a lot of fun, but they take up too much space to stay assembled in your play area all the time. Unless you have lots of room, don't spend a lot of money on car sets with huge tracks. Remember that toys that require adult help because they are complicated will only get played with when an adult is available. That may not be as often as you like.

3. Toys should be challenging. Of course, playing isn't supposed to be work, but if a toy is too easy to master—like a video game that only has one screen—you'll probably get bored with it quickly. When you shop, look for toys that may be a little bit complicated. Chances are you'll learn something from them.

4. Toys should be original. Watch out for new versions of old toys—you could be buying the same toy you already have, only with a different package and a new name. If you already own a racecar set, make sure that the one you're thinking of buying does something that your old one doesn't do. You'll also find many copycats among handheld video games.

5 TIPS FOR TOY SHOPPERS

Toys are a multibillion-dollar industry in America, meaning there are many different companies out there trying to get your attention—and your money. You'll get more for your money if you keep these pointers in mind when you shop for toys.

1. Compare prices. If you compare prices for the same toy at different stores, you'll find a difference of 5, 10, or even 20 dollars, depending on the toy. Call a few stores before you make your purchase or check newspaper ads for sales and bargains. You could save enough money to buy a whole other toy!

2. Test the toy before you buy. This may not always be possible, since stores don't have display models for everything they sell. Ask a friend who already has the toy if you can try it out, or just get other opinions from kids you know or by consulting a computer forum. In the case of home video games, you can try out the arcade version, but be careful: These can often be *very* different from one another.

3. Don't buy something just because it looks great on TV. Toys rarely work in real life the way they do in commercials, which we think is *very* unfair. TV commercials use special effects, and let's face it: the kids in the commercials are being paid to look like they're having a great time. (See

"6 Ways in Which Advertisers Try to Get You to Buy Toys," which follows this list.) Pictures on boxes often are also misleading. If you can, try to get a look at the real thing before you buy it.

4. Check warranties. In many cases, if the toy breaks down after you've played with it a few times, you can get your money back—but only on the toys that have warranties and for which you have held onto the warranty (sometimes on the box; sometimes inside). Even if you lose these or throw them out by mistake, large toy stores and department stores will usually try to help you if you are able to show that there was something wrong with the toy when you got it.

5. Find out whether batteries are included with the toy. It's always frustrating to rush home to play with a new toy, only to discover that you'll have to make another shopping trip to get the necessary batteries. Read the writing on the box before you head home for the fun.

6 WAYS IN WHICH ADVERTISERS TRY TO GET YOU TO BUY TOYS

According to the law, the items you buy at a store are supposed to look just as they do in an advertisement. Unfortunately, that's not the way it always works out. Here are some of the ways in which advertisers cheat. If you wind up being the victim of unfair advertising, do something about it. Start by taking a look at "7 Things You Can Do If You Get Ripped Off," page 60.

1. Advertisers make the product look better on TV than it does in real life. For example, when you see a toy oven "that really bakes," the advertiser shows perfectly scrumptious-looking golden cookies coming out the oven door. But chances are, those cookies were baked in a professional oven. Yours won't look like those!

2. With hobby kits, advertisers may make you think something will take just minutes to finish, but often there are many steps and you have to wait a full day between steps.

3. They *do* let you know when toys require assembly. What they *don't* tell you is that assembly may be very complicated, involving more than 40 parts and badly written instructions.

4. They make you think the toy makes sounds or creates effects that are really just part of the TV commercial. This is especially true of ads for video games and space toys. More often than not, the sounds you hear are *not* coming from the toy.

5. They try to make you feel like you're not being loyal to your favorite TV character if you don't rush out and buy the toy with his or her picture all over it. They sometimes do this by showing lots of kids playing with the toy, so you'll feel like the only kid in the world who doesn't have it.

6. They make things look bigger than they really are. Sometimes they do this by packing small toys in large boxes that are mostly filled with cardboard. (Don't forget to recycle this stuff!) Or they show you a picture of the toy standing by itself, so you're not really sure how large it is.

TOY PRICES, 1897

In 1897, Sears Roebuck and Company called themselves "the cheapest supply house on earth." Their hefty catalog, which listed everything from ladies' underwear to farm equipment, didn't have a toy section, since most kids made their own toys back then. But the following items appeared in the catalog at prices that make us want to turn back the hands of time.

1. A pair of steel-blade ice skates: 62¢
2. The Spalding Official Boys' League baseball: 72¢
3. The Spalding boys' catcher's mitt: 20¢
4. Toy wagons made of solid steel: starting at $1.15
5. Rocking horses called "shoo-fly horses": 75¢
6. A deck of Tally-Ho playing cards: 13¢
7. The Brass Band harmonica, advertised as "the king of harmonicas": 22¢
8. Girls' 20-inch, two-wheel bicycles: $29.00
9. Girls' toy brooms: 9¢
10. Steel toy safe, ancestor of the piggy bank: 25¢

20 KINDS OF MARBLES

Marbles have been around since ancient times and have fascinated children, artists, and collectors. You can still buy ordinary marbles at any toy store—or you can pay thousands of dollars for the rarest ones!

1. Aggies
2. Bird's eggs
3. Bumblebees
4. Cat's-eyes
5. Clearies
6. Clouds
7. Comics
8. Corkscrews
9. Cub scouts
10. Flames
11. Gooseberries
12. Indians
13. Lutzes
14. Micas
15. Onionskins
16. Oxbloods
17. Popeyes
18. Purees
19. Rolled commies
20. Root beer floats

THE CRAYON HALL OF FAME, PART 1

8 Colors That Crayola Stopped Making in 1990

1. Blue gray
2. Green blue
3. Lemon yellow
4. Maize
5. Orange red
6. Orange yellow
7. Raw amber
8. Violet blue

THE CRAYON HALL OF FAME, PART 2

8 New Colors

1. Cerulean
2. Dandelion
3. Fuchsia
4. Jungle green
5. Royal purple
6. Teal blue
7. Vivid tangerine
8. Wild strawberry

7 GAK TIPS

You can squish it, stretch it, inflate it, splat it, and make it slurp, but can you make it last? No! Gak, a gooey and slippery ooze, is more than half liquid. Every time you play with it, it looses moisture, and this causes the Gak to dry up and shrink. There are a few things you can do to make your Gak last longer.

1. Add a teaspoon of water to its container after each time you use it.

2. Snap the lid of the container back on by pressing down of the center of the lid so that air is forced out.

3. Keep Gak off cloth surfaces. Cloth will soak liquid out of Gak.

4. Don't let your Gak get too hot or cold.

5. Keep your Gak clean.

6. The less you use it the fresher it will stay.

7. Don't feed it after midnight.

PLAY-DOH HISTORY

Squish it. Squeeze it. Turn it into anything. You've probably been playing with the stuff all your life. But did you know that the Playskool company, which makes Play-Doh, still keeps the top-secret formula under lock and key—or that there was a time when our government conducted experiments to find out whether Play-Doh could be used for military purposes? (The answer was no!) Here's a history lesson you won't learn in school.

1956: In Cincinnati, scientists experimenting with soap and cleaning solutions discover Play-Doh, a nontoxic modeling compound that's easy to mold. They sell the stuff in one color—off-white—in department stores in 1½-pound cans.

1957: Three new colors are added—red, yellow, and blue. The first TV advertisements appear for Play-Doh on *Captain Kangaroo* and *Ding Dong School*.

1958: Now you can buy the

handy four-pack of Play-Doh, with a can for each color.

1959: Play-Doh introduces the first "accessories" to help kids make Play-Doh objects, the Pixie-Pak and the Little Baker's Set. Future accessories will include the Play-Doh Forge Press, the Play-Doh Fuzzy Pumper, Shape Makers, the Play-Doh Zoo Set, Funny Frogs, and the Bake 'N Cake Shop, among others. Later on, these products will be based on popular TV and film characters, such as those from *Star Wars, The Bionic Woman, The Care Bears,* Disney's *Duck Tales, Beetlejuice,* and the Hanna Barbera cartoon characters.

1960: The Play-Doh Boy is born, to be used in advertising.

1963: Mini-cans of the stuff go on sale for the first time.

1964: Play-Doh is introduced in England, France, and Italy.

1972: Play-Doh manufactures its 5 millionth can.

1976: A man in Virginia creates a replica of Monticello with 2,500 bricks made of Play-Doh. His effort is recorded in Play-Doh history as the most ambitious use of Play-Doh ever.

1979: Play-Doh is first sold in a three-pound container.

1980: National Play-Doh Day is celebrated for the first time on September 16.

1983: Four bright colors are added to the original four, and now Play-Doh comes in the Rainbow 8-Pack.

1987: Glow-in-the-dark Play-Doh is sold as part of the Real Ghostbusters Playset.

1991: Play-Doh celebrates its 35th birthday as one of America's most popular toys.

1992: Sparkling Play-Doh, with glitter mixed into it, is sold for the first time.

THE G.I. JOE OATH OF HONOR

G.I. Joe was named after a character in the movie *The Story of G.I. Joe* and was the world's first "action figure," manufactured by Hasbro Toys. Thirty years later, the term "G.I. Joe" refers not only to one toy but to a whole line of toys representing every branch of the U.S. armed forces and even some foreign ones. He's been through a lot of wars but still believes the same things he did when he started out. G.I. Joe always:

1. Defends the rights of others and neutralizes evil wherever it exists

2. Maintains good health by eating the right foods, getting plenty of PT (physical training), and staying away from drugs and alcohol

3. Obeys the law and does the right thing

4. Answers the call for help from those who need it.

YOU'VE COME A LONG WAY, BARBIE!

In 1959 Ken and Barbie Handler, who founded the Mattel toy company, introduced one of the most successful toys ever—the Barbie doll. By the time Barbie turned 25 in 1984, 200 million Barbie dolls and other members of her family had been sold worldwide, and over the years, kids had purchased more than 20 million of her fashions annually. Barbie has lots more competition these days than she did back in 1959, but she's managed to stay among the favorites, mostly due to Mattel's introduction of new developments over the years. Here are some of them.

1. In 1961 Barbie was no longer presented as just a glamour doll. Bar
stewardess o
kits—a nur
even an astro
years!

2. Barbie
veloped. Ech
with heavy e
the other ha
she first wor

3. In 196

4. In 196
time, made

5. In 196
could use to

6. In 196

7. In 1971 Barbie got her own motorized stage, which made the Live Action Barbie dance.

8. In 1976 Barbie smiled for the first time, when Olympic-hopeful Gold Medal Barbie was introduced.

9. In 1979, Kissing Barbie came with puckered lips and a button in the back so that she could give "real" kisses.

10. In 1981 Black Barbie was introduced. She wore an Afro and a bright red African style dress. Mattel took this one off the market because many people complained that the doll didn't represent black people realistically.

11. In 1984 Barbie's "family" had grown to include Ken, Skipper, P.J., Christie, Tracy, Todd, and a host of other friends.

12. In 1989 UNICEF Barbie sold in four versions: Oriental, Hispanic, black, and white.

13. In 1990 Ken got his ear pierced; Earring Magic Ken quickly became a collector's item.

14. In 1993, Native American Barbie, complete with long black braids and beaded dress, came and then quickly went. Native Americans accused Mattel of racism, and Mattel responded by removing the doll from toy shelves.

15. In 1994, Barbie celebrated her 35th birthday with special Barbie boutiques in toy department stores.

THIS SPUD'S FOR YOU

The Life Story of Mr. Potato Head

1952: Mr. Potato Head is born as a kit with eyes, ears, mouth, a pipe, and noses. You had to have your own potato!

1953: Mr. Potato Head meets and marries Mrs. Potato Head. They honeymoon in Boise, Idaho, the potato capital of the United States.

1964: Mr. and Mrs. Potato Head get their plastic bodies, which now come with the kits.

1966: Mr. Potato Head becomes Jumpin' Mr. Potato Head, with a head that moves up and down. All Mrs. Potato Head gets is a vacuum cleaner, a floor polisher, and a bell, to let Mr. Potato Head know when it's time to eat.

1974: At the age of 22, Mr. Potato Head has gained a lot weight. In fact, he's doubled in size. (Guess that little dinner bell really works!)

1983: Mr. Potato Head now comes with his own storage compartment for all his extra parts.

1985: Four people vote for Mr. Potato Head for mayor of Boise. He loses the election in a landslide.

1987: At the suggestion of those who know smoking is unhealthy, Mr. Potato Head gives up smoking and loses the pipe.

8 TOYS THAT WERE POPULAR IN THE 1950s AND ARE STILL POPULAR TODAY

1. Barbie dolls
2. Erector building sets
3. Etch-a-Sketch
4. The Hula Hoop
5. Lincoln Logs
6. Pogo sticks
7. Silly Putty
8. The yo-yo

23 CONSTRUCTION TOYS

The following construction sets are available for kids aged 3 to 14.

1. Better Bloks
2. Bigger Better Blocks
3. Bric Builders
4. Brik
5. Buildem Blocks
6. Builderific
7. Capsela
8. Duplo
9. Erector
10. Girder and Panel Building System
11. Googolplex
12. Kids at Work
13. K' Nex
14. Lego
15. Lincoln Logs
16. Lunapark Gear Set
17. Main Street Build & Play Set
18. Meccano
19. Mega Bloks
20. Paul Bunyan Log Builders
21. Tinker Toys
22. Tootsietoy Wood Blocks
23. Wood Builders

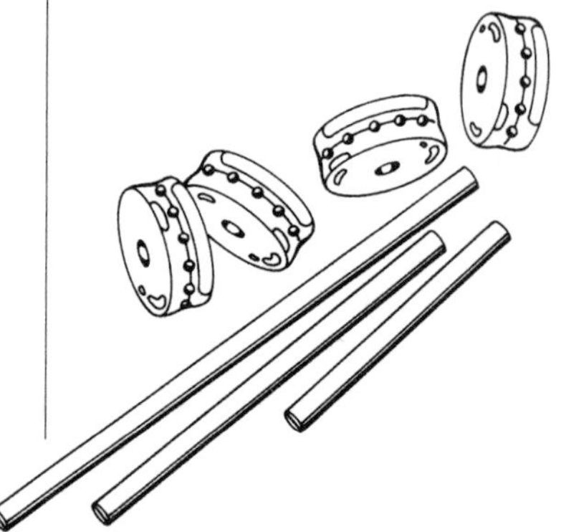

20 BOARD GAMES BASED ON BOOKS, TV SHOWS, AND MOVIES

1. The Babysitters Club
2. Barney
3. Batman
4. Cheers
5. Clarissa Explains It All Game
6. Escape from Frankenstein
7. Family Feud
8. Full House
9. Home Alone
10. Jeopardy!
11. Jurassic Park
12. Last Action Hero
13. The Lion King
14. Mighty Morphin Power Rangers
15. The Ren & Stimpy Show Log Cereal Game
16. Revenge of Dracula
17. Saturday Night Live
18. The Shadow
19. Star Trek, The Next Generation (three different games)
20. X-Men (two different games)

THE 10 HIGHEST-SCORING WORDS IN SCRABBLE

All of these are seven-letter words, so you also get a 50-point bonus if you can make any of them. Of course, we assume that you know what these words mean.

1. BEZIQUE
2. CAZIQUE
3. JAZZILY
4. QUARTZY
5. QUETZAL
6. QUIZZED
7. ZEPHYRS
8. ZINCIFY
9. ZINKIFY
10. ZYTHUMS

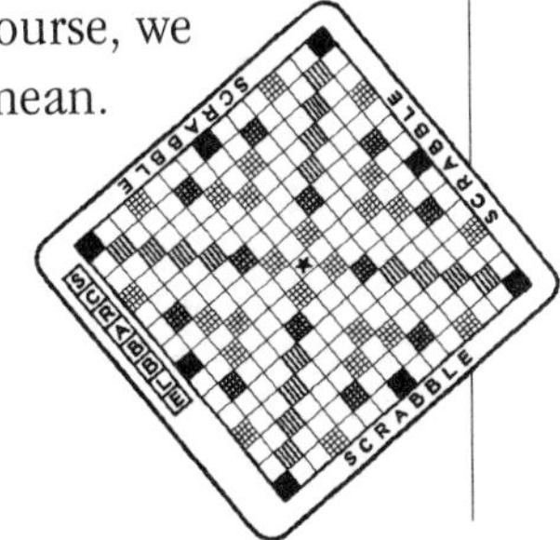

39 THINGS THAT KIDS COLLECT

1. Action figures
2. Advertising signs
3. Animal figures
4. Autographs of famous people
5. Barbie dolls
6. Baseball cards
7. Birds' nests
8. Buttons, badges, patches, and pins

9. Bookmarks
10. Books
11. Bottle caps
12. Butterflies
13. CDs and cassette tapes
14. Chess sets
15. Comic books
16. Dolls and dollhouses
17. Dried flowers
18. Gum wrappers
19. Horse figurines
20. Hot Wheels cars
21. Insects
22. Keys
23. Leaves
24. Maps
25. Marbles
26. Matchbox cars
27. Miniatures
28. Models
29. Movies on video
30. Paper dolls
31. Postcards
32. Posters
33. Rocks
34. Seashells
35. Stamps
36. Stickers
37. Teddy bears
38. Troll dolls
39. Video games

THE MOST LANDED-ON SQUARES IN MONOPOLY

The board game Monopoly was first invented in 1936. Today it is available in 23 different languages, each of which uses the local currency for its play money: In South America you play for rands, in Peru you play for sols, and in Austria you play for schillings. Monopoly is the best-selling copyrighted game of all time, having sold more than 1 billion sets. The following are the squares people land on most often when they play the game, so be sure to buy the properties if you have a chance to do so.

1. Illinois Ave.
2. Go
3. B&O Railroad
4. Free Parking
5. Tennessee Ave.
6. New York Ave.
7. Reading Railroad
8. St. James Place
9. Water Works
10. Pennsylvania Railroad

14 BOARD GAMES—BESIDES MONOPOLY—THAT TEACH YOU HOW TO HANDLE MONEY

1. The Allowance Game (Lakeshore Learning Materials)
2. Ax Your Tax (Parker Brothers)
3. The Game of Life (Milton Bradley)
4. Hotels (Milton Bradley)
5. Interplay Rat Race (Waddington)
6. The Inventors (Parker Brothers)
7. Money Card (Schaper)
8. Power Barrons (Milton Bradley)

9. Rags to Riches (Computer Market Simulation)
10. The Reward Game (National Center for Financial Education)
11. Roup (Porter Planet-3)
12. $peculation (Cayla)
13. Stocks and Bonds (Avalon Hill)
14. Trump the Game (Milton Bradley)

75 AUTOGRAPHS TO COLLECT

If you're an autograph hound, here are some special autographs to be on the lookout for. These are often sold by professional autograph dealers for high prices, so if you're lucky enough to bump into Steven Spielberg or Arnold Schwarzenegger at the mall, be sure to (politely) ask for an autograph. For more information, check out *Autograph Collector Magazine,* 510-A South Corona Mall, Corona, CA 91719-1420; (909) 734-9636.

1. Paula Abdul
2. Muhammad Ali
3. Christina Applegate
4. Roseanne Barr
5. Drew Barrymore
6. Christie Brinkley
7. David Bowie
8. Clint Black
9. Jon Bon Jovi
10. Matthew Broderick
11. Jeff Bridges
12. George Burns
13. Jennifer Capriati
14. Mariah Carey
15. Nicholas Cage
16. Dana Carvey
17. Phoebe Cates
18. Connie Chung
19. Wilt Chamberlain
20. Eric Clapton
21. Bill Clinton
22. Hillary Clinton
23. Cindy Crawford
24. Tom Cruise
25. Billy Crystal
26. Bill Cosby
27. Danny DeVito
28. Laura Dern

29. Robert De Niro
30. Richard Dreyfuss
31. Sheena Easton
32. Clint Eastwood
33. Gloria Estefan
34. Jodi Foster
35. Harrison Ford
36. Michael J. Fox
37. Debbie Gibson
38. Whoopi Goldberg
39. Al Gore
40. Tom Hanks
41. Whitney Houston
42. Janet Jackson
43. Latoya Jackson
44. Michael Jackson
45. Mick Jagger
46. Michael Jordan
47. Michael Keaton
48. Spike Lee
49. Rob Lowe
50. Marky Mark
51. Reba McEntire
52. Eddie Murphy
53. Tatum O'Neal
54. Sinéad O'Connor
55. Luke Perry
56. Lou Diamond Phillips
57. Jason Priestley
58. Martha Plimpton
59. Winona Ryder
60. Roy Rogers
61. Arnold Schwarzenegger
62. Steven Seagal
63. Brooke Shields
64. O. J. Simpson
65. Christian Slater
66. Steven Spielberg
67. Bruce Springsteen
68. Barbra Streisand
69. Patrick Swayze
70. Sylvester Stallone
71. Kiefer Sutherland
72. Kathleen Turner
73. Donald Trump
74. Jean-Claude Van Damme
75. Vanilla Ice

TIPS FOR GETTING CELEBRITIES TO RESPOND TO YOUR LETTERS

1. Send a photo of yourself. Celebrities will find it impossible to resist your adorable face!

2. Include a self-addressed stamped envelope. That

makes it easier for the celebrity to send something back.

3. Explain early in your letter (maybe even the first sentence) **why you are writing.** Do you have a question? Are you looking for an autograph? Say so.

4. Don't write a very long letter. These people *don't* have a lot of time.

5. Make sure your letter is neat and easy to read. If someone has to struggle to read what you write, they'll probably give up and throw it away.

6. Don't send anything that you expect to get back. Chances are, you won't.

11 TIPS FOR TRADING CARD COLLECTORS

Collecting trading cards can be a very enjoyable hobby for kids and adults. It's a great way to learn about your favorite sport or hobby and make new friends. It can also be exciting to find out that a card in your collection is worth a lot more than what you paid for it. Here are some tips from the pros.

1. Keep cards away from food and liquids.

2. Don't store cards in places that are very hot or damp.

3. You should store your cards in a notebook with plastic pages, place them in a plastic sleeve, or shield and keep them in a storage box. Storage supplies are available at trading card and comic stores.

4. Never hold cards together with rubber bands. This will damage the cards and reduce their value.

5. Sort cards by manufacturer, year (set), and number, not by team or players.

6. Establish a friendly relationship with your local card shop owner. He'll be more willing to help you and you will learn more about collecting. Never handle cards in the shop without permission.

7. If you buy cards in sets, you will usually spend less money than if you bought the cards one at a time.

8. Have a written list of the cards you're interested in acquiring whenever you are shopping or trading, so you don't wind up getting something you already have.

9. The best to collect are cards with mistakes on them.

10. Always buy, sell, and trade *fair*.

11. Even if you lose interest in collecting, don't throw any cards away. Store them properly. You may become interested in them at a later date—when they'll be more valuable.

TIPS FOR STORING COMIC BOOKS

Most paper has acid in it; acid makes paper age (it turns brown and crumples easily). We can't stop the aging process, but we can slow it down. Take good care of your comics if you want them to be worth more later on. Here's how.

1. Protect each comic book in its own acid-free plastic bag. (These and the other supplies mentioned here are available from comic book dealers. Check your yellow pages.)

2. The comic books, in their bags, should be stored vertically (standing up), not lying on top of each other. They should be stacked in special acid-free boxes.

3. Store the boxes in a cool (40°–50°), dark place with a relative humidity of 50°. Avoid heat, ultraviolet light, and dampness.

4. Keep your collection away from polluted air and dust.

5. Mylar bags should be changed every two or three years.

84 THINGS YOU CAN USE TO MAKE A COLLAGE

Here's something to do when there's nothing to do: Make a collage. All you need are a stiff piece of paper or board, some colorless glue, and your imagination. Choose from the items listed below or find others. Your collage can even center around a theme. For instance, if you were going to make a collage for someone who works as an accountant, you might use some play money, the stock market section of the newspaper, some pennies, and the person's business card. A get-well collage might consist of some Band-Aids, vitamins, a toy thermometer, and your special message spelled out in pasta alphabet letters. Be creative!

1. Absorbent cotton
2. Acorns
3. Aluminum foil
4. Band-Aids
5. Beads
6. Birthday cake ornaments
7. Bobby pins
8. Bottle caps
9. Bows
10. Business cards
11. Buttons
12. Candy wrappers
13. Carpet scraps
14. Cereals and grains
15. Clay
16. Coins
17. Colored mints
18. Comic strips
19. Confetti
20. Cranberries
21. Dried beans
22. Dried leaves
23. Egg shells
24. Fabric scraps
25. Feathers
26. Foil hearts
27. Foil stars

28. Food labels
29. Glitter
30. Graph paper
31. Inexpensive plastic toys
32. Jelly babies
33. Keys
34. Loose-leaf paper hole reinforcements
35. Maps
36. Newspaper
37. Nuts
38. Nuts and bolts
39. Paper clips
40. Paper doilies
41. Paper plates
42. Pasta
43. Pebbles
44. Pencil shavings
45. Pictures cut out of magazines
46. Pipe cleaners
47. Plastic animal eyes
48. Plastic flowers
49. Play money
50. Popped corn
51. Popsicle sticks
52. Postage stamps
53. Postcards
54. A report card
55. Ribbon
56. Rose petals
57. Rubber bands
58. Rubber-stamped impressions
59. Sand
60. Screws
61. Seeds
62. Sequins
63. Sheet music

64. Shells
65. Snapshots
66. Soda can tops
67. A special date circled on a calendar
68. Sponges
69. Spools of thread
70. Sports emblems
71. Stickers
72. Store receipts
73. String
74. Styrofoam bits
75. Ticket stubs
76. Tinsel
77. Toothpicks
78. Twigs
79. Twist ties
80. Vitamins
81. Wallpaper scraps
82. Wire
83. Wrapping paper
84. Yarn

10 GREAT GIFTS THAT COST UNDER $10

1. A poster of someone's favorite movie or TV star. Or find a film developer who can enlarge any snapshot to poster size. Who would resist a life-sized portrait of *you?*

2. Personalized pencils. You can order a dozen pencils with any name or message imprinted on them (like "Happy Birthday") through many large stationery stores and mail-order catalogs. Remember to plan this one in advance, as it usually takes about a month to get the pencils printed.

3. Cold cash, but wrapped and presented with a little imagination. You can put $10 (or less) worth of pennies in a fancy box or tape them together to make a very long "necklace." You can also put the pennies in a fancy jar, tie a ribbon around it, and paint the label "Mad Money" on the front. If the person takes public transportation, you can give them subway or bus tokens.

4. We've all been given birthday or anniversary cakes, but consider a get well cake (nothing too rich) or one that just says "I Love You" or "I'm Sorry," depending on the occasion. If you don't have enough money for a decorated cake, buy a plain one and make your own flag out of a toothpick and a small piece of paper with your personal message to place on the cake.

5. A supply of someone's favorite candy bar.

6. Lottery tickets. Who knows? Your $10 worth of lottery tickets may wind up being worth a million! However, most states that conduct lotteries have age requirements for the purchase of tickets, so get an adult to help you out.

7. An inexpensive pet—like a goldfish—appropriately

named. Name it for the occasion—"Happy Birthday" or "Merry Christmas," for example—or a favorite television or comic strip character. (Very important: Make sure the person really wants to have a pet and that they will take care of it before you make this kind of purchase.)

8. Put on some lipstick, press your lips against a piece of plain paper, and frame your permanent kiss.

9. Write different messages, such as "I Love You" and "Happy Birthday," on pieces of paper, insert them inside balloons, and then blow up the balloons. Your friend will have a bouquet of good wishes.

10. Call up someone using a push-button telephone, and when their answering machine picks up, play "Happy Birthday." Be sure to say your name before you hang up.

1 1 4 1 * 9
1 1 4 1 # 0
1 1 # 0 * 7 4
0 * 0 *

11 GREAT GIFTS THAT DON'T COST ANYTHING

1. A coupon booklet of special favors. You can draw coupons that look like gift certificates, indicating on each one that this certificate is good for one special chore, such as one hour of babysitting, one breakfast served in bed, one whole week of getting your regular chores done on time, or giving the dog a bath. Staple all the coupons together so they look like a little book.

2. An autographed picture of someone's favorite movie or

TV star. (See the list called "Tips for Getting Celebrities to Respond to Your Letters," page 147.)

3. You may not be able to afford to shop in the most expensive store in your neighborhood, but their shopping bags usually don't cost anything! Ask the storeowner for one and explain that the bag is a gift. This is an especially great gift if the shopping bag is real fancy. (Get two and call them "matching luggage!")

4. A personal birthday greeting from the governor of your state. In most states, if you write a letter to the governor in care of your state capitol, within six or eight weeks your friend will receive a birthday greeting, personally signed. The service doesn't cost anything.

5. Tickets to a TV show. These are usually free. Just write to the folks at the show at the address they include in the credits at the end of the program.

6. Dedicate a song to someone over the radio by calling the station and making the request. (Some stations won't do it, but many will.) Of course, you'll want to make sure that the person you're dedicating the song to is listening at just the right time. If you have a tape recorder, you can make a permanent recording of that special moment when your friend's name is announced.

7. Cheerios. Now that might not sound like the world's most exciting gift, but you can make it special by placing a few Cheerios in a small plastic bag, tying a thin ribbon to secure the package, and drawing a small attractive label that says "Bagel Seeds." It's an unusual novelty gift, and if it's really the thought that counts, you should get extra points for this one.

8. Be a slave for a day. That's right—one whole day (or maybe just an hour!) of doing nothing but chores for someone else.

9. The front page of a newspaper printed on the day someone was born. Most large newspapers will send you this if you request it in writing. Many offer the service for free; some may charge a dollar or two.

10. If you can't afford a dozen roses, you can plant flowers instead! What a nice surprise someone will have when those flowers—or vegetables—start to grow.

11. An old sock—stuffed with another old sock—makes a good gift for a pet.

32 OF THE YOUNGEST SPORTS STARS EVER

Sports is one area where you'll seldom be told, "Wait until you grow up." Since the end of World War II, there has been a great increase in the number of sports programs available to kids, and the application of science to sports has resulted in great advances in nutrition and sports technique. So it is hardly surprising that many of these athletes earned their special distinctions in recent years.

1. The youngest international competitor in any sport is Joy Foster, who represented Jamaica in the 1958 West Indies Table Tennis Championships at the age of 8.

2. The youngest jockey is Frank Wooten, who was an English champion between 1909 and 1912. He rode his first winner at the age of 9.

3. The youngest international gymnastics competitor is Anita Jokel, who was 11 when she entered a 1977 international meet in England.

4. The youngest basketball player ever to be signed as a rookie by a major league team is Jorge Lebron, of Puerto Rico. At the age of 14 in 1974, he was signed by the Philadelphia Phillies to play on a farm team.

5. The youngest baseball player to play on a major league team is Joe Nuxhall, who was 15 when he played with the Cincinnati Reds in 1944.

6. The youngest bullfighter is Conchita Cintahn, who became a *rejoeadora* (someone who fights bulls from horseback) at the age of 12.

7. The youngest member of the 111 Mountain Climbing Club is Deborah Wilson, who became a member at the age of 11. In order to do that, she had to climb 111 mountains in the northeastern United States. In addition, Deborah climbed 111 other mountains, all higher than 4,000 feet. She was 3 years old when she first started climbing mountains, and she scaled her first 4,000-foot peak when she was 5.

8. The youngest boxing champion in any weight class is Wilfredo Benitez, who won the world light welterweight title in 1976 at the age of 17.

9. The only girl to ever compete in a Golden Gloves boxing event is Amber Hunt, who was 12 when she competed in 1977.

10. The youngest champion in the history of the U.S. Open Tennis Championship is Tracy Austin, who won at the age of 16 in 1979.

11. The youngest American to pedal a bicycle across the United States is Kirsen Wilhelm, who did so at the age of 9 in 1977. The trip took 66 days.

12. The youngest pair of ice skaters to represent the United States in international competition is Tai Babilonia and Randy Gardner, in 1974, at the ages of 12 and 14 respectively. (See Tai Babilonia's list of skating tips on page 164.)

13. The youngest woman to win an international Grand Championship in judo is Margaret Castro, in 1977, at the age of 17.

14. The youngest person ever to sign a professional soccer contract is Archie Stark, at the age of 14, in 1911.

15. Boris Becker was the youngest tennis player to win at Wimbledon, at the age of 17.

16. Nadia Comaneci was only 15 years old when she won three gold medals in gymnastics at the 1976 Olympics. She was also the first to record a perfect score of 10 in a gymnastic event.

17. Krisztina Egerszegi at the age of 14 is the youngest person ever to win a gold medal in swimming at the Olympics.

18. At age 13, Bobby Fisher was the youngest chess player to ever win a U.S. Junior Chess Championship. At 15 he earned the title of International Grand Master.

19. Shane Gould retired from swimming at 16 after having set five world records in freestyle swimming. He won three gold medals, two silver, and one bronze at the 1972 Olympics.

20. Monica Seles is the youngest tennis player ever to win a Grand Slam title in this century. She won at age 15.

21. The youngest rodeo star is Anne Lewis, who won a world title in barrel racing in 1968 at the age of 10.

22. Richard Daff Jr. is the youngest bowler to score a perfect 300 game. He was 11 at the time.

23. At age 5, Coby Orr of Littleton, Ohio, is the youngest golfer ever to shoot a hole-in-one. The hole was 103 yards from where Coby hit the ball. (Remember, a football field is 100 yards long!)

24. In 1979, Bunny Taylor became the first girl to pitch a no-hitter in Little League baseball. She was 11 at the time.

25. At the age of 14, golfer Gary Gereson of Milford, Indiana, shot a hole-in-one three days in a row.

26. Twelve-year-old Karen Muir of South Africa became the youngest person ever to break a world athletic record. She swam the 100-meter backstroke.

27. Marjorie Gestring won a springboard diving title at the 1936 Olympics. She was only 13 years old.

28. In 1975 Metha Brorsen won a world rodeo title. She was 11 when she and her horse won the barrel racing event.

29. The first girl to win the All-American Soap Box Derby was Karen Stead. She was 11 years old.

30. In 1977, 8-year-old Wesley Paul ran the 26-mile New York City Marathon in three hours, setting a world's record for his age group.

31. Thomas Gregory, at 11, is the youngest person ever to swim the English Channel. It took him 12 hours to swim 21 miles.

32. Eight-month-old Frederick Garcia couldn't walk yet, but did manage to swim well enough to pass the Red Cross water safety beginner's test.

6 KITING TIPS

1. Most people are under the impression that spring is the best time to fly a kite, but the truth of the matter is that kite-flying is a four-season proposition. The best kite-flying weather provides winds traveling at 4 to 18 miles per hour.

2. The best places to fly kites are wide-open spaces, such as beaches, open hillsides, or a stretch of a few acres, such as farmland. Empty parking lots and rooftops are also ideal. But be careful not to get your kite caught on cars or buildings.

3. The best kites, whether they cost $100 or $5 or are homemade, are well-balanced kites. They should be weighted evenly from side to side and have a symmetrical shape and frame.

4. The line you use should be strong. It should be tied to and wound around something, like a stick, a reel, or any kind of winder. Don't just use a ball of string; you're likely to get all caught up in knots, and fumbling will interfere with the smooth sailing of your kite.

5. The best way to launch a kite is to have a friend act as your assistant (a great job for a little brother or sister who wants to help). Have your friend hold the kite (while you hold the line) and tell him or her to walk about 100 feet (about 75 steps) away from you. The wind should be at your back and in the face of your assistant. Your assistant should hold the kite by the center sticks, letting the tail, if there is one, extend to the ground. When the wind seems right, instruct your friend to let go of the kite while you hold the line taut. Now watch the kite rise!

6. If the wind doesn't seem strong enough to support your kite, there are three things you can do: Try a lighter kite; have your assistant launch the kite from a farther position, such as 200 or even 500 feet away from you; give up and accept the fact that some days aren't right for kite-flying.

4 TIPS FOR THROWING A FLYING DISC PROPERLY

1. To throw the disc long distances, take a few short running steps before you throw. The purpose of the run is not to get the disc to fly a greater distance but to put more force into your throwing arm. Try to get your whole body into the throw as you let go. Note that this technique is only used for long-distance throwing.

2. If you're not throwing long distances but are more interested in reaching your target (the other player) accurately, the best position to start from is to stand sideways with your throwing arm toward the target and your other hand behind you—or wherever you need it to give your body good balance. Your feet should be spread apart about as wide as your shoulders, and your knees should be bent.

3. A maneuver called "sighting" can help you reach your target with greater accuracy. That is, before you actually throw the disc, swing your arm with the disc in hand as if you're going to throw it—but don't let go of it. As you do this, try to see if your aim is really as sharp as you want it to be; imagine where the disc would have gone if you had actually let go. Correct your position if you don't think you were right on target. This maneuver will also help you concentrate.

4. When throwing a disc, before you ever let go of it, you need to wrap or curl your wrist around the edge of the disc. As you finally do let go, it's important to unwrap—or uncurl—your wrist very smoothly. It's the uncurling, called "wristing," that puts the spin into your throw.

HOW TO CATCH A FLYING DISC

1. As a disc comes hurling your way, prepare to catch it by standing with your knees bent and your feet about as far apart as your shoulders are wide. Then get up onto the balls of your feet. This position is a good one because you'll be able to move quickly into just the right spot when the disc comes in for its landing.

2. Always look straight ahead when catching so you can see the entire area in front of you. This is important, since you never really know where a disc is going to wind up until it gets there. Looking ahead will keep you prepared for anything.

3. Don't try to catch too soon. Again, flying discs are unpredictable, and you don't know what one is going to do until it does it. Wait to grab the disc until just before you can reach it. This way, if the disc flies to your left but then swings around to your right at the last moment, you won't be reaching out to the wrong side.

EVERYTHING YOU NEED TO KNOW ABOUT BICYCLE SAFETY

Bicycles are fun, a great way to get around, and they provide good exercise. But your bicycle is not a toy—it is a vehicle, as is a car. For your safety and for the safety of others, be sure you know and practice the following guidelines.

1. Buy the right helmet and ALWAYS WEAR IT! You can grumble about it all you want, but you still have to DO IT! In fact, it's a law in ten states and is being considered in many others. Try one on before you buy it to make sure you get a good fit.

2. Buy the right bike. There are three kinds of bikes: high-rise bikes, for younger riders (these have small wheels and high handlebars); single-speed bikes, with coaster brakes (these are good until you develop strength in your hands); and multispeed lightweight bikes, which are great for high speeds and long distances. Buying a bike that is right for you will mean that you can manage the ride better

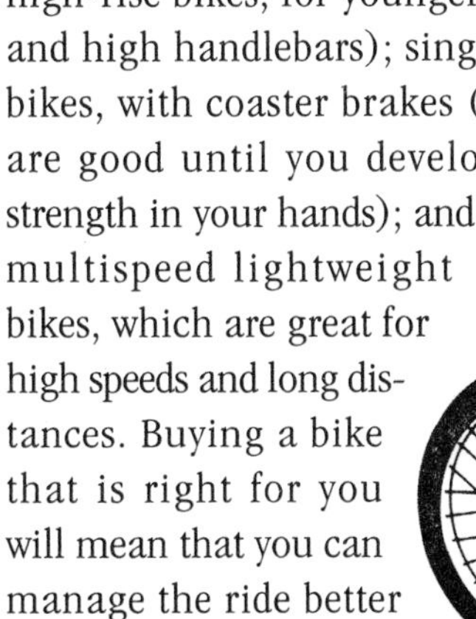

and more safely.

3. Size it up. It's important that the bike you choose is the right size for you. In general, a good rule to follow is that when you sit on the seat, you should be able to balance the bicycle with the tips of your toes. You should also be able to reach the pedal in its lowest position with the tips of your toes while sitting in the seat. If you are between eight and ten years old, your bicycle should most likely be a 24-inch; if you're eleven or older, try a 26-inch wheeler.

4. Keep your bike in proper working order. Keep a constant check that everything is operating as it should. Before riding, check your brakes, make certain the tires are properly inflated, and test the lights and horn or bell.

5. Learn hand signals—they are important. You should know and use these signals just as adults use them when driving cars.

Left turn: Left arm straight out to your side.
Right turn: Left arm raised up in a salute.
Slowing or stopping: Left arm in downward position.

6. Obey all traffic signs and signals.

7. Ride in the same direction as traffic.

8. Pedestrians always have the right of way.

9. Never carry passengers on your seat. Bicycles are built for one.

10. Never wear loose or long clothing that can get caught in the wheels as you ride.

11. Beware of parked cars. Be alert when you ride by parked cars in case a door is suddenly opened.

12. Be a smart "groupie." When riding with a group of friends, never ride more than two abreast and make sure to watch the rider in front of you.

13. Handle with care. Always ride with both hands on the handlebars, except when signaling.

14. Watch out for slippery surfaces. Damp roads are slippery. Ride more slowly under these circumstances and brake slowly and earlier than you normally would.

15. Avoid top-overs. You can do this by being especially careful around drain gates, soft road edges, gravel or sand, leaves (especially when wet), potholes, ruts and uneven paving, and any obstacles that might be in your path.

16. Be a night owl. This means keeping your eyes open and acting wisely. Avoid wearing dark-colored clothing (motorists can see bright colors better) or clothing that might cover up your rear light. Also, make sure your reflectors and lights are working, and carry extra batteries just in case.

10 THINGS YOU SHOULD KNOW WHEN SELECTING A MARTIAL ARTS SCHOOL

Martial arts schools are not difficult to find these days, but choosing the right school must be done carefully. A good school should not only train you physically but should also teach you courtesy, respect for others, patience, and how to avoid a fight.

1. Don't choose a school because it is closest to home. Visit as many schools in your area as you can.

2. Observe a class and see whether the kids are enjoying themselves. If the kids are not getting along, there might be a problem. If the school won't let you sit in on a class, don't even consider joining.

3. If there are more than 15 kids per instructor, you won't get the attention you will need. A class of about 10 students is ideal.

4. Instructors should have at least five to six years of training experience. You can ask for this information.

5. Talk to kids that train in the school. They'll give you great information.

6. Don't be impressed by a lot of trophies that may be on display. Anyone can go to a hobby shop and buy a trophy.

7. Don't choose a school that tries to pressure you into signing up for a long period of time.

8. If students are awarded black belts after only two or three years of training, this is not a very serious school. A legitimate black belt takes at least five to eight years to earn.

9. The instructor should emphasize nonviolence and respect for others in the class. Ask students at the school or one of their parents about this.

10. Explore the different styles of martial arts that are being taught and choose the one that appeals to you. Martial arts magazines are a good place to start your research.

TAI BABILONIA'S TIPS ON HOW TO FALL WHILE ICE SKATING WITHOUT HURTING YOURSELF

Tai Babilonia should know: she fell frequently while she was practicing to become a world champion figure skater.

1. When you realize you're going to fall, put your arms out behind you so your body doesn't hit the ground first.

2. Don't stiffen your body. Stay loose.

3. Go with the fall—don't fight it.

10 TIPS FOR BUYING ICE SKATES

If you're having difficulty skating, one of the reasons could be that your skates do not fit properly. A skate that is not made well will not give your foot the support it needs. Skates should be of good quality, properly fitted, and comfortable. Here are some guidelines you can follow when buying skates.

1. Your skates should either be the same size as your ordinary shoes or slightly smaller.

2. The boot should be laced loosely and tried on while you are sitting down. When you stand up, there should be enough room for your toes to move slightly. The heel and ball of your foot, however, should not be able to move at all. Make sure that your toes are not uncomfortable.

3. Grip the boot by the back of the heel. Pull up and down. You should hear suction and a snap.

4. Walk on the skate. There should be no motion of the heel.

5. If the skate seems too narrow, you can sometimes adjust the fit by the way you lace up. You can also try on a boot that is a half size larger.

6. The boots should be made of top grain leather. The counter, which is the part of the boot that your foot rests on, should be waterproof and have a cup that holds your heel in place.

7. The upper portion of the boot should be a soft leather that will allow your ankle to bend backward and forward.

8. The boot should have a full lining. The hooks and eyelets should be securely fastened.

9. Blades should be made of high-tempered steel and be able to hold an edge well.

10. Never try to break in a new pair of skates by walking on them without the blades.

HOW TO FALL WHILE ROLLER-SKATING

Chances are you aren't thinking of taking up roller-skating just so you can fall, but falling is something worth learning and practicing. After all, even professionals lose their balance at times, and practicing the proper method for falling will minimize the damage if and when it happens to you. These falling guidelines are recommended by the Roller Skating Rink Operators Association.

1. Start practicing by standing up and bending your knees until you are in a squatting position.

2. Lean back and to the side and let yourself fall on your rump. Keep your arms forward and your hands up.

3. Always try to fall onto the softer part of your body by trying to sit as you feel yourself falling. Never break the fall with your hands or elbows.

4. To get up after a fall, sit up and then get on your knees. Rest your weight on one knee and then draw up the other leg so that you're on your feet again in a squatting position. With your weight centered over both skates, raise your body by straightening your knees.

5. When recovering from a spill on the skating floor, try to get up facing the other skaters so that you aren't suddenly pushed forward by an oncoming skater.

8 ROLLERBLADING SAFETY TIPS

Skating in traffic is never recommended. However, if you have to skate in the street to get where you are going, please follow these safety guidelines.

1. Always look up! And always be aware of what is going on around you.

2. Always stay off to the side of the road or on the sidewalk.

3. Never skate against traffic; always go with the flow.

4. Watch for car doors opening and cars pulling out of parking spaces and into the road.

5. Never wear headphones. You need to be able to hear all of the street sounds around you.

6. Never hold on to a moving vehicle to "skitch" a ride.

7. Never zigzag. This will confuse drivers and pedestrians.

8. If you are approaching a parked car, notice the direction that the tires are pointed in. If they are turned out toward the street, be very cautious. This could mean that the car is about to pull out into the street.

6 WAYS TO MAKE SURE YOUR SKATEBOARD IS SAFE

If you make the mistake of riding on a board that is unsafe, you are asking for trouble. Here are some safety measures that you should be aware of.

1. Make sure that your wheels work properly. Your wheels should spin freely. Use a bearing spray to clean dust and dirt off the wheels.

2. If your wheels seem too tight, it would be helpful to loosen the bearing nut.

3. Before you go riding, place your board on a flat surface and give it a little push. If the board does not roll in a straight line, something is wrong. Take it back to the shop and have them check out the problem for you.

4. Wheel wobble can be extremely dangerous. If your wheels begin to wobble, use your skate key to tighten the truck bolt so that there is pressure between the bolt and the truck plate.

5. To prevent your wheel from wearing down unevenly, you should rotate your wheel every four to six weeks. Rotate from front right to rear left, front left to rear right, rear right to front left, and rear left to front right.

6. If the deck of your board shows any signs of cracking, you should bring it back to the shop for repair, especially if the cracks are deep.

CHAPTER FOUR

FOOD

17 TABLE MANNERS TO GET YOU THROUGH FANCY MEALS

Your first formal meal can be a frightening experience, especially if you're uncomfortable about various rules of etiquette. Here are some things to remember that will help you get through:

1. It's all right to eat asparagus with your fingers.

2. When you take a piece of candy from a boxed assortment, you should also take the frilly little cup that the candy comes in. (Also, you should only take one piece at a time.)

3. If you have to remove something from your mouth, like a bone or something you can't swallow, place your napkin to your mouth and spit it into the napkin as inconspicuously as possible.

4. It's bad manners to sneeze at the table. If you need to sneeze, excuse yourself and go someplace else.

5. It's all right to eat parsley and other decorations, but you don't have to.

6. If you hate what's being served, take a small portion anyway and nibble at it if you can. If you are asked why you're not eating the stuff, say it's delicious but that you had a big lunch.

7. If someone asks you to pass the potatoes and you haven't taken any for yourself yet, pass them first and then request the bowl so that you can serve yourself.

8. It's never polite to take the last piece of anything.

9. At a formal meal, when someone asks you to pass the salt, it's most polite to pass the salt and pepper if they're on the table together.

10. If you're eating spaghetti and you're left with those long strands hanging out of your mouth, it's best to suck them all in rather than to bite down, with the ends dropping back into your plate.

11. When eating fruits with pits, such as grapes and cherries, it's all right to remove the pits from your mouth with your fingers.

12. Don't be the first to start eating after the food has been served. Wait until the head of the house has begun. While you're waiting to begin, you can put salt, pepper, and butter on your food.

13. If everyone seems to be doing something that you're not used to doing and that you know is wrong, do it anyway. You don't want anyone to feel uncomfortable.

14. If you're uncomfortable with your surroundings and can't think of anything to say, just smile a lot when someone looks at you.

15. If someone puts something on your plate that you'd rather die than eat, just leave it there.

16. It's okay to use a small piece of bread to push tricky foods like peas onto your fork. (Or you can pretend that you are clumsy and don't know about the bread trick in order to avoid eating the peas!)

17. It is always polite and kind to thank your hosts for inviting you.

AND YOU THOUGHT BRUSSELS SPROUTS WERE BAD!

23 Delicacies You Might Not Want to Try

While most of us consider hamburgers and french fries a pretty good meal, there are those adventurous souls out there who seem always willing to try something new. The following are gourmet delicacies somewhere in the world, even throughout parts of the United States. Many of these taste just like chicken...NOT!

1. Alligator
2. Ant eggs
3. Antelope
4. Bird's nest soup
5. Buffalo
6. Butterflies
7. Camel
8. Caterpillar grubs
9. Dirt (In Nigeria it's seasoned with vinegar and salt before eating. As if that makes a big difference!)
10. Goliath beetles
11. Grasshoppers
12. Ground billy goat
13. Iguana flesh
14. Kangaroo
15. Locusts
16. Moose à la mode
17. Moose nose
18. Raccoon pie
19. Rattlesnake
20. Roast bear
21. Seaweed
22. Squirrel
23. Thousand-year-old eggs (They're really only about eight weeks old and are eaten raw.)

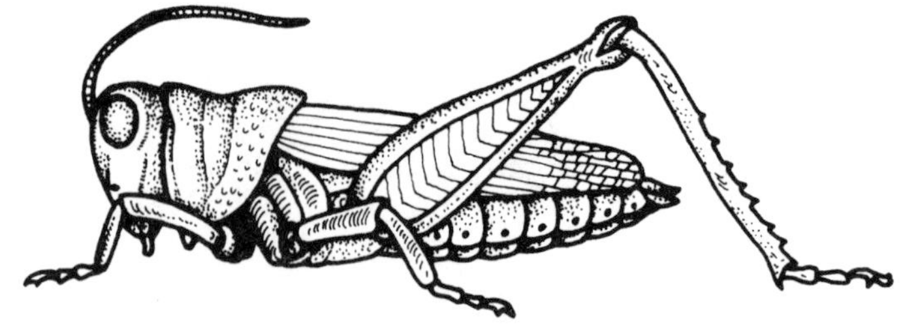

LUNCH COUNTER LINGO

Waiters and waitresses didn't always write your restaurant order down on a pad and pass it back to the kitchen. Back in the 1850s, when restaurants were much smaller than they are now, the waiter would simply call your order to the cook. Now yelling out "Gimmie an order of beef stew" would be understandable enough, but Americans like to spice up their language, and so a list of code words developed over the years. Beef stew became "bossy in a bowl"; a banana split became known as a "houseboat" for its shape; and two poached eggs on toast were referred to as "Adam and Eve on a raft." ("Wreck 'em," called the waitress if those eggs were to be scrambled.) The new lingo, or household Greek, as it was known, must have made the day's work more interesting for all. Too bad these terms have all but disappeared.

1. Axle grease: butter

2. Belch water: plain soda water

3. Blast: to heat up

4. A bowl of birdseed: a bowl of cereal

5. Burn the British: a toasted English muffin

6. Burn the pup: a hot dog

7. Campers: people who sit at a table for a long time without ordering anything

8. CB: a cheeseburger

9. CJ: a cream cheese and jelly sandwich

10. A crowd: three of whatever is ordered, as in "a crowd of cowboys," which means three western omelettes

11. Crumbs: children, because they leave so many

12. Dog biscuits: crackers

13. 80: a glass of water

14. 86: We're out of it.

15. Eve with the lid on: apple pie
16. Five: a large glass
17. 41: lemonade
18. 51: a cup of hot chocolate
19. 55: a glass of root beer
20. Fly cake or roach cake: a slice of raisin pie
21. Grass: lettuce
22. Keep off the grass: without lettuce
23. MD, hold the nail: Dr Pepper, no ice
24. Moo juice: a glass of milk
25. Nervous pudding: Jell-O
26. Paint it red: with ketchup
27. Put out the lights and cry: liver and onions
28. Radio: tuna salad sandwich on toast
29. Suds: a glass of root beer
30. Warts: olives

THERE'S NO SUCH THING AS A FREE LUNCH

5 Very Expensive Lunch Boxes

Old lunch boxes, which some people collect, have sold for very high prices. Here are some examples of really expensive lunch boxes obtained from *The Official Price Guide to Lunch Box Collectibles.*

1. Mickey Mouse, 1935, $1,000
2. Star Trek, 1968-69, $250
3. Bullwinkle, 1963, $200
4. Benny & Cecil, 1963, $150
5. Lost in Space, 1978-79, $145

12 FOODS YOU SHOULD EAT BEFORE A TEST

These foods won't make you smarter than you are, but studies show that they can help you keep alert by fighting the effects of carbohydrates (candy, bread, sugar), which tend to make you more calm or "sleepy."

1. Apples
2. Broccoli
3. Fish (especially oysters)
4. Grapes
5. Lean beef
6. Lowfat yogurt
7. Nuts
8. Peaches
9. Peanuts
10. Pears
11. Skim milk
12. Turkey breast

6 FOOD FIRSTS

1. When the machine that Clarence A. Crane was using to produce a new kind of mint candy malfunctioned and accidentally punched a hole in the center, the first Life Saver was invented.

2. George Crum, an Adirondack Indian chief, worked as a chef and was rather proud of his french fries. When one of his customers complained that they were too thick, Chief Crum grabbed the nearest potato and carved the thinnest slice he could. He fried it and served it up to the customer, who thought it was great. That's how potato chips were born.

3. Antoine Feuchtwanger sold sausages in the United States in the 1880s. But they were served so hot that he actually gave his customers gloves to wear, so they wouldn't be so difficult to hold. This proved highly impractical, so Mr. Feuchtwanger replaced the gloves with sliced rolls, thus inventing the hot dog.

4. In 1902, vendors sold ice cream at the St. Louis World's Fair and ran out of dishes. Ernest Hamwi, a pastry vendor, came to the rescue: he came up with a cone-shaped pastry to hold the ice cream. These were the very first ice cream cones.

5. In 1905, 11-year-old Frank Epperson combined soda water with a flavored powder, mixed it up with a wooden stick, and then forgot about it, leaving it outdoors overnight. When he awoke the next morning, he found that he had invented the popsicle!

6. In 1920, Bruce Murrie and Forest Mars decided to invent a new kind of chocolate candy for soldiers, so they came up with something that wouldn't get their trigger fingers sticky. They used their own initials to name the new candy; that's how M&M's came to be.

HAVE IT YOUR WAY

7 Really Big Foods

1. The biggest frankfurter ever was prepared by the German Butcher's Guild in 1601. It was over a half-mile long.

2. In 1979, students at Smith College made the biggest ice cream sundae ever. It contained 1,800 gallons of ice cream, 150 pounds of fudge, 75 pounds of sprinkles, 90 pounds of walnuts, 12 gallons of cherry halves, and one dozen cans of whipped cream. (Burp.)

3. The world's largest Boston cream pie was baked in

honor of Boston's 350th birthday. It weighed an astounding 3,800 pounds.

4. In 1974, the largest Easter egg was made by a group of Australians. It weighed more than 600 pounds and measured more than six feet high.

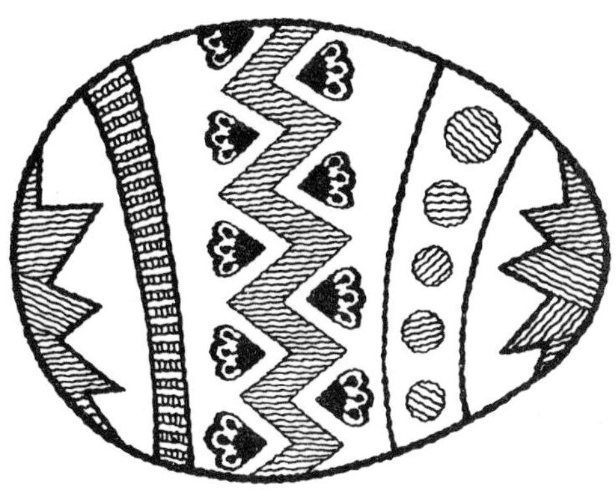

5. The largest main-course dish was often prepared for weddings in Arab countries. Here's how it was made: cooked eggs were stuffed into fish; the fish were stuffed into cooked chickens; the chickens were stuffed into a roasted sheep; the sheep was stuffed into a whole camel; then the entire thing was cooked. Imagine having to do the dishes after that meal!

6. The world's largest chocolate chip cookie weighed 475 pounds and was baked by the chef Franz Eichenauer.

7. If you had lived 200 years ago, you could have indulged in a slice of the biggest meat pie ever, created by one Sir Henry Gray. His masterpiece was 9 feet in circumference and weighed 200 pounds. Here are the ingredients:

2 bushels of flour
20 pounds of butter
4 geese
2 turkeys
2 rabbits
2 wild ducks
2 woodcock
6 snipe (a kind of bird)
2 curlews (a kind of bird)
2 oxen's tongues
4 partridges (hold the pear trees!)
7 blackbirds
7 pigeons

THE TEN MOST POPULAR JUNK FOODS

You know that they are not exactly the healthiest foods you could be eating, but they sure taste great. So great that nearly $8 billion dollars a year is spent on junk food. Here is a list of your favorites, starting with the most popular.

1. Pizza
2. Chicken nuggets
3. Hot dogs
4. Cheeseburgers
5. Macaroni and cheese
6. Hamburgers
7. Spaghetti and meatballs
8. Fried chicken
9. Tacos
10. Grilled cheese sandwiches

7 PIZZA FACTS

1. Pizza is the most popular of all fast foods.

2. Americans eat enough pizza every day to cover an area equivalent to 90 acres of land.

3. The average person eats 60 slices of pizza every year.

4. The most popular toppings are: pepperoni, mushrooms, extra cheese, sausage, green pepper, and onion (in that order).

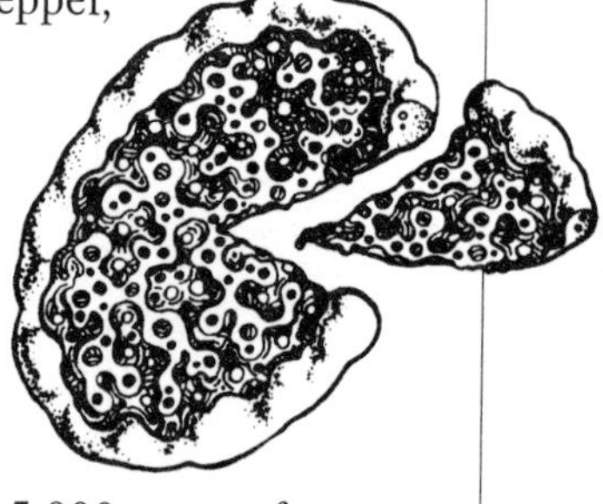

5. The least favorite topping is anchovies.

6. There is a magazine called *Pizza Today.*

7. The largest pizza ever was made by a man named Lorenzo Amato. His pie, made on October 11, 1989, covered 5,000 square feet.

18 ICE CREAM FLAVORS YOU'VE PROBABLY NEVER HEARD OF

1. American Beauty: contains the petals of real roses!

2. Arab Lunch: the only ice cream we've heard of that contains cheese, in addition to dates and honey

3. Azuki Bean: made from a Japanese sweet bean

4. Easter Egg: coconut cream, toasted pecans, and caramel

5. Girl Scout Cookie: not made by *real* Girl Scouts!

6. Hard Hat: whiskey and crème de menthe

7. Have a Date, Honey: honey and dates

8. I Yam What I Yam: sweet potatoes!

9. Jungle Princess: pineapple, mango, and coconut

10. Nesselrode: contains nine different flavors, including rum, brandy, lemon, and pineapple

11. Pickle: no kidding!

12. Sabra: a chocolate and orange Israeli liqueur

13. Soursop: a tangy ice cream that gets its flavor from a tropical fruit known as the custard-apple

14. Star Wars: vanilla ice cream with swirls of multicolored marshmallows

15. Strawcot: strawberry and apricot

16. Turtle: tastes better than it sounds, with vanilla ice cream, toasted pecans, and caramel

17. Veggie: spinach, carrots, tomatoes, and twelve other vegetables (Yechhhh!)

18. Wedding Bells: strawberry and champagne

THE TOP 15 ICE CREAM FLAVORS

According to the International Association of Ice Cream Manufacturers, these are the flavors that kids of all ages prefer.

1. Butter almond
2. Butter pecan
3. Cherry
4. Chocolate
5. Chocolate chip
6. Chocolate marshmallow
7. Chocolate/vanilla combination
8. Coffee
9. French vanilla
10. Maple nut
11. Neapolitan
12. Rocky road
13. Strawberry
14. Vanilla
15. Vanilla Fudge

THE 10 BEST-SELLING HÄAGEN-DAZS ICE CREAM FLAVORS

1. Belgian Chocolate
2. Caramel Cone Explosion
3. Choc Choc Chip
4. Cookie Dough Dynamo
5. Cookies and Cream
6. Macadamia Nut Brittle
7. Pralines and Cream
8. Strawberry
9. Vanilla
10. Vanilla Chocolate Fudge

THE 10 BEST-SELLING BEN & JERRY'S ICE CREAM FLAVORS

1. Cherry Garcia
2. Cherry Garcia Frozen Yogurt
3. Chocolate Chip Cookie Dough
4. Chocolate Fudge Brownie
5. Chocolate Fudge Brownie Frozen Yogurt
6. Chunky Monkey
7. English Toffee Crunch
8. Mint with Cookies
9. New York Super Fudge Chunk
10. Wavy Gravy

BAD NEWS ABOUT MOVIE SNACKS

The next time you go to the movies and order a snack at the candy counter, be careful! What you get may be a lot more then what you wanted. Here's a calorie count.

1. Buttered popcorn (medium) = three meals: scrambled eggs, bacon, and home fries for breakfast, Spam on rye for lunch, and a 6-ounce steak, baked potato, and slice of cheesecake for dinner (1,538 calories total)

2. Unbuttered popcorn (medium) = 1 double cheeseburger with large fries and a chocolate shake (1,240 calories)

3. Goobers (3.5 ounces) = 3 cheese enchiladas, an order of refried beans, and nachos with an onion dip (810 calories)

4. Milk Duds (5 ounces) = 1 frozen 12-inch pizza with pepperoni (360 calories)

5. Peanut M&M's (3 ounces) = 4 slices of white bread, each with a pat of butter (424 calories)

6. Raisinets (3.5 ounces) = A plate of spaghetti with white clam sauce and 2 brownies for dessert (570 calories)

7. Junior Mints (5.5 ounces) = 2 hot dogs on rolls with mustard (560 calories)

8. Twizzlers (5 ounces) = 12 rice cakes (480 calories)

CALORIE CONTENT OF FAST FOOD FAVORITES

1. Arthur Treacher's fish (2 pieces)—355 calories
2. Burger Chef's Big Chef burger—569 calories
3. Burger King's Double Whopper with Cheese—951 calories
4. Burger King's french fries (large size)—331
5. Gino's Cheese Steak—469 calories
6. Hardee's Big Twin—447 calories
7. Jack in the Box Jumbo Jack hamburger—461 calories
8. Kentucky Fried Chicken Original Recipe Chicken (one drumstick)—117 calories
9. McDonald's Egg McMuffin—353 calories
10. McDonald's french fries (large size)—362 calories
11. McDonald's Quarter Pounder with Cheese—518 calories
12. Pizza Hut Thick n' Chewy cheese pizza (two slices of a medium pizza)—450 calories
13. Taco Bell taco—159 calories
14. Wendy's double hamburger with cheese—797 calories
15. Wendy's french fries—327 calories
16. White Castle double cheeseburger—305 calories

CANDY IS DANDY

American kids eat an average of four pounds of the stuff a week. Here are some of their favorites and the years in which the candies were first sold.

1. Almond Joy (1947)
2. Baby Ruth (1921)
3. Butterfinger (1923)
4. Cracker Jack (1896)
5. Hershey Bar (1894)
6. Hershey's Kisses (1907)
7. M&M's (1920)
8. Milky Way (1923)
9. Mounds (1921)
10. Reese's Pieces (1978)
11. Snickers (1930)
12. 3 Musketeers (1932)
13. Tootsie Roll (1896)

CANDY IS NOT SO DANDY AFTER ALL

Calorie and Fat Content of 11 Candy Bars

	CALORIES	FAT GRAMS
Almond Joy (1.76 oz)	250	14
Good & Plenty (1.8 oz)	191	0
Hershey's milk chocolate (1.55 oz)	240	14
Junior Mints (1.6 oz)	192	5
Kit Kat (1.5 oz)	230	12
Life Savers (.9 oz)	88	0
M&M's peanut (1.74 oz)	250	13
Mr. Goodbar	240	15
Sugar Daddy (2 oz.)	218	1
Tootsie Roll (2.25 oz)	252	6
York Peppermint Pattie (1.5 oz)	180	4

THE 10 BEST-SELLING BRANDS OF CANDY IN THE U.S.

1. Butterfinger
2. Brach's
3. Hershey's
4. Hershey's Kisses
5. Kit Kat
6. Life Savers
7. M&M's
8. Milky Way
9. Reese's
10. Snickers

THE 10 BEST-SELLING BRANDS OF POTATO CHIPS

1. Eagle Ripples
2. Eagle Thins
3. Herr's
4. Keebler O'Boises
5. Lay's
6. Pringles
7. Private Label
8. Ruffles
9. Utz
10. Wise

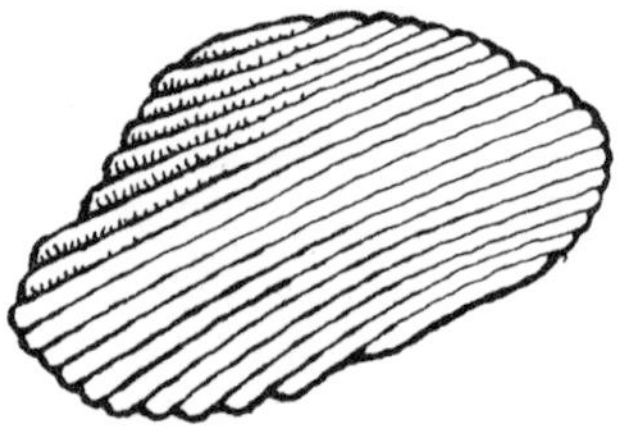

THE 10 BEST-SELLING BRANDS OF GUM

1. Bubblicious
2. Carefree
3. Dentyne Cinn A Burst
4. Freedent
5. Trident
6. Wrigley's
7. Wrigley's Big Red
8. Wrigley's Doublemint
9. Wrigley's Extra
10. Wrigley's Juicy Fruit

THE FREQUENCY OF COLORS FOUND IN A ONE-POUND BAG OF M&M'S

1. Dark brown (151)
2. Yellow (95)
3. Red (94)
4. Green (86)
5. Orange (71)
6. Light brown (28)

14 NAMES FOR SUGAR

If you're reading food labels to avoid sugar, you should know that all of the following *are* forms of sugar.

Barley malt syrup
Brown sugar
Corn syrup
Dextrose
Fructose
Honey
Lactose
Maltose
Maple Syrup
Molasses
Raisin syrup
Raw sugar
Sorghum
Turbinado sugar

10 TIPS FOR BAKING THE BEST CHOCOLATE CHIP COOKIES EVER

Americans bake more than 7 billion chocolate cookies each year. If you're one of those who have contributed to that statistic, keep these tips in mind. You can use them with any recipe.

1. Don't use an old cookie sheet. Old, dented cookie sheets will give you badly shaped cookies, plus they absorb heat faster, which leads to the bottoms of the cookies getting burned.

2. Use a rubber spatula rather than a plastic one. The rubber kind bends to conform with the curved sides of the bowl, so you can mix all the good stuff into the batter.

3. Use an oven thermometer to measure the heat in your oven. Chocolate chip cookies are very sensitive to high temperatures, and your cookies will benefit from a true oven reading. (The recipe you use will give you the correct temperature.)

4. Transfer your cookies to a cooling rack once they're baked. Cookies need evenly circulated air once they're out of the oven, and a cooling rack is your best bet.

5. Use chocolate chips that aren't too sweet. Bittersweet chocolate is best, because the flavor contrasts with the sweetness of the sugar.

6. Cover your cookie sheet with aluminum foil before you use it. That way your cookies won't spread out too much while they bake, and you'll get nice thick ones.

7. If you decide to cut your own chocolate chips from a chocolate bar rather than use the morsels that come in packages, don't cut the pieces too thin or you'll get brittle, hard little chips instead of big chewy soft ones.

8. If your recipe calls for vanilla, use real extract of vanilla, not imitation vanilla.

9. You can substitute honey for sugar in your recipe. Use three-quarters as much honey as you would sugar.

10. After you've mixed the batter, leave it in the refrigerator for about twelve hours before you actually get down to the baking.

36 THINGS YOU CAN ADD TO CHOCOLATE CHIP COOKIES

Once you're happy with a basic chocolate chip recipe, it's time to get creative. Consider adding any of the following (in whatever quantity your palate fancies) to your batter. Use your imagination to come up with even more ideas.

1. Allspice
2. Almond extract
3. Candied ginger
4. Chopped, candied orange peel
5. Chopped dates
6. Chopped prunes
7. Cinnamon
8. Coconut extract
9. Cream cheese
10. Crumbled graham crackers
11. Crushed peppermint sticks
12. Crushed Wheaties
13. Granola
14. Grated orange rind
15. Honey
16. Instant coffee
17. Lemon juice
18. Lemon rind
19. M&M's
20. Mashed banana
21. Mashed potato chips
22. Molasses
23. Nutmeg
24. Nuts (any kind)
25. Oatmeal
26. Orange juice
27. Peanut butter

28. Pumpkin seeds
29. Raisins
30. Reese's Pieces
31. Rice Krispies
32. Shredded coconut
33. Sliced maraschino cherries
34. Sour cream
35. Sunflower seeds
36. Wheat germ

HOW TO TELL WHAT'S INSIDE ASSORTED CHOCOLATES

Assorted chocolates can be fun—when you get the one you want. And you'll be happy to know that there is a way to tell what's inside without sticking your finger through the bottom, which can be gross, especially when you get the squooshy ones you don't like. The secret is knowing what those squiggles on the tops of the chocolates mean. You see, manufacturers have a code, and each of those funny designs actually is a symbol for what the chocolate is filled with.

1. Fudge

2. Orange

3. Nougat

4. Truffle

5. Marshmallow

6. Caramel Cream

12 NONALCOHOLIC COCKTAILS

When you're out with your parents and they order fancy alcoholic drinks with exotic names like "piña colada" and "black Russian," you don't have to settle for a plain Coke. Here are some just-as-fancy drinks that you can try. Or make them at home to share with your friends. (And the next time you think of setting up a lemonade stand, consider selling some of these instead.)

1. The Goldfish. Pour 3 ½ cups orange juice over ice. Fill the rest of the glass with club soda and add an orange slice.

2. Mellow Yellow. In a saucepan, combine 1 ⅜ cups sugar with 1 ⅜ cups water. Bring to a boil. Add 1½ cups grapefruit juice, 2 ⅜ cups pineapple juice, and 1½ cups lemon juice. Chill and then serve. This recipe makes enough for four people.

3. The Purple People Eater. Combine 3 ½ cups lemonade with 1 ½ cups grapefruit juice. Serve over ice. (A variation of this drink, which we call the Red Riding Hood, calls for 3 ½ cups cranberry juice mixed with 1½ cups orange juice, also served over ice.)

4. The Texas Cow. Add a splash of grenadine to a glass of milk. (To make a Heifer, add the grenadine to chocolate milk instead.)

5. Tutti-frutti Shake. Blend 1⅓ cups chilled apricot or strawberry juice with ⅔ cups of cold milk. Serve over ice. You'll have enough for four people.

6. Egg Noggin. In a shaker, mix 4 cups of chilled milk, 4 eggs, 4 tablespoons honey, 1 teaspoon vanilla, some grated orange or lemon rind, and 1¼ cups cracked ice. Mix well. Pour into four glasses and sprinkle some nutmeg on top of each. If you want to get real fancy, add some vanilla ice cream or yogurt or 1 to 3 teaspoons of smooth peanut butter to the batch before mixing.

7. Cherry Bing. Dilute one pint cherry juice and 4 ounces orange juice in 10 ounces of water. Stir to blend. Add ice cubes and serve.

8. Florida Cocktail. In a shaker combine 3½ ounces grapefruit juice, 1 tablespoon lemon juice, 2 ounces sugar syrup, and a pinch of salt. Fill the rest of the shaker with ice. Shake well. Strain over crushed ice, then add 1 ounce of seltzer to each glass and decorate with a mint leaf.

9. Ginger Peach Cocktail. Combine 8 ounces peach juice, 8 ounces orange juice, and 4 ounces lemon juice. Stir well. Add 1 pint ginger ale, pour into eight glasses, and add a chunk of whole ginger to each.

10. Mock Manhattan. Start with a shaker containing a few ice cubes. Add the following: 2 ounces orange juice, 2 ounces cranberry juice, a few drops of lemon juice, a few drops of maraschino cherry juice, and a dash of orange bitter. Shake well. Strain over ice and decorate with a cherry.

11. Raspberry Delight. Scoop 3 ounces of raspberry sherbet into a glass. Add some ice and fill the rest of the glass with ginger ale. Garnish with a few fresh raspberries. Sip through a straw.

12. Shirley Temple. Fill a champagne glass with ginger ale. Add a few drops of grenadine. Stir. Add one or two cherries.

I HATE VEGGIES!

Well, now you have seven fewer vegetables to hate—the following are really fruits.

1. Cucumbers
2. Eggplant
3. Gherkins
4. Okra
5. Pumpkins
6. Squash
7. Tomatoes

5 JELL-O FLAVOR FLOPS, FLUKES, AND FAILURES

Those marketing whizzes at General Foods aren't perfect. In past years, they've produced some unusual flavors and discovered—duh!—that no one *really* wants to eat quivering blobs of iridescent glop that tasted like:

1. Apple
2. Cola
3. Celery
4. Mixed vegetable
5. Salad

16 POPCORN FLAVORS

1. Apple
2. Banana
3. Butter
4. Butterscotch
5. Caramel
6. Cheese
7. Chocolate
8. Cinnamon
9. Fudge
10. Honey
11. Peach
12. Piña colada
13. Pistachio
14. Raspberry
15. Vanilla
16. Watermelon

15 FOODS THAT FURTHER FLATULENCE

In other words, they make you fart. Don't eat them before your piano recital. By the way, if you do "let one rip" in the presence of others, the polite thing to do is to say "Excuse me" and go on with what you were doing. If someone else does it, ignore it.

1. Apples
2. Avocados
3. Beans
4. Brussels sprouts
5. Cabbage
6. Corn
7. Cucumbers
8. High-fiber cereals
9. Lima beans
10. Melons
11. Peas
12. Prune juice
13. Radishes
14. Raisins
15. Turnips

CHAPTER FIVE

BOOKS, MAGAZINES, THE COMICS, AND CYBERFUN

JACQUELINE KENNEDY'S ADVICE TO YOUNG READERS

You may know that Jacqueline Kennedy was the First Lady married to President John F. Kennedy, but did you know that she was a book editor too? Before she passed away in 1994, the Commission on Literature of the National Teachers of English asked Ms. Kennedy to share her best advice to young readers. Here are some of the points she made.

1. "Read for escape, read for adventure, read for romance, but read the great writers." She added that "the great writers will always be easier to read and more enjoyable than any others, for it is these writers who can stir your imagination best and open your world to the new experiences that books hold in store. The best writers will also help you develop your own language skills."

2. Ms. Kennedy recommended that young people read the works of Edgar Allen Poe, Jack London, Jules Verne, and Ernest Hemingway.

3. Poetry is important, too. "Rhythm is what should first seize you when you read poetry." Ms. Kennedy recommended "The Congo" by Vachel Lindsay, "Tarantella" by Alfred Noyes, "The Fog" by Carl Sandburg, and the poetry of Countee Cullen, e. e. cummings, Emily Dickinson, and Siegfried Sassoon.

4. "If you read, you may want to write," suggested Ms. Kennedy, pointing out that great painters learned to paint by copying others. You, too, may want to try to express your feelings by writing about them, and you can learn to do that well by choosing a writer you like and then copying his or her work for practice.

Ms. Kennedy's letter closed with these sentiments: "Once

you can express yourself, you can tell the world what you want from it or how you would like to change it. All the changes in the world, for good or evil, were first brought about by words."

THE TEN BEST-SELLING CHILDREN'S BOOKS OF ALL TIME

1. *The Tale of Peter Rabbit,* Beatrix Potter (1902)
2. *Green Eggs and Ham,* Dr. Seuss (1960)
3. *One Fish, Two Fish, Red Fish, Blue Fish,* Dr. Seuss (1960)
4. *The Outsiders,* S. E. Hinton (1967)
5. *Hop on Pop,* Dr. Seuss (1963)
6. *Dr. Seuss's ABC,* Dr. Seuss (1957)
7. *The Cat in the Hat,* Dr. Seuss (1957)
8. *Are You There, God? It's Me, Margaret,* Judy Blume (1970)
9. *The Wonderful Wizard of Oz,* L. Frank Baum (1900)
10. *Charlotte's Web,* E. B. White (1952)

WINNERS OF THE NEWBERY MEDAL, 1941–1994

Each year, the Association for Library Services to Children, a division of the American Library Association, awards the Newbery Medal for the most distinguished contribution to American literature for children. Here are the books that have won since the year it began, 1941, their authors, and the publishers. If you have any questions about the awards or about children's books in general, write to: The American Library Association, 50 East Huron Street, Chicago, IL 60611.

1941: *Call It Courage,* Armstrong Sperry (Macmillan)
1942: *The Matchlock Gun,* Walter Edmonds (Dodd)
1943: *Adam of the Road,* Elizabeth Gray (Viking)
1944: *Johnny Tremain,* Esther Forbes (Houghton Mifflin)
1945: *Rabbit Hill,* Robert Lawson (Viking)
1946: *Strawberry Girl,* Lois Lenski (Lippincott)
1947: *Miss Hickory,* Carolyn Baily (Viking)
1948: *The Twenty-One Balloons,* William Pen du Bois (Viking)
1949: *King of the Wind,* Marguerite Henry (Rand McNally)
1950: *The Door in the Wall,* Marguerite di Angeli (Doubleday)
1951: *Amos Fortune, Free Man,* Elizabeth Yates (Aladdin)
1952: *Ginger Pye,* Eleanor Estes (Harcourt)
1953: *Secret of the Andes,* Ann Nolan Clark (Viking)
1954: *. . . And Now Miguel,* Joseph Krumgold (Crowell)
1955: *The Wheel on the School,* Meidert De Jog (Harper)
1956: *Carry On, Mr. Bowditch,* Joan Lee Latham (Houghton Mifflin)
1957: *Miracles on Maple Hill,* Virginia Sorenson (Harcourt)

1958: *Rifles for Watie,* Harold Keith (Crowell)
1959: *The Witch of Blackbird Pond,* Elizabeth George Speare (Houghton Mifflin)
1960: *Onion John,* Joseph Krumgold (Crowell)
1961: *Island of the Blue Dolphins,* Scott O'Dell (Houghton Mifflin)
1962: *The Bronze Bow,* Elizabeth George Speare (Houghton Mifflin)
1963: *A Wrinkle in Time,* Madeleine L'Engle (Farrar)
1964: *It's Like This, Cat,* Emily Neville (Harper)
1965: *Shadow of a Bull,* Maia Wojciechowska (Atheneum)
1966: *I, Juan de Pareja,* Elizabeth Borton de Trevino (Farrar)
1967: *Up a Road Slowly,* Irene Hunt (Follet)
1968: *From the Mixed-Up Files of Mrs. Basil E. Frankweiler,* E. L. Konigsburg (Atheneum)
1969: *The High King,* Lloyd Alexander (Holt)
1970: *Sounder,* William H. Armstrong (Trophy)
1971: *Summer of the Swans,* Betsy Byars (Viking)
1972: *Mr. Frisby and the Rats of NIMH,* Robert C. O'Brien (Atheneum)
1973: *Julie of the Wolves,* Jean Craifhead George (Harper)
1974: *The Slave Dancer,* Paula Fox (Bradbury)
1975: *M. C. Higgins, the Great,* Virginia Hamilton (Macmillan)
1976: *The Grey King,* Susan Cooper (Atheneum)
1977: *Roll of Thunder, Hear My Cry,* Mildred D. Taylor (Dial)
1978: *Bridge to the Teribithia,* Katherine Paterson (Crowell)
1979: *The Westing Game,* Ellen Raskin (Dutton)
1980: *A Gathering of Days,* Joan W. Blos (Scribner)
1981: *Jacob Have I Loved,* Katherine Paterson (Crowell)
1982: *Dicey's Song,* Cynthia Voight (Atheneum)
1983: *The Glorious Flight: Across the Channel with Louis*

Bleriot, Alice and Martin Provensen (Viking)

1984: *Dear Mr. Henshaw,* Beverly Cleary (Morrow)

1985: *Hero and the Crown,* Robin McKinley (Greenwillow)

1986: *Sarah, Plain and Tall,* Patricia MacLachlan (HarperCollins)

1987: *The Whipping Boy,* Sid Fleischman (Greenwillow)

1988: *Lincoln,* Russell Freedman (Ticknor & Fields)

1989: *Joyful Noise,* Paul Fleischman (HarperCollins)

1990: *Number the Stars,* Lois Lowry (Houghton Mifflin)

1991: *Maniac Magee,* Jerry Spinelli (Little, Brown)

1992: *Shiloh,* Phyllis Reynolds Naylor (Macmillan)

1993: *Missing May,* Cynthia Rylant (Orchard Books)

1994: *The Giver,* Lois Lowry (Houghton Mifflin)

BOOKS THAT CELEBRITIES LIKED WHEN THEY WERE YOUNG

The Commission on Literature of the National Teachers of English asked a group of celebrities to name the books that had most influenced them when they were children. Here are some of the responses.

1. Mayim Bialik

Are You There God? It's Me, Margaret, Judy Blume
Blubber, Judy Blume
Tales of a Fourth Grade Nothing, Judy Blume

2. Carol Burnett

Jane Eyre, Charlotte Brontë
Roget's Thesaurus
The Yearling, Marjorie K. Rawlings

3. Betsy Byars

The Adventures of Mabel, Harry T. Peck
Uncle Wiggily stories, Howard R. Garis

4. Bill Cosby

The Adventures of Huckleberry Finn, Mark Twain
Aesop's Fables, Aesop
The Bible

5. Paula Danziger

A Separate Peace, John Knowles
The Catcher in the Rye, J. D. Salinger
Pride and Prejudice, Jane Austen

6. John-Paul Gosselaar

Arrowsmith, Sinclair Lewis
The *Betsy, Tacy, and Tibb* books, Maud Hart Lovelace
The Citadel, A. J. Cronin
East of Eden, John Steinbeck
In Dubious Battle, John Steinbeck
Madeleine, Ludwig Bemelmans
Of Mice and Men, John Steinbeck
The Red Badge of Courage, Stephen Crane

7. Louis L'Amour

The Count of Monte Cristo, Alexandre Dumas
Kim, Rudyard Kipling
Treasure Island, Robert Louis Stevenson

8. Linda Lavin

Doctor Doolittle, Hugh Lofting
Island Stallion, Walter Farley
Stuart Little, E. B. White

9. George Lucas

Mutiny on the Bounty, Charles Nordhoff and James N. Hall
Swiss Family Robinson, Johann D. Wyss
Treasure Island, Robert Louis Stevenson

10. Mickey Mantle

The Adventures of Tom Sawyer, Mark Twain

11. Walter Matthau

David Copperfield, Charles Dickens
King Arthur and His Knights, Sir Thomas Malory
The Wind in the Willows, Kenneth Grahame

12. Joan Rivers

Mary Poppins, P. L. Travers
Nancy Drew Mysteries, Carolyn Keene
The Secret Garden, Frances Hodgson Burnett

13. Maurice Sendak

Chicken Little, Beverly C. Burgess
A Child's Garden of Verses, Robert Louis Stevenson
Pinocchio in Africa
The Prince and the Pauper, Mark Twain
Toby Tyler, James Otis

14. Abigail Van Buren ("Dear Abby")

For Whom the Bell Tolls, Ernest Hemingway
The Human Mind, Karl Menninger
Lust for Life, Irving Stone

15. Herve Villechaize

Around the World in Eighty Days, Jules Verne
Twenty Thousand Leagues Under the Sea, Jules Verne
Uncle Tom's Cabin, Harriet Beecher Stowe
Any other books by Jules Verne
The works of Jack London

16. Dionne Warwick

The works of Charlotte Brontë
The works of Charles Dickens
The works of Henry Wadsworth Longfellow

EDWARD ASNER LISTS 7 BOOKS EVERYONE SHOULD READ

Ed Asner has won seven Emmy Awards for his work as an actor, but he is also well known for the work he has done for various political and human causes, including the effort to send medical aid to El Salvador and speaking out against nuclear armament. "These are some of my favorite books," he writes, "and I hope they'll be yours, too."

1. Any books by Samuel Altskeller
2. *Ferdinand the Bull*
3. *Fup,* Jim Dodge
4. *The Last of the Just,* Andre Schwartz-Bart
5. *The Perfect Host,* Theodore Sturgeon
6. *The Scottish Chiefs,* Jane Potter
7. *Stranger in a Strange Land,* Robert Heinlein

5 OF SPIKE LEE'S FAVORITE BOOKS FOR YOUNG READERS

1. *The Egypt Game,* Zilpha Keatley Snyder
2. *A Match of Wills,* Eric Weiner
3. *Monster of the Year,* Stephen Mooser
4. *Philip Hall Likes Me, I Reckon Maybe,* Bette Greene
5. *Yagua Days,* Cruz Martel

6 BOOKS AMY CARTER ENJOYED WHEN SHE LIVED IN THE WHITE HOUSE

Amy Carter was 9 years old when her father, Jimmy Carter, was elected president of the United States. Here are some of the books she read and liked most during her four years in the White House.

1. *From the Mixed Up Files of Mrs. Basil E. Frankweiler,* E. L. Konigsburg
2. *Great Brain,* John Dennis Fitzgerald
3. *King Arthur and the Knights of the Round Table,* Rupert Holland
4. *Robin Hood,* Ann McGovern
5. *Treasure Island,* Robert Louis Stevenson
6. *Watership Down,* Richard Adams

14 BOOKS THAT HAVE BEEN BANNED OR CHALLENGED IN THE PUBLIC SCHOOLS

1. *Are You There God? It's Me, Margaret,* by Judy Blume. This book, along with other Judy Blume books (*Deanie, Then Again, Maybe I Won't, Blubber,* and *Forever*), have been a constant target of the censors, who claim that the books are sexually offensive and amoral. In many communities, students need a permission note from their parents to take these books out of the library.

2. *Our Bodies, Ourselves,* by the Boston Women's Health Book Collective. This important, best-selling health manual for women was banned from a high school in Independence, Missouri, for being "filthy" and for containing "obscene" material about how our bodies work.

3. *Soul on Ice,* by Eldridge Cleaver. This classic work by one of America's most important black writers was removed from a high school district in Island Trees, New York, because it was considered "immoral, anti-American, anti-Christian, and just plain filthy." Fortunately, the book was returned after a 1982 Supreme Court hearing.

4. *The Adventures of Sherlock Holmes,* by Sir Arthur Conan Doyle. Because of references to the occult and spiritualism.

5. *The Diary of Anne Frank,* by Anne Frank. The book, written by a young girl during World War II, was challenged for "sexually offensive" material. One textbook committee in Alabama rejected the book because, they said, it was "a real downer."

6. *Ordinary People,* by Judith Guest. This book, which deals with the mental illness of a young boy, was challenged because one parent found it "obscene and depressing."

7. *The Scarlet Letter,* by Nathaniel Hawthorne. The National Board of Censorship found this classic story by one of America's greatest writers offensive and insisted that it be changed for the film version. A required change was that Hester, the main character, an unwed mother, had to get married.

8. *To Kill a Mockingbird,* by Harper Lee. This classic work dealing with the issue of racism was banned due to the use of the words "damn" and "whore lady."

9. *Merriam-Webster Collegiate Dictionary.* For including "obscene" words.

10. *The Rolling Stone Illustrated History of Rock & Roll,* edited by Jim Miller. This book was challenged in Jefferson

County, Kentucky, because "it will cause our children to become immoral and indecent."

11. *Of Mice and Men,* by John Steinbeck. Due to "profanity and using God's name in vain."

12. *The Adventures of Huckleberry Finn,* by Mark Twain. This book was banned in a number of school districts for a variety of reasons. The book was first removed from library shelves in Massachusetts in 1885 for being "trash and suitable only for the slums." More recently, the book was challenged for its use of the term "nigger."

13. *Alice's Adventures in Wonderland,* by Lewis Carroll. Because of certain references to sex and because the book makes fun of a teacher and a minister.

14. *Charlie and the Chocolate Factory,* by Roald Dahl. A librarian in a Colorado library locked this book away, thinking it encouraged a bad attitude.

12 THINGS YOU CAN DO TO FIGHT CENSORSHIP

1. Find out which books have been banned from your school and read them. Think about why they were censored. You may be surprised to know that some of your best buddies—including Judy Blume and Bart Simpson—have had to deal with censors who felt their work wasn't suitable for young people.

2. Talk to your friends about starting a group to fight censorship. Learn about how censorship works and how your school and library are affected by it.

3. Write letters to newspapers, radio stations, publishers, and members of the local media explaining your opinions on the subject.

4. To learn more about censorship, contact the organization People for the American Way, 1015 18th Street NW, Suite 300, Washington, D.C. 20036.

5. Write to the American Booksellers Association for a complete list of books that have been banned and ask how you can support the annual event called "Banned Books Week" (address: P.O. Box 672, New York, N.Y. 10113).

6. Talk to your parents about censorship and urge them to get involved in the censorship movement in your community.

7. Get your friends and other members of your community to sign petitions against censorship and make sure these are delivered into the hands of public officials who can help. Force them to guarantee their support. If they don't, make sure everyone who signs the petition knows it.

8. Write to your favorite performers and ask what they're doing to help preserve freedom of expression. (When the freedom of one artist is threatened, the freedom of all artists is threatened.)

9. Create art with anti-censorship themes.

10. Create your own T-shirt and get the message on your chest. Here are some ideas for slogans:

11. Support your local library in their anti-censorship efforts. If they aren't doing anything, find out how you can get something started.

12. Read some of the books from the list of banned books on pages 202–204 of this book.

9 LEGENDARY PLACES THAT ANYONE CAN VISIT

Reading can take you places you've never been before. Here's a list of places you might want to visit.

1. Camelot, the magical capital of Logres, which was King Arthur's Kingdom, is a great place to visit if you like enchanted castles. Merlin the Magician built a palace there and decorated it with mystical symbols. To get there, read *The Legend of King Arthur.*

2. Speranza. Plenty of wildlife but no wild beasts, so you're safe. If you like exotic birds and turtles, you'll find this place as awesome as Robinson Crusoe did when he was shipwrecked here in 1659. Directions: read *The Life and Surprising Adventure of Robinson Crusoe* by Daniel Defoe.

3. Lilliput. If you're over six inches tall, you'll feel out of place on this tiny island south of Indonesia. Gulliver sure did when he landed here by mistake. Read about his adventures in *Gulliver's Travels,* by Jonathan Swift.

4. Middle-earth is where elves, dwarfs, and men speak to wizards, and hobbits go on the most amazing journeys. J. R. R. Tolkien wrote of Middle-earth in *The Hobbit, Lord of the Rings,* and other books.

5. Narnia. Created by a lion name Aslan, Narnia is filled with centaurs, fauns, dryads, and a witch. Getting there is complicated: You can only enter through a wardrobe, by magic rings, or by the power of Aslan. It helps if you have a copy of *The Chronicles of Narnia,* by C. S. Lewis.

6. Never-Never Land. Mermaids, pirates, fairies, Red Indians, and adventure—they're here, where Peter Pan takes Wendy Darling to be the mother of the Lost Boys. Read *Peter Pan,* by J. M. Barrie.

7. Oz. Munchkinland is only one region of Oz. Winkie Country, where everyone wears yellow, is another. In Quadling Country they wear red, in Gilliken, purple, and we all know what color they wear in the capital, Emerald City. *The Wonderful Wizard of Oz,* by L. Frank Baum, is very different from the movie!

8. Sleepy Hollow. If you keep your eyes open when you come to Sleepy Hollow, you'll notice that everyone here is just a little bit "dreamy," as if they're in a trance. But try not to lose your head, like poor Ichabod Crane. *The Legend of Sleepy Hollow,* by Washington Irving, makes a great Halloween "vacation."

9. Wonderland. Go to Oxford, England, follow the Thames River, and enter the rabbit hole. Take the long tunnel straight down and you can't miss it. Don't eat or drink anything when you get there, though; strange things can happen. Of course, you can take the easy route by reading *Alice's Adventures in Wonderland* by Lewis Carroll.

13 SEQUELS TO *THE WIZARD OF OZ*

Even if you've seen the movie *The Wizard of Oz* a hundred times, *read the book!* Written by L. Frank Baum in 1900, it remains a classic. But did you know that after Baum wrote the book, he wrote thirteen other books depicting the adventures of his famous characters? You can connect with other Ozmaniacs by joining The International Wizard of Oz Club, 220 North 11th Street, Escanaba, MI 49829.

1. The Land of Oz (1904). Tip, an Ox boy, makes a Pumpkinhead Man, and an old witch brings it to life. They run away to the Emerald City and are "conquered," along with King Scarecrow, by General Jinjur's girl army. Their escape, aided by the Saw Horse, the Woggle-Bug, and the wonderful Flying Gump, makes a lively tale that ends with a real surprise!

2. Ozma of Oz (1907). A storm at sea strands Dorothy on the shores of Ev, where she finds Tik-Tok the Machine Man and Billina the Talking Hen. She also meets her old friends the Scarecrow and Tin Man—and Ozma, the lovely Queen of Oz. But they are soon imprisoned by the tricky Nome King and have a strange adventure in his weird underground castle.

3. Dorothy and the Wizard in Oz (1908). An earthquake plunges Dorothy and her cousin Zed into a magical land in the depths of the earth, where they meet again the jolly Wizard of Oz. After amazing experiences with the Live Vegetables, the Invisible Family, the Gargoyles, and the Dragonettes, they are rescued in the nick of time by Ozma.

4. The Road to Oz (1909). This book tells how to reach Wonderland of Oz over an enchanted road that leads Dorothy into all kinds of adventures. On the way she meets the funny Shaggy Man, Button-Bright (who is not so bright) and Polychrome, the Rainbow's Daughter. At the end of the road is the Emerald City—and Ozma's wonderful birthday party.

5. The Emerald City of Oz (1910). Dorothy finally is invited to live in Oz permanently. But while she is on an Ozian sightseeing tour with her Aunt Em and Uncle Henry, the vengeful Nome King is plotting to tunnel under the surrounding desert and capture the Land of Oz. How the Emerald City is miraculously saved makes an amazing, and delightful, ending.

6. The Patchwork Girl of Oz (1913). Ojo, a little Munchkin boy, sees a Crooked Magician make a ragdoll servant out of a patchwork quilt and bring her to life. Ojo's Unk Nunkie, the zany Patchwork Girl, and the haughty Glass Cat make this one of the best of the Oz stories.

7. Tik-Tok of Oz (1914). Queen Ann of Oogaboo goes forth to conquer the world. Betsy Bobbin and Hank the Mule are shipwrecked on the island of Talking Flowers. The Shaggy Man sets out to seek his long-lost brother. How they all fall into the clutches of the Nome King—and are rescued by Tik-Tok, the intrepid Mechanical Man—is related in this strange and funny tale.

8. The Scarecrow of Oz (1915). Tiny Trot and Cap'n Bill are exploring caves off the California coast when a whirlpool engulfs their boat. They finally reach far-off Jinxland, where King Krewl has made a witch freeze the heart of a lovely princess. Things go from bad to worse before our old friend the Scarecrow arrives on the scene and saves the day.

9. Rinkitink in Oz (1916). Prince Inga of Pingaree is the hero of this perilous quest in the islands of the Nonestic Ocean. Jolly King Rinkitink and his surly goat Bilbil provide the comic relief. They sail off to rescue Inga's parents from the pirates of Regos. How they find, lose, and find again the three magic pearls that are their only hope of success adds up to a thrilling adventure.

10. The Lost Princess of Oz (1917). Ozma is stolen! So are all the magical treasures of Oz, including the Cookie Cook's diamond dishpan. Dorothy and the Wizard head a search party and hunt for the thief until they discover the enchanted Wickerwork Castle and its eerie secret. Who the scoundrel was, where Ozma has been, and where her friends find her will surprise you.

11. The Tin Woodman of Oz (1918). The Tin Woodman, with the Scarecrow and Woot the Wanderer, sets out to find his long-forgotten sweetheart. A wicked Giantess transforms them into a Tin Owl, a Straw-stuffed Bear, and a Green Monkey. How they manage to regain their real forms, and what the Tin Woodman really finds, makes a bizarre and mirth-filled tale.

12. The Magic of Oz (1919). A mischief-bent boy with a magical secret meets the spiteful old Nome King and they decide to invade Oz. Trot and Cap'n Bill, lured by a wonderful Magic Flower, are trapped on a deadly island. Dorothy and the Wizard go off to search for a magic birthday present for Ozma. Their paths all cross, and the result is "mixed magic."

13. Glinda of Oz (1920). Ozma and Dorothy travel to a far-off part of Oz to make peace between the warring Flatheads and Skeezers' glass-domed island city when it mysteriously submerges. Finally Glinda, the Good Sorceress of Oz, and the Wizard pool their magic to bring about a thrilling underwater rescue.

11 BOOKS YOU WILL ENJOY IF YOU ARE INTERESTED IN AFRICAN-AMERICAN CULTURE

1. *All It Takes Is Practice,* by Betty Miles (Knopf, 1976). The arrival of an interracial family in town upsets the quiet lives of Stuart and his fellow fifth graders.

2. *Bizou,* by Norma Klein (Viking, 1983). Bizou, a French child with a black American mother, learns her family roots.

3. *Circle of Fire,* by William H. Hooks (Atheneum, 1982). Three friends—a white boy and two black boys—try to thwart an attack on some Irish gypsies by the Klan.

4. *Go Well, Stay Well,* by Toeckey Jones (Harper, 1980). A white girl in South Africa meets a black girl her own age, and a friendship begins in spite of social pressures.

5. *Iggie's House,* by Judy Blume (Dell, 1970). A black family moves into Iggie's old house.

6. *The Integration of Mary-Larkin Thornhill,* by Ann Waldron (Dutton, 1975). On her parents' order, a white northern girl must attend a black junior high school.

7. *It Ain't All For Nothin',* by Walter Dean Myers (Avon, 1979). A 12-year-old boy is cast adrift in Harlem.

8. *Long Journey Home,* by Julius Lester (Dial, 1972). These six stories based on fact concern slaves and ex-slaves and their lives in a hostile America.

9. *Ludell,* by Brenda Wilkinson (Harper, 1975). A tender story of a girl's year in the fifth grade in a southern segregated school in the mid-1950s.

10. *Return to South Town,* by Lorenz Graham (Harper, 1976). In this fourth volume of a celebrated series, David

Williams, now a doctor, returns to the southern town from which his black family fled years ago.

11. *The Soul Brothers and Sister Lou,* by Kristin Hunter (Scribners, 1968). Louretta Hawkens, a 14-year-old girl, and her friends grow up in an urban ghetto and, in spite of frustration, succeed in creating soul music.

7 BOOKS YOU WILL ENJOY IF YOU ARE INTERESTED IN LATIN CULTURE

1. *Felita,* by Nicholasa Mohr (Dial, 1979). A Puerto Rican family moves from a friendly neighborhood to one in which Spanish is not spoken.

2. *Juan's Eighteen-Wheeler Summer,* by Marian T. Place and Charles G. Preston (Dodd, 1982). A Mexican-American boy spends a summer working with a truck driver to buy a bicycle.

3. *Lupita Manana,* by Patricia Beatty (Morrow, 1981). Two young Mexicans must travel to the United States to find work.

4. *Maria Luisa,* by Winifred Madison (Harper, 1971). Maria Luisa encounters prejudice against Chicanos when she and her younger brother move to San Francisco to live with an aunt.

5. *Sparrow Hawk Red,* by Ben Mikaelsen (Hyperion, 1994). A boy flies an airplane over the Mexican border and lives with the street children there.

6. *Where the Deer and the Cantaloupe Play,* by T. Ernesto Bethancourt (Oak Tree, 1981). A young New York Latin tries to find himself a place in the Wild West.

7. *Yagua Days,* by Cruz Martel (Dial, 1976). Adam Bure visits his parents' homeland, Puerto Rico, for the first time.

6 BOOKS YOU WILL ENJOY IF YOU ARE INTERESTED IN JEWISH CULTURE

1. *Bitter Herbs and Honey,* by Barbara Cohen (Lothrop, 1976). Difficulties and differences are explored in this story of an Orthodox Jewish girl growing up in a New Jersey gentile community in 1916.

2. *Dmitry: A Young Soviet Immigrant,* by Joanne E. Bernstein (Houghton Mifflin, 1981). A Russian-Jewish family leaves the Soviet Union for a life in the United States.

3. *King of the Seventh Grade,* by Barbara Cohen (Lothrop, 1982). Vic Abrams's secure world becomes unstuck when his mother reveals he is not Jewish and therefore will not have a Bar Mitzvah.

4. *The Murderer,* by Felice Holman (Scribners, 1978). A young Jewish boy growing up in the days of the Great Depression is bullied by local boys and accused of murdering Christ.

5. *Stories My Grandfather Should Have Told Me,* by Deborah Brodie (Hebrew, 1977). Twelve stories from a variety of authors that explore many aspects of twentieth-century Jewish life.

6. *The Turning Point,* by Naomi J. Karp (Harcourt, 1976). Hannah and brother Zach encounter anti-Semitism when their Bronx family moves to the suburbs.

3 BOOKS YOU WILL ENJOY IF YOU ARE INTERESTED IN ASIAN CULTURE

1. *In The Year of the Boar and Jackie Robinson,* by Bette Bao Lord (Harper, 1984). This is the story of a Chinese girl who leaves China to join her father in New York in 1947.

2. *Journey Home,* by Yoshiko Uchida (Atheneum, 1975). This is the story of the life of a Japanese-American family after their release from a World War II internment camp.

3. *Sea Glass,* by Laurence Yep (Harper, 1979). An awkward Chinese-American boy moves to a new junior high school and has trouble adjusting.

8 BOOKS YOU WILL ENJOY IF YOU ARE INTERESTED IN NATIVE AMERICAN CULTURE

1. *Indian Hill,* by Clyde Robert Bulla (Harper, 1963). A young Navajo boy and his family must adjust to new ways when they move from the reservation to the city.

2. *Mak,* by Belle Coates (Houghton Mifflin, 1981). Mak is torn between the Indian and white cultures.

3. *Number Four,* by Molly Cone (Houghton Mifflin, 1972). After his brother's death, Benjamin begins to establish his native American identity, as his brother did. Tragedy results in this sensitive and convincing novel.

4. *People of the Dream,* by James D. Forman (Farrar,

1972). This novel concerns the flight of Chief Joseph and his Nez Perce people and the gross injustice inflicted on them.

5. *The Scared One,* by Dennis Haseley (Warne, 1983). This is the story of an Indian boy who is living in fear.

6. *Stone Fox,* by John Reynolds Gardiner (Harper, 1980). Little Willy competes against the Indian Stone Face in the national dogsled races.

7. *When The Legend Dies,* by Hal Borland (Harper, 1963). A Ute Indian boy faces many difficulties growing up in Colorado.

8. *The Whipman Is Watching,* by T. A. Dyer (Houghton Mifflin, 1979). Children who live on an American Indian reservation try to retain their identity in an all-white school.

27 MAGAZINES THAT PUBLISH WORKS BY KIDS

You'll learn *tons* about getting your stories and poems published by consulting a reference book called *Market Guide for Young Writers* by Kathy Henderson. Try the library or ask your local bookstore to order a copy for you from Writer's Digest Books, 1507 Dana Avenue, Cincinnati, OH 45207; 1-800-289-0963. (The book costs $16.95.)

Magazines aim themselves at different kinds of readers, so you may want to find out more about their specific interests before you send in your stories or poems. For instance, your short story about your boat trip to Alaska may be great, but *Lifeprints* won't publish it no matter how good it is since they concentrate on pieces for people who are visually impaired. On the other hand, *Stone Soup* would probably be very interested in your adventure.

See the list on page 227 for general instructions on sending material to magazines. Good luck!

1. *The Acorn*
1530 7th St.
Rock Island, IL 61201

For kids in grades K through 12, publishes fiction, nonfiction, and black and white drawings on any subject, including personal feelings about anything.

2. *American Girl Magazine*
8400 Fairway Place
Middletown, WI 53562

A glossy magazine with a section on kids' poems, tips, and suggestions. No short stories.

3. *Calliope*
7 School St.
Petersborough, N.H. 03458

Publishes only short poems and letters by kids but often holds creative writing contests.

4. *Chalk Talk*
1550 Mills Rd., RR2
Sidney, BC V8l 3s1, Canada

Written for kids and by kids aged 5 to 14. Publishes fiction, nonfiction, poetry, crafts, puzzles, and whatever else you can think of. Originality counts more than ability here.

5. *Child Life*
1100 Waterway Blvd.
P.O. Box 567
Indianapolis, IN 46202

Publishes poetry, stories, and jokes for kids aged 9 to 11. The magazine is mostly about health and nutrition, but your submissions don't have to be about these subjects.

6. *Children's Digest*
   1100 Waterway Blvd.
   P.O. Box 567
   Indianapolis, IN 46202

Another health-oriented magazine, this one for preteens, that publishes stories, poems, and jokes by kids. Your submission may be on any subject.

7. *Creative Kids*
   P.O. Box 6448
   Mobile, AL 36660

One of the best we've come across! Publishes stories, poetry, plays, and photography by and for kids aged 5 to 18. Get this magazine to find out what talented kids are up to.

8. *Creative With Words*
   P.O. Box 223226
   Carmel, CA 93922

Another excellent magazine with plenty of space for submissions from young people. Sometimes, when they can't publish your work, the editors will take the time to offer opinions. (This is rare! Usually you'll get a standard rejection letter that basically says "thanks but no thanks.")

9. *Flying Pencil Press*
   P.O. Box 7667
   Elgin, IL 60121

Not really a magazine, *Flying Pencil* publishes creative works by young people aged 8 to 14 in book form from time to time. Each edition has a different theme, so find out what themes they're working on before you send anything in.

10. *Highlights for Children*
803 Church St.
Honesdale, PA 18431

The magazine is for kids aged 2 to 12 but publishes short stories, factual articles, jokes, plays, and art (color and black and white) by older kids.

11. *How On Earth!*
P.O. Box 3347
West Chester, PA 19381

"Teens supporting compassionate ecological living." Publishes anything concerning ecology, ethics, animal and global issues, by and for people aged 12 to 20. This is a nonprofit magazine completely run by volunteers.

12. *Ink Blot*
7200 Burmeister
Saginaw, MI 48609

A monthly newsletter especially designed for the voices of new, young writers. Submit nonfiction essays, short stories, poetry, or black and white art.

13. *Kid's Korner Newsletter*
P.O. Box 413
Joaquin, TX 75954

This newsletter by kids and for kids publishes fiction, nonfiction, and art on any subject.

14. *Kids N' Sibs*
191 Whittier Rd.
Rochester, N.Y. 14624

A newsletter that allows kids to share the views and experiences of disabled kids and their siblings. The publication is free.

15. *Boodle: By Kids, for Kids*
P.O. Box 1049
Portland, IN 47371

Each issue contains *lots* of stories, articles, poems, and mazes sent in by kids. Doesn't like anything "sad or depressing."

16. *Kopper Bear Press*
P.O. Box 19454
Boulder, CO 80303

A real publishing company looking for high-quality fiction, nonfiction, poetry, essays, and even full-length novels by young authors. If you ask for it, they'll give you their opinion of your work.

17. *Listen, Celebrating Positive Choices*
P.O. Box 7000
Boise, ID 83707

A magazine that promotes physical and mental health also accepts short essays and poems for their "Listening" column.

18. *The Mcguffy Writer*
5128 Westgate Dr.
Oxford, OH 45056

Short stories, essays, poems, songs, and black and white art by kids under age 12.

19. *Meryln's Pen: The National Magazine of Student Writing*
P.O. Box 1058
East Greenwhich, R.I. 02818

Publishes just about anything by kids in grades 7 through 10. Encourages expressions that come from personal experience.

20. *New Moon*
P.O. Box 3587
Duluth, MN 55803-3587

"The magazine for girls and their dreams" was created by girls and is written for girls aged 8 to 14. Offers a wide variety of topics, from stories, biographies, and daydreams, to book, movie, and electronics reviews. This publication promotes the idea that all of us, *all over the globe,* are connected. Highly recommended.

21. *Skipping Stones*
P.O. Box 3939
Eugene, OR 97403

Publishes writing and art by kids aged 7 to 18. In addition to stories, poems, and art, they also publish jokes, recipes, magic tricks, science experiments, toys, games, and movie and book reviews.

22. *Skylark*
Purdue University Claumet, 2200
169th St.
Hammond, IN 46323

Mostly written by adults, but each issue has 15 to 20 pages of prose, poetry, and art by writers and artists aged 8 to 18. Focuses on publishing well-stated opinions on many subjects.

23. *Spark!*
1507 Dana Ave.
Cincinnati, OH 45207

This magazine, which encourages creativity in kids aged 6 to 12, publishes kids' submissions in their "Show and Tell" column.

24. *Spring Tides*
Savannah Country Lower School
824 Stillwood Dr.
Savannah, GA 31419

Publishes stories and poems, with or without illustrations, in black and white or color. By kids aged 5 to 12.

25. *Stone Soup*
P.O. Box 83
Santa Cruz, CA 95063

One of the most famous magazines for kids, probably because it's often used in schools. Includes stories, poems, personal experiences, book reviews, and art by children under age 13.

26. *'TEEN*
P.O. Box 488990
Los Angeles, CA 90048-5515

A glossy magazine like the ones you see on the newstand but with a feature called "In Your Own Words," where readers send in thoughts and poems about their lives.

27. *The Writer's Slate*
P.O. Box 734
Garden City, KS 67846

Original poetry and prose by kids in grades K–12 published three times a year, including one issue that includes only the work of contest winners. Illustrated submissions are okay.

26 SPECIAL-INTEREST MAGAZINES YOU MIGHT WANT TO SUBSCRIBE TO

The magazines listed here publish articles by kids and for kids. Be sure to see the list "27 Magazines That Publish Works by Kids" on page 215.

1. *Biography Today*
   Omnigraphics, Inc.
   Penebscot Building
   Detroit, MI 48225
   Profiles newsmakers in fields such as entertainment, politics, sports, and literature.

2. *Boys' Life*
   Boy Scouts of America
   1325 W. Walnut Hill Lane
   P.O. Box 15079
   Irving, TX 75015-2079
   All about scouting for boys

3. *Business Kids*
   1300 1st. NW, Suite 1080 East
   Washington, D.C. 20005
   Profiles teens who own their own businesses.

4. *Cobblestone*
   7 School St.
   Petersborough, N.H. 03458
   Each issue concerns a particular theme related to American history.

5. *Disney Adventures*
   Walt Disney Publications
   500 South Buena Vista
   Burbank, CA 91521-0001
   For kids aged 7 to 14. Articles on music, movies, trends, games, travel and adventure

6. *Dolphin Log*
   Cousteau Society Membership Center
   870 Greenbriar Circle
   Suite 402
   Chesapeake, VA 23320
   Exploration of oceans, rivers, waterways, and marine life

7. *Faces*
   7 School St.
   Petersborough, N.H. 03458
   Articles submitted are

about the customs and cultures of different races around the world.

8. *Falcon Magazine*
P.O. Box 15936
North Hollywood, CA 91615-5936
Articles, games, and lots of interesting stuff for kids who care about nature and conservation

9. *Home Education*
P.O. Box 1083
Tonasket, WA 98855
Nonfiction articles and interviews about kids who are educated at home

10. *Kidsports*
P.O. Box 8488
Coral Springs, FL 33075
Posters, games, fiction, and fact about sports

11. *Little Leaguer*
Little League Baseball Inc.
P.O. Box 3485
Williamsport, PA 17701-0485
Baseball-related articles

12. *National Geographic World*
1145 17th and M St. NW
Washington, D.C. 20036-4688
Publishes artwork, photos, and poems about the natural world.

13. *National Wildlife*
National Wildlife Federation
8925 Leesburg Pike
Vienna, VA 22184
Photos and articles about wildlife, conservation, and ecology

14. *Nintendo Power*
Nintendo of America, Inc.
4820-150th Ave. NE
Redmond, VA 98052
Game reviews, tips, and stories

15. *Odyssey*
7 School St.
Petersborough, N.H. 03458
Publishes scientific articles related to a particular theme.

16. *Owl*
255 Great Arrow Ave.
Buffalo, N.Y. 14207-3082
Articles and photos on animals, science, and nature

17. *Plays*
120 Boylston St.
Boston, MA 02116
Original one-act plays and programs for kids interested in theater

18. *Ranger Rick*
National Wildlife Federation
8925 Leesburg Pike
Vienna, VA 22184
Science, conservation, and study via articles, photos, and stories

19. *Sassy*
Lang Communications
230 Park Ave., 7th Floor
New York, N.Y. 10169-0005
Articles related to girls' lives, relationships, and problem-solving

20. *Sports Illustrated for Kids*
P.O. Box 830609
Birmingham, AL 35283-0609
Articles, games, comics, and loads of inside information about your favorite sports stars

21. *Superscience Blue*
Scholastic, Inc.
2931 E. McCarty Street
Jefferson City, MO 65102-3710
Science and technology news and experiments

22. *3-2-1 Contact*
P.O. Box 53051
Boulder, CO 80322
Science, technology, nature study, and current events

23. *U*S* Kids*
Children's Better Health Institute
P.O. Box 7036
Red Oak, IA 51591
True-life stories about nature, pets, and family life

24. *YM*
Young Miss
Gruner & Jahr
685 Third Ave., 30th Floor
New York, N.Y. 10017-4024
Fashion and beauty related articles

25. *Zillions*
P.O. Box 54861
Boulder, CO 80322-4861
One of the most interesting magazines we've come across, with lots of articles on how to get the most for your money

26. *Zoobooks*
Wildlife Education, Inc.
3590 Kettner Blvd.
San Diego, CA 92101-1139
Each issue covers a particular animal or group of animals.

10 TIPS FOR YOUNG WRITERS

Lots of kids have learned that writing is one of the most rewarding hobbies you can have. It's a great way to explore ideas, practice communicating, and save your thoughts for later reference. It's also a lot of fun. Here are some ideas that might help you along the way.

1. Write about things you really know about instead of spending a lot of time trying to come up with exotic subjects and situations. If you write from your own experience—and from the heart—your story will be a lot more believable.

2. If you think your own life is boring and not worth writing about, remember that different people have different experiences, and your life may very well be what other readers can only dream about. Also pay attention to what goes on around you, even the "boring details." These could help to make your story more realistic.

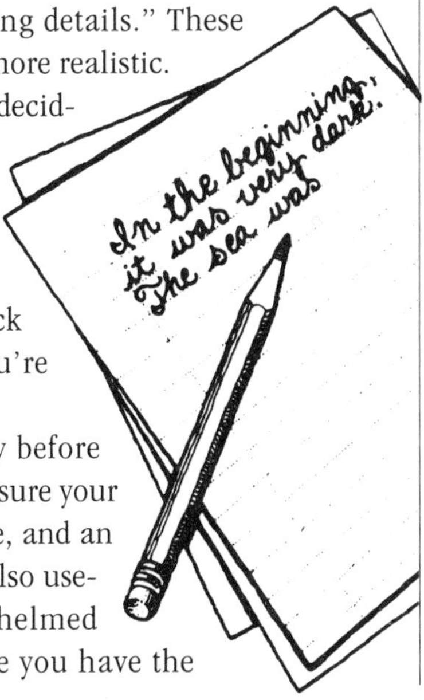

3. If you're having trouble deciding how to begin (lots of writers have the same problem), just start writing from the point at which you feel comfortable. You can always go back and add a beginning when you're done.

4. Try to outline your story before you start writing it. Then make sure your story has a beginning, a middle, and an end. The outline technique is also useful for writers who are overwhelmed with all they want to say. Once you have the outline done, you can just write the story one part at a time.

5. After you've finished your first version of the story, which is commonly called a "first draft," review what you've done. Ask yourself if you've used exactly the right words to get your point across. Use a thesaurus to find other words that mean almost the same thing. Also, use a dictionary to check spelling before you write a final version of the story. And keep in mind that many writers go through numerous versions before they are satisfied with that they've written. Paula Danziger once said that she wrote four different endings for *The Cat Ate My Gymsuit* before she finally found one that seemed right.

6. Even if you're not ready to write a story, you can still work on your writing skills by keeping a diary of everything you see and hear and practicing putting those observations into words. You can use those observations later if you need ideas for details.

7. Don't worry about getting your stories published. Most kids' stories never get into print, but you shouldn't let this discourage you. Your writing will serve as great practice for the stories or books you may write when you get older, and in the meantime, you can enjoy the experience and dream about the future.

8. Don't be shy about sharing your stories with friends and family. This is sometimes hard, especially if you're afraid that others won't like what you've written. Right now, it's important that you like what you've written. But be open-minded, too. It's often hard to take criticism about something that's so personal, but others may have good ideas that will help you improve your craft in the future. So listen to what they say and then be as objective as you can in deciding if what they're saying makes sense.

9. Enjoy yourself! No matter how serious you are about what you are doing, it will come out a lot better if you can relax a little and take pleasure from the experience. Writing is hard work, but the roads you travel in the course of doing it and the doors it opens can serve as some of the most gratifying experiences in your life.

10. Learn to write by reading a lot—everything you can find. Reading the works of others will give you ideas and teach you all about the variety of styles that there are. Thomas Rockwell, who wrote *How to Eat Fried Worms,* believes in this method. As he put it, "The best way to learn to write is to write a lot and read a lot."

10 TIPS FOR SUBMITTING YOUR WORK TO MAGAZINES FOR PUBLICATION

If you're an aspiring writer, you've probably daydreamed about seeing your name in print. Maybe you will someday. But until that happens, keep trying, and keep trying new things. What you do before you become successful is just as important as what you do afterward. Here are some ways to present yourself professionally to publishers. If they take you seriously, maybe they'll give you their opinions, which is *very* helpful. Also, check out a book called *The Young Person's Guide to Becoming a Writer* by Janet E. Grant.

1. Do not send money to anyone in return for publishing work.

2. Be sure that the work you submit is original, which means that you wrote it by yourself and that none of it was copied.

3. Only submit your best work. Keep working on your piece until you're sure it says exactly what you want it to say.

4. Make sure you send your work to the appropriate publication. No matter how good your story is, you'll get turned down if a magazine never publishes that kind of story. For this reason, write to magazines and contests for their exact guidelines before you send in anything. Send a self-addressed stamped envelope with your request.

5. Some submissions require that a parent or guardian fill out a certain form. Follow this and other rules very carefully.

6. Write or type your entry on one side of 8½-by-11 sheets of paper. If you write by hand, use lined paper. If you type, double-space. Be neat but remember that even the most professional-looking essay won't get published if it's not a good essay. (Generally, if you're under 13, you're not expected to type.)

7. On the first page of your work, include your name, address, phone number, and the date.

8. Do not tell an editor your life story unless you are asked to do so.

9. Always make a copy of anything you send before you send it. *Most magazines and contests do not return the copy you send them.*

10. Most magazines don't pay kids for submissions. Send your work in anyway. Young writers need all the experience they can get, and it *is* fun to see your name in print.

11. Learn that failing is what comes before success—and *keep trying!*

12. Be patient. It may take *months* before you get a response from a magazine.

Upton Sinclair, one of America's most famous writers, supported his family at the age of 15 by writing short stories and jokes for magazines. Even when he left home two years later, he continued to send money home to his parents. Two of Sinclair's most famous books are *The Jungle* and *Dragon's Teeth.*

11 CONTESTS FOR CREATIVE KIDS

Use the addresses given here to send away for more information on contest rules and deadlines. Hey, you never know!

1. Cricket League Contests
P.O. Box 300
Peru, IL 61354

Each month, the magazine holds contests on different themes in four categories: poetry, short stories, art, and photography. There are two age groups: 4 to 9 and 10 to 14.

Prizes: They vary. Most winning entries are published in the magazine.

2. If I Ran the World Contest
1530 7th Street
Rock Island, IL 61201

Essays are limited to 200 words in four grade categories: K to 2; 3 to 5; 6 to 8; 9 to 12. The contest encourages kids to think about making the world a better place to live.

Prizes: Winner is published and gets a one-year subscription to *The Acorn* magazine.

3. Kentucky State Poetry Society Contests
℅ Louise Logan
HC63
P.O. Box 699
Greenup, KY 41144

Open to kids everywhere, a variety of annual poetry contests include categories for grades 1 to 3 and 4 to 6.

Prizes: First-place winners are published, plus there are varying cash prizes and certificates.

4. My Favorite Teacher
1530 7th Street
Rock Island, IL 61201

Each year, one winning essay of no more than 200 words is selected from these grade categories: K to 2; 3 to 5; 6 to 8; 9 to 12.

Prizes: The winner and the favorite teacher each get a one-year subscription to *The Acorn* magazine, and the winning entry is published.

5. National Geographic World
1145 17th and M Streets NW
Washington, D.C. 20036-4688

Aiming to inspire curiosity about the world around us, the contests are geography-related. There are two grade categories: K to 5 and 6 to 9. Sponsored by *National Geographic* magazine.

Prizes: A $5,000 college scholarship is awarded in each category, plus the winner's school receives another $5,000 worth of *National Geographic* educational products.

6. National Written and Illustrated By...
Awards Contests for Students
Landmark Editions, Inc.
1402 Kansas Avenue
Kansas City, MO 64127

Kids have to write and illustrate their own books to enter this contest. For ages 6 to 9, 10 to 13, and 14 to 19.

Prizes: Winners go to Kansas City and participate in preparing their books for publication. They also receive royalties on the sales of their books.

7. Paul A. Witty Outstanding Literature Award
℅ Cathy Collins
Texas Christian University

P.O. Box 32925
Fort Worth, TX 76129

Elementary, junior high, and high school entries are judged separately in two categories: prose and poetry.

Prizes: $25 and plaques to winners, plus merit certificates to others.

8. Publish-a-Book Contest
Raintree/Steck-Vaughn
P.O. Box 27010
Austin, TX 78755

Annual contest for kids in grades 4 to 6 on a specific theme, which is announced each fall.

Prizes: The winning book is published and the author gets a $500 advance plus royalties and 10 free copies of the book.

9. Quill and Scroll International Writing/Photography Contest
University of Iowa
Iowa City, IA 52242-1528

High school and junior high school students compete in different categories, including editorial, editorial cartoon, investigative reporting, news, features, sports, advertising, and photography.

10. *Read* Writing and Art Awards
245 Long Hill Road
Middletown, CT 06457

Read magazine invites students in grades 6 to 12 to compete in separate contests for short stories, essays, and art.

Prizes: First-place winners receive $100 each and their work is published. Second-place winners get $75 each; third-place winners get $50. All winners receive colorful certificates of excellence.

11. *Writing Contests*
The Writing Conference, Inc.
P.O. Box 664
Ottawa, KS 66067

This one is sponsored by The Writing Conference, which tries to get people interested in reading and writing. Students in grades 3 to 12 enter poems and essays on topics that are assigned each year.

Prizes: They vary.

11 SUPERHEROES AND THEIR SUPERPOWERS

1. Batman. He is superpowerful and supersmart. Gets around in his Batmobile with his sidekick, Robin. Batman lives in his laboratory, the Batcave. He also owns a Batplane and lassos criminals with his Batarang.

2. Captain Marvel. The following powers were given to him by a 3,000-year-old wizard: Solomon's wisdom, Hercules' strength, Atlas' stamina, Zeus' power, Achilles' courage, and Mercury's speed.

3. Flash. Became the fastest man on earth when he was hit by a bolt of lightning.

4. Incredible Hulk. When Bruce Banner gets upset, he turns into the Hulk, who has green skin, weighs 1,000 pounds, and is seven feet tall. His strength, which he acquired when he was caught in a nuclear explosion, is incredible.

5. Matter-Eater Lad. He can eat anything, and he has often saved his pals by munching jail bars, caved-in rocks, and other seemingly indigestible obstacles.

6. Popeye. Just give him a can of spinach and Popeye turns into a human dynamo who can beat up anyone or anything.

7. Sabraman. A popular superhero in Israel, Sabraman can shoot radioactive rays from his eyes, cross oceans in a split second, and surround himself with a magic field that prevents anyone from attacking him.

8. Siopawman. If you've never been to the Philippines, you've probably never heard of Siopawman, since that's where he's popular. Bullets and blows can't hurt him, and he's kind of ugly, with a big nose, a fat body, and a bald head. He wears an "S" on his chest like Superman. His enemies are all criminals, like Jelloman, who quiver with fear at the very thought of Siopawman.

9. Spiderman. When he was bitten by a radioactive spider, Peter Parker turned into a superhero with the power to climb walls and act like a human spider. His web-shooters spin rope lines, and he can grow new arms.

10. Superman. He can fly faster than a speeding bullet, leap tall buildings in a single bound, and travel to the very edges of the universe. He has superhearing and X-ray vision, not to mention his superstrength, with which he can lift a whole railroad train. His breath can blow supercold. Superman's only weakness is that he is vulnerable to kryptonite, especially the green variety.

11. Wonder Woman. Wonder Woman was born with her incredible strength, which allowed her to tear a tree out by the roots when she was 3 years old and to run as fast as a deer by the time she turned 5. Her metal bracelets protect her—bullets bounce off them. She has a radio in her headband; her belt keeps her honest; and her invisible robot plane can travel at the rate of 3,000 miles per hour. (When Wonder Woman needs her plane, she summons it by sending thought waves out to it.)

THE JUSTICE SOCIETY OF AMERICA

Back in the 1940s, when America was at war, comic book characters, too, were busy keeping the world safe, fighting for "truth, justice, and the American way." To this end, the Justice Society of America was formed. These were its members:

- Aquaman
- Atom
- Batman
- Black Canary
- Dr. Fate
- Dr. Midnight
- Flash
- Green Lantern
- Hawkman
- Hourman
- Red Tornado
- Johnny Thunder
- Martian Manhunter
- Mr. Terrific
- Sandman
- Spectre
- Starman
- Superman
- Wildcat
- Wonder Woman

POPEYE'S VITAL STATISTICS

Height: 5 feet, 6 inches
Weight: 158 pounds
Hair: red
Biceps: 7 inches
Forearm: 20 inches
Chest, expanded: 60 inches
Thigh: 7 inches
Calf: 20 inches
Spinach capacity: 36 tons

OLIVE OYL'S VITAL STATISTICS

Height: 5 feet, 10 7/8 inches
Weight: 96 pounds, 3 ounces
Neck: swan
Nose: pickle
Arms: long
Shoe size: 14AAAAAA

16 LANDMARKS IN VIDEO GAME HISTORY

Marcus Webb is the editor of *Replay* magazine, a publication for people who work in the coin-operated amusement world. Following is his pick of the major events in the evolution of video games over the past 20-plus years.

1972: Nolan Bushnell, founder of Atari, creates his first smash: Pong. This simple two-player game—like tennis in slow motion—features sliding paddles that intercept a white ball as it glides across the screen. A revolution in entertainment is under way.

1978: Star Fire, by Exidy, is the first video game with a four-color screen. (But it doesn't really have a color screen: It cheats by placing a layer of colored plastic over the black and white monitor!)

1980: Bally/Midway introduces Pac-Man. The game is such a smash that the Pac-Man character (a smiley face in profile, his mouth wide open; see "16 Smileys," page 250) soon appears on the cover of *Time* magazine.

1981: Mario (of Brothers fame) makes his first appearance in a wacky game, Donkey Kong. This year the success of arcade games such as Space Invaders and Galaxian make video a $7.25 billion (that's with a "b") industry, making more money this year than the record and movie businesses combined.

1982: Ms. Pac-Man, the first of six spinoffs of the original, appears; it goes on to sell more copies than any other arcade game and is still earning money today. This year also sees the first interactive laser disc games, where players' choices determine which of many cinema-quality animated scenes will play. The most popular of this type is Dragon's Lair, which in 1994 was reborn as a CD-ROM game.

1983: President Ronald Reagan endorses video games as "teaching tools." Speaking to a group of math and science students, he says, "Many young people develop incredible hand, eye, and brain coordination in playing these games.... Watch a twelve-year-old take evasive action and score multiple hits while playing Space Invaders and you'll appreciate the skills of tomorrow's pilots." (Reagan reminded his audience, however, "Friends and homework still come first.") No doubt some of the kids weaned on video games flew fighter planes in the Gulf War a decade later.

1984: Data East releases Karate Champ, the first martial arts head-to-head game. A year later, the top three games were all fighting games. The trend continues today, with fighting games blowing away their competitors.

1985: SEGA releases Hang On, its first simulator game. The game features a full-size motorcycle with a monitor mounted on the handlebars and controls in the handgrips and foot pedals.

1986: Gauntlet, by Atari, a Dungeons and Dragons–type fantasy adventure, is the first game to introduce a new perspective: Players look down on the characters from above as they run from room to room in a castle. Also this year, Nintendo launches its first home system just in time for Christmas.

1987: Taito releases the first Double Dragon, which stays on the list of top ten arcade games for an unheard-of two years. The level of violence (a woman gets punched, for example) draws concern from adults.

1989: FBI anti-drug messages appear on the "attract screens" of arcade games. Teenage Mutant Ninja Turtles by Konami is one of the year's big hits, as is the first version of Capcom's Street Fighter. Nintendo introduces Game Boy.

1990: The first CD-ROM video game appears, called It Came From the Desert, by Cinemaware. The game features live-action, fifteen-frames-per-second digital video footage and computer animation of giant ants. Actors exchange witty dialogue (He: "Ants the size of gas trucks!" She: "I don't even like little ants at picnics!") as they battle the mutants with pistols, flamethrowers, tanks, and fighter planes. Also this year, in Chicago, Virtual World Entertainment creates the first simulator center, Mech War, in which players sit in "pods" equipped with screens. Each screen shows the field—a post-apocalyptic landscape—from the individual player's point of view. Between four and sixteen players manipulate their huge robots around the field, trying to destroy each other in a high-tech version of Capture the Flag.

1991: The era of true VR—virtual reality—begins. A company called Virtuality creates 'Dactyl Nightmare, the first VR game, in which players wear helmets that respond to their head movements. They move around a three-dimensional platform in space, lobbing grenades at their opponents (another player or the computer) while ducking the onslaught of digital pterodactyls.

1992: The first five Virtual Reality Centers—arcades devoted to VR games and simulators—open in St. Louis, New York, and other cities.

1993: The U.S. government demands that the video game industry create a "voluntary" rating system to indicate the amount of sex and violence in a game.

1994: SEGA test markets the Sega Channel, a cable station that allows subscribers to access and download up to 50 different games directly into their Genesis systems.

10 IMPORTANT DATES IN PINBALL HISTORY

If you're a pinball wizard interested in competing in a tournament, you can call Chris Warren, Chairman of the Pinball Promotion Committee for the AMOA (Amusement and Music Operators Association), at 406-442-7088 for more information.

1775: Bagatelle, a pin game, is introduced in Europe. A pin game is basically a box with a bunch of pins, or obstacles, sticking up from the bottom. You drop a ball in the top, then whack and shake the box while trying to get the ball to fall through various holes. Some holes are worth more points than others. Bagatelle (the word means "little thing" or "trifle"; today it's pronounced "bag-uh-telly") was a smash hit in coffee shops and other eighteenth-century hangouts.

1929: Whoopee, the first copyrighted game of Bagatelle, is marketed in the United States by George Deprez and the In and Out Game Company of Chicago. Whoopee doesn't advance the Bagatelle concept very much. It too is simply a box covered with glass; you drop the metal ball in and shake the box around. Different versions have different arrangements of pins and holes. There is no art or design on the Whoopee box other than the name of the game. In some places, the game was used for gambling.

1934: The first "tilt" feature appears on an electric pin game, Signal, manufactured by Bally. As every frustrated pinballer knows, tilt mechanisms shut the game off if you get too rough. This innovation added years to the life of a machine, since these games tend to be subject to lots of abuse.

1947: Humpty Dumpty, created by the D. Gottlieb Co., is the first to use flippers—six of them, to be precise. (Technically, machines without flippers were known as "pin games"; once flippers evolved, they became "pinball," or, to be really accurate, "flipper pinball.")

1954: Super Jumbo, also by Gottlieb, is the first game for more than one player. In this game two players take turns and their scores are tallied by separate counters on the back panel.

1966: Capersville by Bally is the first game to use multiple balls. Certain targets trap up to three balls and then release them simultaneously.

1975: Spirit of '76 by Micro Games is the first all-electronic pinball machine. This one uses digital scoring instead of the revolving mechanical reels that were common up to that time. (Don't confuse this game with The Spirit of '76, released by Gottlieb in the same year.)

1979: Gorgar, the first talking pinball game, is released by Williams. Besides grunting and groaning, the monster Gorgar taunts players with such phrases as "Me Gorgar—beat me!" and "Hurt Gorgar!" (Bonus factoid: In 1933, Contact, a battery-operated pin game by Pacific Amusement Manufacturing, introduces sound—bells and buzzers—to the game.)

1980: The Black Knight by Williams is the first game to feature a multilevel playing field. (Two years later, Gottlieb's Haunted House goes one better and introduces the three-level field.)

1992: The Addams Family by Bally becomes the best-selling pinball machine in history. The fast, complicated action, the wide variety of targets, and the fidelity to the movie all contribute to the machine's vast popularity.

COMPUTER AND VIDEO GAME RATINGS

A lot of the flak about video games comes from people who worry that pixellated violence might escalate into the real thing. The government put pressure on software developers to come up with a video game rating system.

Actually, they came up with two. The Entertainment Software Rating Board—which includes some of the big cheeses from Nintendo, Sega, Sony, and other cartridge and CD-ROM game guys—created a system like that of movie ratings. Games are labeled according to the age of the appropriate audience. Depending on the game, the labels may include descriptions of the content, such as "realistic blood and gore" or "use of tobacco and alcohol" or "contains gambling."

RATING	REPRESENTS	MEANING
EC	Early Childhood	Suitable for ages 3 and up, with no material that parents would find inappropriate. Some games may require reading or other skills.
KA	Kids to Adults	Suitable for ages 6 and up. Appealing to people of many ages and tastes. May include minimal violence, some comic mischief, or crude language.
T	Teen	Suitable for ages 13 and up. May include violent content, profanity, and mild sexual themes.
M	Mature	Suitable for ages 17 and up. May include more intense violence, profanity, and more mature sexual themes than products in the teen category.
AO	Adults Only	Suitable only for adults. May include graphic depictions of sex and violence. Not intended to be sold or rented to people under 18.

Meanwhile, makers of computer-based games created the Recreational Software Advisory Council. This group uses a scale of 1 to 4 to rate the levels of violence, nudity and sex, and profanity. Game makers fill out a questionnaire; the answers are analyzed by a computer, which then spits out the rating. In this system, age doesn't count.

NETIQUETTE

14 Rules of On-Line Courtesy

Computer forums and chat lines are great ways for you to share information and ideas, meet new people, and have a lot of fun to boot. With the information super highway becoming more and more a part of our lives, a new kind of community is forming. Thousands of kids are already hooked into (and hooked on!) computer networks like CompuServe, America Online, and Prodigy. In the years ahead, chances are you'll be plugged directly into that vast computer network called the Internet. Whether you realize it or not, right now you are a citizen of a global village—and you'll want to be a good neighbor.

Swapping messages in forums and chatting live online is no different from sending letters or talking with a group of people at a party. There are right ways and wrong ways to go about it. No one likes someone who interrupts, who hogs the conversation or who changes the subject, or who is intolerant of other people's opinions or mistakes. So you don't come off looking like a complete feeb, here are some expert tips to make yourself welcome on computer forums.

1. Listen before you leap. Plunging into a forum discussion is like trying to jump in while your buddies are turning the jump rope. If your timing and rhythm are off, you'll get tangled up—and no one will have any fun. Take some time just to read a lot of the messages on the message board before sending any of your own. Before joining in a live forum, just listen in for a while. You'll learn a lot by watching how the pros handle themselves.

2. Get your FAQs straight. FAQs are "frequently asked questions." Everyone who's new to the online world has a lot of questions. Chances are, you're not the first person to wonder how to download a file or send a message to a pen pal. Before taking up another person's time with a question that's been asked a squillion times already, check to see if the forum's library has a FAQ file that contains answers to basic questions. Access it and read it carefully. Then, if you still don't understand something, or if you need other information, feel free to post a message to other members.

3. Don't send test messages. There's no need to waste time (and money) sending messages like "Hello! Just testing to see if this works." Better to go ahead and say what you want to say. When you get a response, you'll know the system is functioning—and you won't take up valuable cyberspace in the process. (Sometimes people on forums waste so much time saying "Hi" and "Hello" to each other that they never say anything important. There are even some forums that have the rule No hi!)

4. Stay "on topic." If everybody in the forum is discussing pets, it's impolite to say, "Hey, did anybody see that new Power Rangers episode yesterday?" And pose questions to the appropriate forum. A forum on on-line skating is no place to start discussing the way-cool fatalities in the latest war 'n' gore game.

5. Think twice; post once. Once you've sent a message, you can't take it back. Before you hit the "send" button—and experience that twinge of regret an ohnosecond later (see "Top 14 Techno-Jargon Terms" list on page 246), read over what you've written. If there's a chance it might be misunderstood, or that it might hurt someone else's feelings, or that it might make you look like a total dweeb, erase it. After all, that's what the "DEL" key is for.

6. Watch your tone of voice. If you call your best buddy a dweeb, he'll know from your smile or that playful punch on the arm that you're just giving him a hard time. On-line, though, you don't have that luxury. Words on computer screens don't always carry the teasing or joking tone of voice you intended. If your joke might be misinterpreted, you can soften it a little by using an expression like "grin" or a "smiley" (see the list on page 250). Be careful, though—some grouchy people really hate those things.

7. DON'T USE ALL CAPITAL LETTERS WHEN YOU WRITE! It looks like you're shouting, and that's what people will think IF YOU WRITE LIKE THIS.

8. Watch your temper. There's a great temptation to be real snotty when we're talking to people whose faces we can't see and whose names we don't know. If someone makes a goof or says something clueless, it's all too easy to say "What an idiot!" (or worse). In computer talk, this is known as "falming." All too often, forum discussions wind up as insult wars. This is an utter waste of time for everyone. If you *must* respond with a strong comment, do everyone a favor: At least give a little warning by writing "Flame" or "Flame on!" before launching your tirade. Or ask your fellow net-neighbor to continue the discussion privately, via E-mail (or Instant Messages on America Online), instead of mucking up the public forum. And you'd better be sure of your facts, or you'll risk getting flamed yourself. Better yet: Just chill out. Thumper's mother was right: If you can't say something nice, clam up.

9. Don't correct people's grammar or spelling. Nobody's perfect. Some forum users are better typists than others. Other people are in a hurry to post their comment and will send messages without bothering to clean them up. Remember, too, that on-line services let you talk with people from all kinds of places and backgrounds. Some people may not even be from your country, and may not be adept at using English as you are. Be tolerant of other people's errors, and hope that others will be tolerant of yours!

10. Do correct your own grammar or spelling! Try to clean up your own act as much as possible. Nobody likes struggling to read sloppy writing, whether it's off a piece of paper or a computer screen. Do the proofreading. You'll be more likely to receive responses to your postings if you look like a careful and conscientious writer and not some slob.

11. Don't believe everything you read. Some people use the forum to create new identities for themselves. They pretend to be smarter, richer, better looking, older, or younger than they really are. Just because they sign their message "Shaq" or "Chelsea Clinton," it doesn't mean that's who is on the other end of the wire. Computer forums are open to everyone—and unfortunately, that sometimes means that a few creeps and losers will be hanging out.

12. Don't be a spoiler. If you're talking about a great movie you saw or a book you read, don't ruin it for others by giving away the surprises. If you just gotta say something to make your point, give fair warning: Print the word "Spoiler!" before your comment.

13. Don't assume your E-mail will be kept private. You may think your remarks to another person are no one else's business, but once you've posted a message, you have no control over what might happen to it. If you're using a school's system or your parents' computer service account, your notes might wind up in some unexpected places—like the principal's office or your mom's boss's desk. You may even find your flames included in a Top On-Line Insults list in the next edition of this book!

14. Share what you know. After a few weeks on-line, you'll be an old pro. If you see messages from people who are struggling to catch up, help them out. Maybe you've discovered some great new way to make your computer dance and do tricks. Tell others! Remember, the info highway is a two-way street.

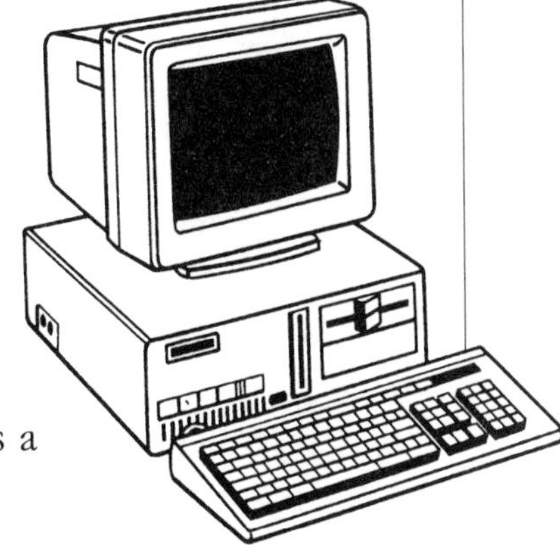

TOP 14 TECHNO-JARGON TERMS

Use these handy words and phrases to impress your friends (and confuse your parents!):

1. Bio-break (noun)—Techie for "using the toilet." *Usage:* "I just drank three cans of Pepsi, and man, do I gotta take a bio-break!"

2. Bi-star (adjective)—Describing two things that are apparently inseparable. Based on the astronomical term "binary star configuration," referring to two stars caught in each other's gravitational pull. *Usage:* "Computer hacking and Cheez-Its are totally bi-star!"

3. Bit Flip (noun)—A 180-degree personality change. *Usage:* "Karen's done a major bit flip since she started going out with that geek Ryan."

4. Bozon (noun)—A unit of stupidity. *Usage:* "That kid's science project has a pretty high bozon count."

5. Byte-bonding (verb)—To make friends by talking about computers and technology; especially to talk about stuff that nontechies don't get. *Usage:* "We byte-bonded when we swapped passwords to get to level 954 of UltraSuper Mario Second Cousins Once Removed."

6. Feeb (noun) (from "feeble")—An incompetent person. *Usage:* "He's a total feeb when it comes to executing the kick-punch-slash-puke move in Feet of Strength IV."

7. Knowbot (noun)—Librarians of the future; software programs you will be able to use to dig up any information you want on the info highway. *Usage:* "I got my knowbot to track down some phat codes so I could get the blood to spurt purple in Mortal Combat XIV."

8. LRF support (noun)—"Little Rubber Feet." An official-sounding but nonexistent feature of computer hardware or programs. Used when giving ROM brains a hard time. *Usage:* "Okay, this computer has a Quadzillion DX800 Processor with a Googolbyte hard drive—but does it have LRF support?"

9. Mouse potato (noun)—Computer zombie; the wired generation's version of the couch potato. *Usage:* "When Juan got his multimedia computer he turned into a mouse potato big-time."

10. Notwork (noun)—A network that doesn't. *Usage:* "My mom was complaining that the computers in her office are hooked up to the notwork."

11. Ohnosecond (noun)—A unit of time; that minuscule fraction of a second during which you realize you've just made a BIG mistake, like deleting your entire homework assignment without saving it. *Usage:* "It took an ohnosecond for Jake to core-dump his notes for the whole semester."

12. ROM brain (noun)—A person who spews out a steady stream of ideas and opinions but who can't receive any input from the outside world. *Usage:* "I can't stand having that ROM brain Matt in my science class. No one else gets a chance to talk!"

13. Techno-hippies (noun)—Derisive term for older-generation computer freaks regarded by young hackers as parental party crashers. *Usage:* "I knew the dude who butted into our video game chatline last night was a techno-hippie when he started raving about the 'classic simplicity' of Pong."

14. Thrash (verb) (from the manual to the CD-ROM game Myst)—To click madly around an interactive computer screen hoping to find an object that will do something—anything. *Usage:* "I thrashed every pixel on that image, but the secret passage wouldn't open."

22 ON-LINE ACRONYMS

An acronym is an abbreviation made up of the first letters of the words. Two common acronyms that actually graduated into honest-to-Pete real words are *laser* (Light Amplification by Simulated Emission of Radiation) and *scuba* (Self-Contained Underwater Breathing Apparatus).

Acronyms (pronounceable and otherwise) are popular in the computer world because they save precious time, space, and bytes.

1. **BRB:** Be right back
2. **BTW:** By the way...
3. **FAQs:** Frequently asked questions
4. **FUBAR:** [Fouled] up beyond all recognition
5. **FWIW:** For what it's worth
6. **FYI:** For your information
7. **GDR:** Grinning, ducking, and running (after making a smart remark)
8. **IAE:** In any event
9. **IMCO:** In my considered opinion
10. **IMHO:** In my humble opinion
11. **IMO:** In my opinion
12. **IOW:** In other words
13. **NRN:** No response necessary (to prevent lots of "thanks for the message!" messages)
14. **OIC:** Oh, I see!
15. **OTOH:** On the other hand
16. **PITA:** Pain in the ASCII
17. **ROF,L:** Rolling on floor, laughing
18. **RSN:** Real soon now
19. **RTFM:** Read the [flippin'] manual!
20. **SNAFU:** Situation normal, all [fouled] up
21. **TAL:** Thanks a lot
22. **TIA:** Thanks in advance

BONUS LIST: 12 ACRONYMS THAT DON'T EXIST BUT SHOULD

1. **HDYWTDT:** How do you work this dratted thing?
2. **ICTIA:** I can't take it anymore.
3. **IGU:** I give up.
4. **MPADMC:** My parents are driving me crazy.
5. **NGA:** No geeks allowed.
6. **POD:** Party on, dude.
7. **SHMUK:** Shows how much you know.
8. **TIC:** This is cool.
9. **TS:** This sucks.
10. **TWYT:** That's what you think.
11. **UFB:** Utter (freaking) baloney.
12. **WCTC:** Who cut the cheese?

14 INTERESTING E-MAIL ADDRESSES

1. **Beavis:** beavis@mtv.com
2. **Jordan Brady (MTV host):** 73112.731@compuserve.com
3. **Butthead:** butthead@mtv.com
4. **Adam Curry (MTV VJ):** acurry@mtv.com,adam@mtv.com
5. **Coke machine:** fingerdrinkdrink.csh.rit.edu
6. **Dogs:** listserv@pecvm.bitnet
7. **Bill Gates (America's wealthiest businessman):** billg@microsoft.com

8. **Kites:** kites-request@harvard.harvard.edu
9. **Ross Perot (ex-Presidential candidate, one of America's richest men):** 71511.460@compuserve.com
10. **Santa Claus:** santa@north.pole.org
11. **Santa's elves:** elves@north.pole.org
12. **Star Trek reviews:** listserv@cornell.edu
13. **Super Nintendo:** snes-request@spcvxa.spc.edu
14. **The White House:** http://www.whitehouse.gov (You don't get to communicate with them, but you do get a tour of the place.)

16 SMILEYS

Smileys are also known as emoticons and are used by computer hacks to bring a little humor to the world of high technology. To decipher a smiley, turn the page sideways.

TOP

:-)	Basic smile
;-)	A wink and a smile
:-(	A frown
(-:	User is lefthanded
8-)	User is wearing sunglasses
:-]	User is a vampire
:-E	User is a buck-toothed vampire
:'-(	User is crying
:-#	User wears braces
O :-)	User is an angel
:-D	User is laughing
:-X	User's lips are sealed
=):-)=	User is Abe Lincoln
d:-)	User likes baseball
<<<<<(:-)	User sells hats
@@@@@@@:)	User is Marge Simpson!

BOTTOM

10 WAYS TO USE ON-LINE SERVICES TO GET HELP WITH YOUR HOMEWORK

If you thought it was tough studying history now, check out this factoid: Some future-minded folks predict that by the year 2010, the amount of information in the world will *double every 70 days!* That means that on the last day of your school year there will be *four times* as many facts to keep straight as there were on the first day! Someday soon, "knowbots" will be available to track down information for us. For now, though, if you want to keep up —better get wired!

1. Join forums, chat lines, and bulletin boards. Ask other kids in your grade for help.

2. Post messages asking for responses from experts in the field. Many professionals are glad to share what they know, especially to help promote the cause of education.

3. Scour electronic encyclopedias—plenty of good, basic information.

4. Search databases—magazines, newspapers—for up-to-the-minute facts. Sometimes these searches can be costly, especially if you download many articles. But when doing research on current topics, they're hard to beat.

5. Explore other facets of the reference sections. Depending on your service, you can get book and movie reviews, information about health and medicine, an astounding array of government facts and statistics—just about anything you can imagine. And a lot of it is available for no extra charge!

6. One picture is worth a thousand bytes (give or take a million). Clip art, screen-capturing programs, or on-line image libraries might have just the pix you need to make your point visually.

7. Check out shareware forums for programs that can jazz up your work: phat fonts, powerful presentation programs, even sound bites. Chances are someone out there has created just the tool you need.

8. Plug in to your local library. In some communities you can tap directly into your library's computer to find out what's available. Knowing whether the library carries a certain book or a periodical, and if it's there on the shelf, can save you time, trips, and trouble.

9. Beg, plead, and cajole your parents to turn your home computer into a direct Internet node. (Fat chance!)

10. Fool around! Sometimes playing with the computer can lead you into unexpectedly rich areas—databases, discussion groups, resources—that you might not have found otherwise. Follow your hunches and see where they lead.

WINNERS OF THE 1994 CYBERMANIA AWARDS

The first awards for electronic gaming and interactive entertainment were given out in November 1994. Viewers were able to vote for the best overall game while the show was being aired on TBS using the Prodigy network. These were the winners:

1. Best Action Adventure: Doom

2. Best CD Game: The Seventh Guest

3. Best Portable Game: Disney's Aladdin

4. Best Comedy: The Wacky World of Miniature Golf

5. Best Art and Graphics: Myst

6. Special Award for Best Achievement in Virtual

Reality: Iwerks Entertainment
7. Best Musical: Explorer/Peter Gabriel
8. Best Simulation or Strategy Game: Sim City
9. Best Interactive Sports Video: Caesar's World of Boxing
10. Best Female Actor: Grace Zabriskie, Voyeur
11. Best Male Actor: Robert Culp, Voyeur
12. Best Game: Mortal Kombat

7 THINGS THAT MAKE A GAME LAME

1. Not enough blood
2. Based on a Saturday morning cartoon
3. Not enough blood
4. Too easy to beat
5. Not enough blood
6. Gets old too fast
7. Not enough blood

8 PROBLEMS YOU MAY HAVE WITH CD-ROMS

(*and How to Get Around Them*)

1. Bum wrap. What they say about books is true of discs: You can't judge a ROM by its cover. Some ROMs come in the coolest packages—weird shapes, dazzling graphics, holograms. But most of these boxes contain two things—air and a disc—and they get thrown away as soon as they're opened. What they say about people is also true of discs: It's what's inside that counts.

2. Byte bait. Imagine that you could just reach through your television set and grab anything you see advertised. Well, some CD-ROM samplers, catalogs, and software clubs work pretty much that way. These free (or almost free) discs contain tons of fully working software programs, plus jazzy samples to whet your appetite. To access the full program, all you have do is call the manufacturer and give them an account number (such as any credit card your parents happen to have handy). The operator then gives (or rather, *sells*) you an "unlocking code" that lets you copy the program onto the hard drive, and you're up and running.

Having all those programs sitting there waiting for you on the disc is a big (and expensive) temptation. If you sample something you think you'd like, don't just pick up the phone. Show the program to your mom or dad. Talk about what the program does and how you'd use it. Best of all, find out if any of your friends—at school or on-line—use and like the program. Go to the software store and ask for a complete demonstration—and see if there's another program that does the same thing but costs less.

3. Click—and drag. In a way, plain old books are "interactive" simply because you have to do something—turn the page—before you can go to the "next level." Some CD-ROMs are no more interactive than that. You click and the next thing happens; or you click and get the next page of text, or you click and see a boring poor-quality video clip, then return to where you were in the game. Multimediocrity—yawn. In a game, true interactivity means you get to make choices that profoundly affect the outcome. In a reference work, interactivity means being able to search for related information quickly and easily. Not every ROM that claims to be "fully interactive" really is. Read reviews; talk to friends; do some digging before getting sucked into making a bad purchase.

4. Damage control. When the compact disc first appeared, people boasted that it was an indestructible and permanent way of storing data. Not true. Discs are almost as prone to skips and scratches. A piece of lint or a bubble in the coated playing surface is enough to cause your laser beam to wander aimlessly and your system to crash. If your ROM came in a cardboard sleeve, it's even more vulnerable to damage. As irritating as they are to handle, plastic jewel boxes are a better way to store discs. You can buy spare ones at most computer or music stores. Always ask about the store's return policy before buying. Unless you have a receipt, you may not be able to take back a disc that's faulty, even if it looks like someone used it for target practice.

5. Medium mismatch. Just because you *can* play a Beethoven symphony on a kazoo doesn't mean you *should.* Some ROMs should never have been made, because ROM isn't the right medium for the content. There are a bunch of ROMs, for example, that have endless clips of people telling jokes or that contain recycled bits from TV shows. When the jokes fall flat—as they usually do—you half expect an icon to pop up of someone shrugging his shoulders and saying, "I guess you had to be there." Before buying, apply the "why bother" test: Ask yourself, "Does this stuff really belong on a ROM?"

6. Once is not enough. With ROM games and discs costing as much as they do, they need to have a high "multiplay" potential. A game should have several possible endings (the more the better), while a science or nature program should have information you can use now and in the future—not just in the fifth grade but in the eighth and ninth as well. Apply the "how often" test: Ask yourself how many times you might use the disc in the course of, say, a year. Ideally, a disc will "grow" with you. As you get older and smarter, you can get more out of it.

7. Shovelware schlock. When ROMs were first invented, people exclaimed, "And they can hold the equivalent of 500 books!" Sure enough, it wasn't long before discs came out that contained—you guessed it—the complete texts of 500 books. Other discs are out there that cram 900 ho-hum shareware games onto their shiny surfaces, or that contain 22,000 pieces of pretty lame clip art. Such discs are known as "shovelware"—which means they contain anything and everything the makers can shovel into them, like digital landfills. To make things worse, these ROMs often have no decipherable interface that lets you search for what's on the disc, so you'll spend forever looking for what you want. Don't buy a ROM just because you're impressed by its bulk. Quantity does not always mean quality.

8. System snarls. The hotshots who make ROMs usually create them using the latest high-tech equipment—power processors, mega-RAMs of memory, countless colors. Sometimes they then "dumb down" the disc so it'll run on as many pokey little home systems as possible. But not always. A lot of discs won't work unless you, too, have high-end graphics or special sound cards. Before plunking down your money, know the components (and the limits) of your computer system. Write down the information and bring it with you to the software store, and read the fine print on the ROM box. If your system isn't up to the task, you have three choices: Bug your parents to upgrade your machine, put up with crummy (or no) performance—or do without the disc.

BEST-SELLING PC GAMES (DOS, WINDOWS)

(List Price $20 or More)

RANKING THROUGH JUNE 1994	TITLE	MANUFACTURER	RANKING 1993*
1	SimCity 2000	Maxis	4
2	Myst (CD-ROM)	Broderbund	–
3	Star Wars Rebel Assault (CD-ROM)	Lucas Arts	10
4	Microsoft Flight Simulator	Microsoft	1
5	5 Ft 10 Pack (CD-ROM)	Sirius	–
6	The 7th Guest (CD-ROM)	Virgin	3
7	X-Wing	Lucas Arts	2
8	Wolfenstein 3-D	GT Interactive	5
9	Links-386 Pro	Access	6
10	Master of Orion	MicroProse	–
11	Microsoft Arcade	Microsoft	–
12	Elder Scrolls: The Arena	Bethesda Software	–
13	X-Wing Mission Disc #2 B-Wing	Lucas Arts	12
14	Leisure Suit Larry VI	Sierra On-Line	–
15	Aces Over Europe	Sierra On-Line	16
16	Police Quest IV	Sierra On-Line	19
17	Indy Car Racing	Virgin	–
18	Links-Pebble Beach	Access	–
19	Gabriel Knight	Sierra On-Line	–
20	Commanche Maximum Overkill	Nova Logic	9

* = May represent previous version of game

NOTE TO DOOM FANS

Where on this list, you may be wondering, is that ultra-popular interplanetary shoot 'em up? Surely after so many people spent so much time plasma-blasting all the demons of hell, DOOM must have ranked someplace. Well, you're right. According to the data experts, DOOM would be number one on the list— with the number-two game ranking a distant second. But many people were using demo copies of the game that they got free via download from a computer network or that they bought for a few bucks at a software store. The games listed here sold for at least $20.

BEST-SELLING MACINTOSH GAMES

RANKING THROUGH JUNE 1994	TITLE	MANUFACTURER
1	Myst (CD-ROM)	Broderbund
2	SimCity 2000	Maxis
3	Pathway Into Darkness	Bungee
4	Chessmaster 3000	Software Toolworks
5	SimCity	Maxis
6	Jeopardy! with Alex Trebeck	Gametek
7	The 7th Guest (CD-ROM)	Virgin
8	FA-18 Hornet	Graphic Simulations
9	PGA Tour Golf II	Electronic Arts
10	PGA Tour Golf	Electronic Arts

The five best-selling Mac games in 1993 were:

1. Prince of Persia (Broderbund)
2. Microsoft Flight Simulator (Microsoft)
3. SimCity 2000 (Maxis)
4. Civilization (Microprose)
5. King's Quest V/Red Baron Bundle (Sierra On-Line)

TOP NINTENDO ENTERTAINMENT SYSTEM (NES) GAMES

1. Kirby's Adventure
2. (*tie*) Jurassic Park; Mega Man 6; Tetris 2
3. Teenage Mutant Ninja Turtles: Tournament Fighters
4. Ren & Stimpy Show: Buckaroo$
5. Tecmo Super Bowl
6. Mario is Missing!
7. Tecmo NBA Basketball
8. WWF: King of the Ring
9. Battletoads Double Dragon: the Ultimate Team
10. Mario's Time Machine
11. Bubble Bobble Part 2
12. Zoda's Revenge: Startropics II
13. Jungle Book
14. Star Trek: The Next Generation
15. Flintstones 2
16. Bram Stoker's Dracula
17. Tiny Toon Adventures 2: Trouble in Wackyland
18. Mighty Final Fight
19. Pugsley's Scavenger Hunt
20. Battleship
21. Cliffhanger
22. (*tie*) Bonk's Adventure; Mickey's Adventures in Numberland
23. (*tie*) Beauty and the Beast; Monopoly; Rescue Rangers 2
24. (*tie*) Black Bass; Last Action Hero

TOP SUPER NINTENDO SYSTEM GAMES

The information in the following group of lists is based on rentals at major video chains.

1. Mortal Kombat
2. Disney's Aladdin
3. Ken Griffey Jr. Presents MLB
4. Super Metroid
5. (*tie*) Clayfighter; Mega Man X
6. Street Fight II Turbo
7. MLBPA Baseball
8. Super Empire Strikes Back
9. Super Street Fighter II
10. Tecmo Super Bowl
11. Lethal Enforcers
12. Jurassic Park
13. (*tie*) Saturday Night Slam Masters; Teenage Mutant Ninja Turtles: Tournament Fighters
14. (*tie*) Clay Fighter Tournament Edition; Jungle Book
15. NHL Hockey '94
16. (*tie*) Stunt Race FX; Super Mario All-Stars
17. Rock & Roll Racing
18. (*tie*) John Madden NFL '94; World Heroes
19. Cool Spot
20. Star Trek: The Next Generation
21. Rocko's Modern Life
22. (*tie*) Bugs Bunny Rabbit Rampage; NBA Show-down; Robocop vs. The Terminator
23. Final Fight Guy
24. Mortal Kombat II
25. (*tie*) FIFA International Soccer; Maximum Carnage
26. (*tie*) Capcom's MVP Football; Tetris 2; Zom-bies Ate My Neighbors
27. (*tie*) Captain America & The Avengers; Double Dragon V; WWF Royal Rumble
28. (*tie*) Alien vs. Predator; Bubsy in: Claws Encoun-ters of the Furred Kind
29. Konami NFL Football
30. (*tie*) Goof Troop; World Heroes

TOP SEGA GENESIS GAMES

1. Mortal Kombat
2. NBA Jam
3. Street Fighter II Special Champion Edition
4. Disney's Aladdin
5. Eternal Champions
6. Sonic the Hedgehog 3
7. World Series Baseball
8. Temco Super Bowl
9. Sonic Spinball
10. Virtual Racing
11. Lethal Enforcer
12. Jurassic Park
13. John Madden NFL '94
14. NBA Action '94
15. Jungle Book
16. Bill Walsh College Football
17. (*tie*) NBA Showdown; NHL Hockey '94
18. Shinobi III: Return of Ninja Master
19. (*tie*) ESPN Baseball Tonight; Robocop vs. The Terminator
20. (*tie*) General Chaos; Temco NBA Basketball; X-Men
21. Mortal Kombat II
22. Super Street Fighter II
23. Maximum Carnage
24. (*tie*) Barkley: Shut Up & Jam!; MLBPA Baseball
25. (*tie*) Bubsy in: Claws Encounters of the Furred Kind; FIFA International Soccer
26. (*tie*) Double Dragon V; Joe Montana NFL Football '94
27. ESPN Sunday Night Football
28. (*tie*) College Football's National Championship; Incredible Hulk; R.B.I. '94; Rocket Knight Adventures
29. (*tie*) Lotus II R.E.C.S.; Micro Machines; Winter Olympic Games
30. (*tie*) Jammit; Splatterhouse 3; Star Trek: The Next Generation; Streets of Rage 3; Top Gear 2

TOP SEGA CD GAMES

1. Mortal Kombat
2. Tomcat Alley
3. Star Wars 3D: Rebel Assault
4. Joe Montana NFL Football
5. Rise of the Dragon
6. Jurassic Park
7. Mad Dog McCree
8. Sonic CD
9. NHL '94
10. Ground Zero, Texas
11. Dragon's Lair
12. WWF Rage in the Cage
13. Dark Wizard
14. (*tie*) Batman Returns; Lethal Enforcer
15. Jaguar XJ220
16. Dracula Unleashed
17. Mansion of Hidden Souls
18. Third World War
19. Spider-Man vs. The Kingpin
20. Final Fight
21. Bram Stoker's Dracula
22. (*tie*) Formula 1 GP; Prize Fighter Video Boxing; Sewer Shark
23. AH-3 Thunderstrike
24. Adventures of Willy Beamish
25. Road Avenger
26. (*tie*) Robo Aleste; Silpheed
27. (*tie*) Heimdall; Road Avenger 2
28. (*tie*) Bill Walsh College Football; Night Trap
29. (*tie*) Microcosm; Night Trap
30. (*tie*) ESPN Sunday Night Football; Stellar Fire
31. Who Shot Johnny Rock?
32. European Racers
33. (*tie*) FIFA International Soccer; Lunar—The Silver Star
34. (*tie*) After Burner III; Dune
35. (*tie*) Cobra Command; Formula 1 World Championship; Revenge of the Ninja; Wing Commander

10 GORIEST FATALITIES IN MORTAL KOMBAT II

RANK	CHARACTER	FATALITY	DESCRIPTION
1	Baraka	Stab	Skewers opponent with an upward thrust of his bladelike hands
2	Kung Lao	Slice	Slices opponent in half (vertically) with his razor-edged hat
3	Kitana	Kiss of Death	Blows a kiss; opponent's chest swells until the body bursts
4	Mileena	Inhale	With her mega-breath she inhales her opponent, digests him, and spits out the bones
5	Scorpion	Toasty	Rips off his mask to reveal his skull; shoots flames and incinerates victim
6	Shang Tsung	Life Force	Draws back his arm and sucks out the opponent's life force, leaving him a withered shell of his former self
7	Sub-Zero	Deep Freeze	Emits a freezing blast of arctic air to immobilize the opponent, who shatters into pieces

8	Liu Kang	Dragon	Morphs into a dragon and takes a significant chunk out of opponent
9	Johnny Cage	Torso	Grabs opponent's waist and rips him in half
10	Jax	Head Pop	Squeezes opponent's head until it pops like a balloon

CHAPTER SIX

TV, MOVIES, AND MUSIC

HOW TO USE YOUR *WHOLE* BRAIN WHEN YOU WATCH TV

Actually, you don't *need* your whole brain to understand most of what's on TV. On the other hand, if you find yourself watching something that *deserves* your whole brain:

1. Look up words in the dictionary that you haven't heard before.

2. Ask questions about the opinions you hear on TV.

3. Think about why the characters do what they do. Analyze their personalities.

4. Think about how the story is developing. What will happen next?

5. Talk to friends about what you saw on television and share your opinions.

COUNTRIES WITH THE MOST VCRs

1. United States: 66,560,000
2. Japan: 30,095,000
3. Germany: 21,770,000
4. Brazil: 20,669,000
5. United Kingdom: 16,354,000
6. France: 13,417,000
7. Italy: 8,851,000
8. Canada: 6,995,000
9. Spain: 5,866,000
10. Former USSR: 5,648,000

15 CELEBRITIES WHO HAVE APPEARED ON *THE SIMPSONS*

That is, they did voiceovers for characters based on themselves.

1. Aerosmith
2. Wade Boggs
3. Albert Brooks
4. Danny DeVito
5. Smokin' Joe Frasier
6. Sara Gilbert
7. Kelsey Grammar
8. Neil Patrick Harris (Doogie Howser)
9. Michael Jackson
10. Jon Lovitz
11. Luke Perry
12. Michelle Pfeiffer
13. The Red Hot Chili Peppers
14. Brooke Shields
15. Kathleen Turner

THE BEST TV MOMS

Entertainment Weekly recently came up with a list of the best TV moms and the worst TV moms based on readers' comments. Here are the best TV moms and the reasons why people think so:

FIRST PRIZE

1. Roseanne Conner (Roseanne), *Roseanne.* The best thing about Roseanne is that she's honest with her kids about the realities of the kind of life the family leads. (But see below—she also made it to the "Worst TV Moms" list!)

2. Ma Kent (K. Callan), *Lois & Clark: The New Adven-*

tures of Superman. Even though she's only Superman's adoptive mother, she encourages her kid to find out more about his real background.

3. Dr. Michaela Quinn (Jane Seymour), *Dr. Quinn, Medicine Woman.* A great role model and a perfect reminder that women made many more contributions to history than TV lets us know.

4. Marge Simpson, *The Simpsons.* A classic TV mom, modern and old-fashioned all at the same time. Even though she stays home with the kids, she's an independent person. She puts up with Homer's stupidity because she knows he loves her, and she's patient with Bart.

5. Jill Taylor (Patricia Richardson), *Home Improvement.* She's firm with her boys and keeps them in line, but she's never crabby. She also protects her kids from the goofy ideas that their dad sometimes comes up with, and when dad gets angry at the kids, she reminds him that "boys will be boys."

THE WORST TV MOMS

1. Murphy Brown (Candice Bergen), *Murphy Brown.* She never spends time with her son and just seems to use him as a "prop" on the show. When she's too busy to think about her baby, she just hands him to someone else.

2. Peg Bundy (Katey Segal), *Married with Children.* She runs around in sexy sweaters and tight pants all the time, which is probably how Kelly (Christina Applegate) got to be such a slut. She also has a lousy relationship with her son, Bud (David Faustino).

3. Roseanne Conner (Roseanne), *Roseanne.* Roseanne may get points for being honest with her kids, but sometimes she's too honest. When she gets really angry she says nasty, sarcastic things to the kids. It's no surprise, then, that the kids, Becky, Darlene, and D.J., can be pretty nasty when they want to be.

4. Marilyn Larson (Marilyn Kentz) and **Carol Kellogg** (Carol Kristensen), *The Mommies.* All these moms ever seem to do is torture their spoiled children with their nasty wisecracks!

5. Cindy Walsh (Carol Potter), *Beverly Hills 90210.* She's nice but somewhat dumb and never seems to know what's going on with her kids. She's setting a lousy example for them!

26 TV NETWORK ADDRESSES

"Fifty-seven channels and nothing's on," sang Bruce Springsteen in 1992. If you feel that way, too, write to the television networks and let them know. You can also use these addresses to find out more about your favorite show or TV personality.

1. ABC
77 West 66 Street
New York, N.Y. 10023-6298

2. American Movie Classics (AMC)
150 Crossways Park West
Woodbury, N.Y. 11797

3. Arts & Entertainment Network (A&E)
235 East 45 Street
New York, N.Y. 10017

4. Black Entertainment Television (BET)
1232 31 Street, Northwest
Washington, D.C. 20007

5. Bravo
150 Crossways Park West
Woodbury, N.Y. 11797

6. Cable News Network (CNN)
One CNN Center, Box 105366
Atlanta, GA 30348

7. Cable-Satellite Public Affairs Network (C-SPAN)
400 North Capitol Street, Northwest
Suite 65D
Washington, D.C. 20001

8. CBS, Inc.
51 West 52 Street
New York, N.Y. 10019

9. Cinemax
1100 Avenue of the Americas
New York, N.Y. 10036
10. CNBC
2200 Fletcher Avenue
Fort Lee, N.J. 07024
11. The Discovery Channel
7700 Wisconsin Avenue
Bethesda, MD 20814-3522
12. ESPN
ESPN Plaza
Bristol, CT 06010
13. The Family Channel
100 Centerville Turnpike
Virginia Beach, VA 23463
14. Fox Television
205 East 67 Street
New York, N.Y. 10021
15. Home Box Office
1100 Avenue of the Americas
New York, N.Y. 10036
16. Lifetime Television
Lifetime Astoria Studios
34-12 36 Street
Astoria, N.Y. 11106
17. Madison Square Garden Network (MSG)
2 Pennsylvania Plaza
New York, N.Y. 10121
18. The Movie Channel
1633 Broadway
New York, N.Y. 10019
19. MTV
515 Broadway
New York, N.Y. 10036
20. NBC
30 Rockefeller Plaza
New York, N.Y. 10112
21. Nickelodeon
515 Broadway
New York, N.Y. 10036
22. Showtime
1633 Broadway
New York, N.Y. 10019
23. The Sports Channel
150 Crossways Park West
Woodbury, N.Y. 11797
24. Turner Broadcasting System (TBS)
One CNN Center, Box 105366
Atlanta, GA 30348
25. Turner Network Television (TNT)
One CNN Center, Box 105366
Atlanta, GA 30348
26. The USA Network (USA)
1230 Avenue of the Americas
18th Floor
New York, N.Y. 10020

DOUBLE DARE SUPER SLOPPY SUPPLIES

If you've ever watched the Nickelodeon TV show *Double Dare,* you know that it can get *really* messy. Between 1991 and 1993 the super sloppy game show toured the United States. How messy was it? Here's a list of the materials they used in their stunts:

16,800 gallons of Gak
3,000 cans of whipped cream
67,200 eggs
1,600 gallons of pudding
3,520 pies
20,736 paper towels to clean it all up

THE TEN BEST TV SHOWS FOR KIDS

According to *TV Guide,* the best TV programs for school-age kids are the following:

1. *ABC After-School Specials.* Stories deal with the real-life problems and concerns of kids in an honest manner.

2. *CBS School-Break Specials.* Young people's concerns are dealt with in an entertaining and realistic way.

3. *Reading Rainbows* (PBS). A highly informative and entertaining program, hosted by Levar Burton of *Star Trek: The Next Generation* fame.

4. *Are You Afraid of the Dark?* (Nickelodeon). Kid's tell scary (but not *too* scary) stories around a campfire.

5. *Beakman's World* (CBS: The Learning Channel). Kids are taught science in a highly entertaining and often amusing way.

6. *Clarissa Explains It All* (Nickelodeon). Clarissa, the show's main character, is an intelligent and good-natured teen dealing with the everyday problems of being a teenager.

7. *Ghostwriter* (PBS). A "haunted" computer leaves messages for a group of enterprising kids and enables them to solve crimes.

8. *Name Your Adventure* (NBC). Real kids have their fantasies come true on this exciting program.

9. *Nick News* (Nickelodeon). A news show that makes current events understandable for kids in an entertaining fashion.

10. *Steven Spielberg Presents Animaniacs* (Fox). Funny, entertaining, and great animation.

THE TEN BEST GROWN-UP TV SHOWS FOR KIDS

1. *Dave's World* (CBS). This family-oriented program demonstrates how parents and kids can solve everyday problems in a loving manner.

2. *Dr. Quinn, Medicine Woman* (CBS). Interesting and understandable plots set in the Old West.

3. *Family Matters* (ABC). What could be funnier than watching Jaleel White as the nerdy Steve Urkel?

4. *The Fresh Prince of Bel-Air* (NBC). Rap star Will Smith launched his acting career on this amusing program.

5. *Lois & Clark: The New Adventures of Superman* (ABC). Kids love the great comic-book action but may be turned off to the romantic scenes.

6. *Roseanne* (ABC). Possibly one of the best family shows ever, it deals with family relationships in an honest, realistic, and often riotously funny way.

7. *seaQuest DSV* (NBC). Great writing, acting, and settings make this a highly watchable program.

8. *The Simpsons* (Fox). This one is a comedy classic that everyone in the family will love.

9. *The Sinbad Show* (Fox). An extremely likable star.

10. *Step by Step* (ABC). Kids seem to really like this show even though some of the plots can be a bit silly.

5 OF STEVE URKEL'S FAVORITE THINGS

In 1990, Jaleel White made his first appearance on TV's *Family Matters* as Laura Winslow's worst nightmare. Audiences loved him, and nerdy Steve Urkel quickly became one of the hottest TV characters of the nineties.

1. His bug collection
2. Cheese
3. Mice
4. His science projects
5. Laura "Smookums" Winslow

4 THINGS MARK-PAUL GOSSELAAR WOULD DO IF HE WASN'T AN ACTOR

Acting since he was 5, Mark-Paul is best-known as "a hunk" to most teen girls and as one of the stars of the original cast of TV's *Saved by the Bell.*

1. Be a lawyer or a businessman
2. Play football
3. Be an architect
4. Have more time for romance

ELIJAH WOOD'S 3 FAVORITE MOVIE DIRECTORS

This is what Jon Avnet, director of the film *War,* has to say about Elijah Wood: "He's the first child actor I've worked with that I think is really an actor. He's not tied to his *cuteness.*"

1. Francis Ford Coppola. He liked *Apocalypse Now* but thought Coppola went overboard on *Bram Stoker's Dracula.*

2. George Lucas, his idol. "He's a director *and* a writer. I enjoy writing, and I know if I can really focus on that and get some good tutoring in English, I can be a really good writer when I get a little older. What's more fun than that? It's creating your own world!"

3. Oliver Stone, even though his mother won't let him see *Natural Born Killers.*

5 THINGS MACAULEY CULKIN LIKES TO DO

This list should give you an idea of what Macauley likes to do when he's off stage—the same things that everybody likes to do.

1. Play dodgeball and soccer, go skateboarding and bike riding

2. Play video games

3. Watch *Full House, Family Matters,* and *Perfect Strangers* on TV

4. Listen to Aerosmith, Metallica, and Guns N' Roses

5. Eat vanilla ice cream with chocolate syrup, no sprinkles

WILLIAM SHATNER LISTS 3 THINGS ABOUT *STAR TREK* THAT HE WISHES WERE REAL

William Shatner became known to millions as Captain Kirk, commander of the *Enterprise* on *Star Trek,* one of TV's most enduring science fiction programs. He's also played the role in the *Star Trek* movie and its sequels.

1. People of different races and beliefs work in harmony for the good of all.

2. If the transporter were real, we could all get around much faster, which would be great.

3. The adventure of being able to travel and explore the universe.

WILLIAM SHATNER LISTS 3 THINGS ABOUT *STAR TREK* THAT HE'S GLAD AREN'T REAL

Off-camera, Shatner is quite content with reality, and he generously offered to share some of his thoughts about his career with our readers. Here are three reasons he gives for preferring reality to the world of *Star Trek.*

1. I'm glad that I do not have the tremendous responsibility that Captain Kirk has as commander of the *Enterprise.*

2. I'm glad the Klingons aren't real because they are not very nice and cause lots of trouble.

3. The boots that I wore on the show were too high and very uncomfortable, so I'm glad they're not real!

3 OF LUKE PERRY'S SECRETS

1. He likes opera (especially *Carmen*).

2. His ear was pierced by a good friend with a diaper pin during a New Year's Eve party.

3. He would like to be stuck in an elevator with Winona Ryder.

6 OF JENNA VON OY'S JOYS

Jenna plays a character named Six on TV's *Blossom.* Here are six things that make her smile.

1. The beach at night
2. Butterflies
3. Chocolate
4. Shopping
5. Sleep
6. Talking on the phone

9 OF EDDIE FURLONG'S FAVES

Eddie Furlong has starred in some of Hollywood's hottest movies. He has had leading roles in *Terminator 2, Pet Sematary 2,* and *Brainscan.*

1. Book: *Shoeless Joe* by Ray Kinsella
2. Candy: Reese's Peanut Butter Cups
3. Cartoon: Ren & Stimpy
4. Favorite thing about being in *T2:* Arnold Schwarzenegger
5. Pastimes: pool, weightlifting, collecting memorabilia from movies I've been in
6. Place I'd most like to visit: France
7. Rock group: U2
8. Snack: Domino's pepperoni and mushroom pizza
9. Sport: basketball

JONATHAN BRANDIS REVEALS THE 4 WORST THINGS ABOUT GROWING UP AS AN ACTOR

Jonathan Brandis starred in the motion picture *Sidekicks,* with Chuck Norris, and in the hit TV show *seaQuest DSV.* As you can see, it wasn't all as glamorous as you might think. Here are some of the problems he experienced.

1. The teachers resented his frequent absences. "To them it didn't matter why—they just cared that I was absent, and they didn't like it."

2. Knowing a lot of different people "but not having time to really get to be friends with too many of them. Acting sure keeps you busy."

3. Moving to Los Angeles at the age of 9. "The kids in L.A. were so different from the kids back east. It took me five years to get used to it here."

4. Kids at school gave him a hard time because he was famous: "This might sound a little egotistical, but there was a lot of jealousy."

WHERE TEEN CELEBS HANG OUT IN LOS ANGELES

If you're in California and you want to do some serious stargazing, here are some good places to hang out.

1. Jerry's Deli
2. California Pizza Kitchen
3. Johnny Rocket restaurants

THE GREAT SATURDAY MORNING HALL OF FAME

Ask any TV addict who grew up in the fifties or sixties, and they'll tell you that the most important day of the week was Saturday. Saturday morning, to be more specific. Unlike today, when Saturday morning television is dominated by cartoon shows, programs back then included adventures, dramas, great westerns, science fiction voyages into the unknown, puppet shows, rock 'n' roll showcases, quiz shows, and a great deal more. Here are some of the best. (While many of these were originally aired on weekdays and in the evening, they all, at one time or another, wound up on the Saturday morning lineup.)

1. *The Adventures of Black Beauty.* The famous horse starred in a half-hour live-action adventure.

2. *The Adventures of Kit Carson.* A great old-time western starring Kit and his sidekick, El Toro.

3. *The Adventures of Rin Tin Tin.* A German shepherd starred in this series, set in Fort Apache (not the one in the Bronx) in the 1880s.

4. *The Adventures of Robin Hood.* The English hero fights evil in Sherwood Forest by robbing from the rich and giving to the poor.

5. *The Adventures of Superman.* The man of steel made his first TV appearance in 1953; the show is still syndicated today.

6. *American Bandstand.* A TV dance party, with Dick Clark hosting, featured the hottest pop stars of the day. Artists such as the Doors, Linda Ronstadt, Simon and Garfunkel, the Supremes, the Temptations, and Stevie Wonder all made their TV debuts on this show.

7. *Andy's Gang.* Andy Devine was emcee of one of the most bizarre kids' shows ever. The "cast" included Froggy the Gremlin (who insulted everyone) and the very weird Midnight the Cat.

8. *Annie Oakley.* The first western heroine had every girl on the block dreaming of horses and six-shooters.

9. *Batman.* The dynamic duo in dangerous doings.

10. *Beany and Cecil.* A 15-minute puppet show featuring the voices of some famous performers of the day, including Spike Jones and Jerry Lewis.

11. *The Big Top.* A live circus showcase with Ed McMahon as one of the clowns.

12. *Bozo the Clown.* A variety show with games, cartoons, and contests hosted by a clown who looked something like the original Ronald McDonald.

13. *Buck Rogers in the 25th Century.* A live-action science fiction adventure about a World War I flier who wakes up after a 400-year nap.

14. *Captain Midnight.* An aviator hero battles enemy agents and gangsters.

15. *Captain Video and His Video Rangers.* One of the first sci-fi TV shows, first broadcasted in 1949.

16. *Circus Boy.* The life and times of Corky, an orphaned boy who joins the circus and rides around on his own elephant.

17. *Commando Cody—Sky Marshal of the Universe.* More live action sci-fi fun. Only 13 episodes were produced, but the show still managed to become one of the most popular of its kind.

18. *Crusader Rabbit.* One of the earliest cartoon shows, first shown in 1949, featured the irrepressible rabbit and his friend, Rags the Tiger.

19. *Dick Tracy.* A live-action detective series based on the famous comic strip character.

20. *Ding Dong School.* Aimed at preschoolers, this show had a "teacher" and a bunch of kids who pretended to be in school. There were games, songs, craft projects, and lots of discussion about being good.

21. *Flash Gordon.* Science fiction set in the twenty-first century and based on the comic strip character.

22. *Fury.* The adventures of a boy and his horse stressed good health, fair play, and good citizenship. Not as boring as it sounds.

23. *The Gumby Show.* We're happy to know that Gumby is alive and well today. A character named Pinky Lee was the host of the show. He sang a ridiculous theme song that everyone loved!

24. *The Heckle and Jeckle Cartoon Show.* Starring two magpies and their pals, Dinky Duck, Gandy Goose, Little Roquefort, and others.

25. *Hopalong Cassidy.* More western fun starring "Hoppy" and his horse Topper.

26. *Howdy Doody.* Buffalo Bob Smith hosted the most popular children's show of the time. Howdy, a boy marionette, and his "father" told about their adventures in Doodyville. The show, which featured games, contests, and sing-alongs, had an audience of kids who were referred to as "the peanut gallery."

27. *Huckleberry Hound.* One of several Hanna-Barbera cartoon series starring the dumb but hardworking dog and his friends, Pixie and Dixie, Jinx, Hockey, and Yogi Bear, who eventually got his own show.

28. *The Incredible Hulk.* In 1978, Bill Bixby and bodybuilder Lou Ferrigno starred in a version of this show. But before that, in 1966, it was a cartoon show.

29. *Jon Gnagy.* A 15-minute program that had an artist demonstrating drawing methods. Kids could buy a Jon Gnagy kit that had all the same materials as those the artist used on TV and a step-by-step book that enabled one to reproduce Gnagy's masterpiece at home. You see lots of shows like this on cable channels now, but Jon Gnagy was the first.

30. *Kukla, Fran and Ollie.* Fran Allison first brought the Kuklapolitan players (puppets, that is) to TV in 1947. The cast included Beulah the Witch, Fletcher Rabbit, Madame Ophelia Ooglepuss, Colonel Cracky, and Clara Coo, among others.

31. *Land of the Giants.* An action adventure about a group of Earthlings stranded in a world of cranky giants.

32. *Lassie.* The famous collie performed heroic acts week after week, saving people from burning buildings, detaining criminals until the sheriff could make the arrests, and somehow always managing to communicate whatever was on her mind.

33. *The Little Rascals.* The Our Gang kids have been getting themselves into trouble on TV since 1954.

34. *The Lone Ranger.* The masked man, with his horse Silver and his trusty companion Tonto, were in the longest-running western series.

35. *Loony Tunes.* This consisted of 191 different cartoons featuring Porky Pig, Daffy Duck, and the rest of the Warner Bros. crew. They're still around today, of course.

36. *The Mickey Mouse Club.* The Mouseketeers, a bunch of kids including Annette Funicello and others who went on to become pop stars and performers, helped host this show, which included cartoons, music, minidramas, and skits starring the Mouseketeers.

37. *My Friend Flicka.* Another boy-and-his-horse drama, this one set at the turn of the century. The show was based on the popular book by Mary O'Hara.

38. *The Paul Winchell and Jerry Mahoney Show.* Winchell, a ventriloquist, starred with his fairly funny dummies, Jerry Mahoney and Knucklehead Smith, who lived up to his name. This show had a studio audience, much like *Howdy Doody.*

39. *Quiz Kids.* This adaptation of a popular radio series had a group of knowledgeable kids answering questions on different subjects. In 1980 Norman Lear revived the format in a show with the same name.

40. *Romper Room.* Still going strong, this one featured kids pretending to be in school. There were musical, instructional, patriotic, and entertainment segments and lots of ads for Romper Room toys.

41. *The Roy Rogers Show.* "The King of Cowboys," Sheriff Roy Rogers, and his wife, Dale Evans, maintained law and order in Mineral City.

42. *Sergeant Preston of the Yukon.* A Canadian Mountie aided by his horse, Rex, and his dog, Yukon King, patrol the Northwest while hunting for his father's murderer.

43. *The Shari Lewis Show.* Shari Lewis, the famous ventriloquist, starred with her family of puppets, Lambchop, Hush Puppy, Charlie Horse, Mr. Goodfellow, and Jump Pup, who still charm us today. Nothing is cuter than Lamb Chop yawning!

44. *Sheena, Queen of the Jungle.* A young girl grows up in the jungle after surviving a plane crash and successfully defends herself and the natives using only a spear and quick thinking.

45. *The Soupy Sales Show.* Comic madness with Soupy, the zany pie-throwing emcee and his puppet friends White Fang and Black Tooth (you only saw their paws), Pookie, and Marilyn Monwolf. Lots of weird humor here, which eventually led to the show being cancelled.

46. *Space Patrol.* Commander Buzz Cory and Cadet Happy battle evil forces in the twenty-first century in this sci-fi action series, which originally aired in 15-minute segments.

47. *The Three Stooges.* The original TV show, starring the inimitable Moe, Larry, and Curly, used recycled clips from their motion pictures. The cartoon spinoff of this show is called *The Robonic Stooges.*

48. *Watch Mr. Wizard.* This show taught you about science by demonstrating experiments. A scientist conducted the experiments in the presence of kids who always acted surprised at the results.

49. *Winky Dink and You.* This show caused major problems in homes all across America. Here's how it worked: An adult host (Jack Barry) talked to cartoon characters Winky Dink and Woofer while drawing pictures of them on a screen. As Barry completed the pictures, the characters would come to life in animated cartoons. In the meantime, kids at home could draw on the same screen by covering their TV screens with a plastic sheet and using special crayons that you could buy for 50 cents. You didn't really need the kit; you could just as easily use cellophane and regular crayons. This show was really fun, but kids got in trouble for writing on their TV screens *without* the plastic sheet!

50. *Wonderama.* This show had four different hosts, starting with Sandy Becker. The show featured games, interviews, civic discussions, weather reports, cartoons, and even drawing lessons with Jon Gnagy. It was the first real variety show for kids.

TV COWBOYS

From Hopalong Cassidy to Zeb Macahan in *How the West Was Won,* TV shows have made stars—whether villains or good guys—of many cowboys. So what's a cowboy, anyway? Well, a look at the guys who ruled the Old West—on TV, anyhow—will tell you that they all made their homes in places like Dodge City or Tombstone or the California frontier in the early to mid-1800s. And they all either chased outlaws or were outlaws themselves. Life on the frontier was rough. Tending ranches and carving out new territory for settlement was how people spent their days. They lived by their wits, their courage, their guns, and—in the case of Bat Masterson—by their canes.

1. Major Seth Adams and Flint McCullough. These two cowboys together ran the Wagon Train from 1958 to 1965. Major Adams (Ward Bond) was the fatherly wagonmaster, and Flint (Robert Horton) was the bold scout. One of the longest-running and best shows.

2. Gene Autry. From 1950 until 1956, *Gene Autry* starred the famous cowboy playing himself. We all loved his famous horse, Champion. Autry was one of the first and all-time best of the singing cowboys, an important part of American folk music. He is loved for his music as well as for his entertaining TV show.

3. The Cartwrights. *Bonanza,* which is still seen on cable TV today, had not one but four cowboy stars. Daddy Ben Cartwright (played by Lorne Greene), Little Joe (Michael Landon, who was best known as the father on *Little House on the Prairie*), Hoss (Dan Blocker), and Adam (Parnell Roberts, who later became the star of TV's *Trapper John*) all lived together on the famous Ponderosa ranch. They were the first TV cowboys to appear in color.

4. Hopalong Cassidy. Hopalong was played by William Boyd, the first TV cowboy, appearing as early as 1945. Today he's still one of the best-loved TV heroes, and reruns of his movies still come on from time to time.

5. Cheyenne. Cheyenne Bodie was played by six-foot-seven Clint Walker and then Ty Hardin, who took over the role. The show was on every other week, alternating with *Sugarfoot* and *Bronco.*

6. Clay Culhane. Played by actor Peter Beck, Culhane was the star of a show called *Black Saddle.* He was a lawyer-cowboy who gave up his guns for his profession. He carried his law books in his saddle bags as he roamed the New Mexico Territory.

7. Matt Dillon. Marshall Matt Dillon, played by James Arness, was the longest-running TV cowboy. His show, *Gunsmoke,* was on from 1955 to 1975 and won many Emmy Awards along the way. Chester, Dillon's sidekick, played by Dennis Weaver, was one of the best-loved cowboys ever.

8. Wyatt Earp. Lawman Earp did his thing on TV in *The Life and Times of Wyatt Earp.* Played by Hugh O'Brien, Earp was the marshall of Dodge City on Tuesdays, even though Matt Dillon already had that job on Saturday nights on a different channel on *Gunsmoke.* Bat Masterson eventually joined Earp on this show, and they fought together.

9. Jesse James. *The Legend of Jesse James* starred Christopher Jones. In typical Hollywood fashion, James was portrayed as a good guy instead of the outlaw he really was.

10. Lancer. The show *Lancer* featured two TV cowboy half-brothers, played by James Stacy and Wayne Maunder, who took care of their father's ranch from 1968 until 1971.

11. The Lone Ranger. A classic. The masked man (played first by Clayton Moore and then by John Hart), his friend Tonto (Jay Silverheels, a Native American), and his famous horse, Silver (played by Silver), chased bad men on TV from 1949 until 1957 and even got to star in a few movies.

12. Zeb Macahan. Zeb Macahan was the main character in *How the West Was Won,* and you might remember him from the movie with the same title. He was a latecomer to the TV cowboy lineup, appearing first in 1978. He was played by James Arness, who had been Matt Dillon on *Gunsmoke.*

13. Bat Masterson. *The Bat Masterson Show* featured a cowboy who was a professional gambler. Masterson, played by Gene Barry, was different from the tough cowboys on other shows. He was cool, charming, and never carried a gun. Instead, he used his brain, and when

that didn't work, he used his famous cane. There was a real Bat Masterson—named William Bartley Masterson—who was actually sheriff of Dodge City. He was known to have been friends with Wyatt Earp.

14. Maverick. Bret Maverick (James Garner) and his brother Bart (Jack Kelley) were the first funny TV cowboys. They were two card-playing rebels who roamed the airwaves from 1957 until 1962.

15. The Rifleman. Starring former baseball star Chuck Connors as rifleman Lucas McCaine, this cowboy had a teenager for a sidekick—his son, played by Johnny Crawford, who recorded a song or two and whom teenage girls considered *very* hot (in a Johnny Depp sort of way).

16. Roy Rogers. Before Roy Rogers opened a chain of restaurants, he was one of the most important of the singing cowboys. Together with his wife, Dale Evans, his horse, Trigger, and his Jeep, which they called Nellybelle, *The Roy Rogers Show* aired on TV from 1951 until 1957.

17. Will Sennett. This granddaddy of all cowboy heroes was played by Walter Brennan; he was the 73-year-old grandfather of Jeff Sennett from the TV show *The Guns of Will Sennett.* When the show was on the air, between 1967 and 1969, *TV Guide* rated it the top show among teens.

18. Sugarfoot. This show alternated with *Cheyenne* and *Bronco.* Tom "Sugarfoot" Brewster, played by Will Hutchins, was a correspondence law student and a poor excuse for a cowboy. He got his nickname because he was even less of a cowboy than a tenderfoot, which is a beginner.

19. The Texas Rangers. The show was called *Laredo,* and it featured four stars: Neville Brand, Philip Carey, Robert Wolders, and Peter Brown. It had a great theme song.

20. The Virginian. Played by James Drury, the Virginian was a mysterious cowboy: No one knew his real name. Based on a novel written in 1902, the Virginian was the first cowboy to have a show run as long as 90 minutes instead of the usual half-hour.

21. Rowdy Yates. Played by Clint Eastwood in the TV show *Rawhide*—way back before *Unforgiven, In the Line of Fire,* or any of the Dirty Harry movies—this cowboy ran cattle cross-country for seven years starting in 1959, when Eastwood was just 29 years old. Yates started out as second in command to the trail boss but got promoted to that job himself in 1965.

22. Zorro. Almost everyone has heard of Don Diego de la Vaga, the famous masked man, and his two wonderful stallions—the black Tornado and the white Phantom—all of whom appeared in the TV series *Zorro.* It can still be seen on some cable stations.

THE 40 MOST POPULAR KIDS' MOVIES OF ALL TIME

These are the movies that were not only the most successful at the theater box office (that made the most money) but were also the movies you rented most and purchased most in video form.

1. *Jurassic Park*
2. *The Lion King*
3. *E.T.—The Extra Terrestrial*
4. *101 Dalmatians*
5. *Star Wars*
6. *Fantasia*
7. *The Jungle Book*
8. *Aladdin*
9. *Home Alone*
10. *Ghostbusters*
11. *Back to the Future*
12. *Beauty and the Beast*
13. *Raiders of the Lost Ark*
14. *Three Men and a Baby*
15. *Return of the Jedi*
16. *Home Alone 2: Lost in New York*
17. *Batman*
18. *The Empire Strikes Back*

19. *Pinocchio*
20. *Who Framed Roger Rabbit?*
21. *Teenage Mutant Ninja Turtles*
22. *Bambi*
23. *Big*
24. *Terminator 2: Judgment Day*
25. *The Terminator*
26. *Cocoon*
27. *Close Encounters of the Third Kind*
28. *Honey, I Shrunk the Kids*
29. *The Wizard of Oz*
30. *Look Who's Talking*
31. *Mary Poppins*
32. *Indiana Jones and the Last Crusade*
33. *Kindergarten Cop*
34. *Alice in Wonderland*
35. *Beethoven*
36. *Gremlins*
37. *Indiana Jones and the Temple of Doom*
38. *The Karate Kid*
39. *Lady and the Tramp*
40. *Superman*

THE 24 MOST POPULAR ANIMATED VIDEO RENTALS, 1994

1. *Pinnocchio*
2. *Sleeping Beauty*
3. *Dumbo*
4. *Lady and the Tramp*
5. *Cinderella*
6. *The Little Mermaid*
7. *Alice in Wonderland*
8. *Beauty and the Beast*
9. *Robin Hood*
10. *Bambi*
11. *An American Tail*
12. *101 Dalmatians*
13. *The Jungle Book*
14. *Peter Pan*
15. *Fantasia*
16. *The Land Before Time*
17. *Aladdin*
18. *The Rescuers Down Under*
19. *Mickey Mouse Commemorative Edition*
20. *Teenage Mutant Ninja Turtles: The Case of the Killer Pizzas*

21. *Teenage Mutant Ninja Turtles: The Shredder Is Splintered*
22. *Teenage Mutant Ninja Turtles: Hot Rodding Teenagers*
23. *The Sword in the Stone*
24. *Winnie the Pooh and Tigger Too*

25 TV AND MOVIE CHARACTERS YOU CAN WRITE TO

1. The Addams Family
   Hanna-Barbera
   3400 Cahuenga Blvd.
   Hollywood, CA 90068
2. Aladdin
   Walt Disney Television Animation
   5200 Lankershim Blvd.
   N. Hollywood, CA 91601
3. Alvin and the Chipmunks
   MWS
   4222 W. Burbank Blvd.
   Burbank, CA 91505
4. Barbie and Ken
   5150 Rosecrans Ave.
   Hawthorne, CA 90205
5. Batman
   Warner Bros. Animation
   15303 Ventura Blvd., #1100
   Sherman Oaks, CA 91403
6. Beavis and Butthead
   MTV
   1515 Broadway
   New York, N.Y. 10036
7. Benji
   Mulberry Square Productions
   10300 N. Central Expressway
   Dallas, TX 75231
8. Bugs Bunny
   Warner Bros. TV
   4000 Warner Blvd.
   Burbank, CA 91505
9. C-3PO and R2-D2
   Lucasfilm
   P.O. Box 8669
   Universal City, CA 91608
10. Donald Duck
    Walt Disney Productions
    500 South Buena Vista St.
    Burbank, CA 91521
11. The Flintstones

Harvey Comics Entertainment
100 Wilshire Blvd., #500
Santa Monica, CA 90401

12. Ghostwriter
Children's Television Workshop
1 Lincoln Plaza
New York, N.Y. 10023

13. G.I. Joe
Marvel Entertainment Group
387 Park Ave. South
New York, N.Y. 10016

14. Kermit the Frog and Miss Piggy
115 East 57th St.
New York, N.Y. 10022

15. Freddy Kreuger
9200 Sunset Blvd., #625
Los Angeles, CA 90069

16. Ronald McDonald
1 McDonald Plaza
Oak Brook, IL 60521

17. Mickey Mouse
Walt Disney Productions
500 South Buena Vista St.
Burbank, CA 91521

18. Ren and Stimpy
Nickelodeon
1515 Broadway
New York, N.Y. 100336

19. Roger Rabbit
Touchstone Pictures
500 S. Buena Vista St.
Burbank, CA 91521

20. Santa Claus
Santa's House
North Pole 30351

21. The Simpsons
Twentieth TV
P.O. Box 900

Beverly Hills, CA 90213

22. Smokey the Bear
Forest Service
Department of Agriculture
The Mall between 12th
and 14th Streets, NW
Washington, D.C. 20250

23. Snoopy
United Features Syndicate
200 Park Ave.
New York, N.Y. 10166

24. Superman
DC Comics
1325 Ave. of the Americas
New York, N.Y. 10019

25. Teenage Mutant Ninja
Turtles
New Line Cinema
116 N. Robertson Blvd., #200
Los Angeles, CA 90048

BUGS BUNNY'S BEST FRIENDS

The most popular rabbit in the world, created by the great Chuck Jones, appeared in his first motion picture, *A Wild Hare,* in 1940. Since then, he has starred in 263 short films, 4 feature films, and 11 half-hour prime-time TV shows. In addition to all this, Bugs Bunny cartoons have appeared on TV continuously for more than 30 years in what has become the longest-running show in TV history. It has been estimated that within a one-week period, more than 100 million people tune in to Bugs and his pals, who include Porky Pig, Sylvester, Tweety, Road Runner, Speedy Gonzales, and, of course, these favorites:

1. Daffy Duck. Daffy is a cowardly, selfish duck who spends most of his time thinking up ways to become rich and famous. Of course, he's so daffy that he always loses his fights to Bugs and winds up spitting, "You're dissss-picable!" Nevertheless, Bugs is amused by Daffy and secretly considers him a friend.

2. Elmer Fudd. We frequently see Elmer, the little hunter, stalking Bugs as he tells us,"Be wery, wery quiet. I'm hunting wabbits! It's wabbit season!" But Bugs knows that Elmer is just an excitable little man who really means no harm. So he plays tricks on poor Elmer, who is always frustrated in the end. Bug's favorite nicknames for Elmer are "Doc" and "Fudsy."

3. Yosemite Sam. Sam is the worst-tempered man in the world. He refers to Bugs as "that rackinfrackin' varmint" and continually announces, "I hates that rabbit!" Still, Bugs who always enjoys a good chase scene, regards Sam as a friendly foe.

15 THINGS YOU PROBABLY DIDN'T KNOW ABOUT SUPERMAN

1. Superman first premiered as a comic book character in Action Comics in June 1938.

2. In 1940, Superman became the star of his own radio program, a serial drama that aired three days a week.

3. It was on the radio program—not in the comic book—that kryptonite, Superman's famous weakness, came into the story.

4. The Superman radio program was originally sponsored by Kellogg's.

5. In the early days, Superman appeared in 17 fully animated color cartoons that were shown in movie theaters.

6. The Superman films starring Christopher Reeve as the man of steel were not the first Superman movies. In 1948, Columbia Pictures produced the first live-action Superman film, called *Superman,* and in 1950 they released *Atom Man Versus Superman*.

7. In 1951 a third film was released, *Superman and the Mole Men,* which starred George Reeves as Superman.

8. In the original legend, Superman's parents were named Jor-L and Lora. A later comic book changed their names to Jor-El and Lara. Similarly, *Daily Planet* editor George Taylor suddenly appeared one day as Perry White.

9. There were 104 *Adventures of Superman* TV episodes, which were produced from 1952 to 1957. One of the first shows to be filmed in color, it immediately became one of the top kids' TV shows in the country. George Reeves played Superman.

10. Superman is the sole survivor of the planet Krypton. The other "super" characters in his comic books all have different origins: Superboy is a clone and Supergirl is a telekinetic shape-shifter from another dimension.

11. Clark Kent asked Lois Lane to marry him in 1990 because he had lost his superpowers and thought he could finally enjoy a normal life. She accepted his proposal (after his powers had returned) in *Superman* #50, which went on sale in November 1990.

12. Because Superman believes he shouldn't keep secrets from the ones he loves, he revealed his identity to Lois Lane in *Action Comics* #667 in January 1991.

13. *Superman* #75, the issue in which Doomsday kills Superman, has sold more than 6 million copies since its release in November 1992. A trade paperback collecting all seven chapters of "The Death of Superman" has sold more than 2 million copies.

14. *Adventures of Superman* #500 is the fastest-selling comic book of all time, selling more than 4 million copies in 36 hours in April 1993.

15. *Lois and Clark: The New Adventures of Superman* debuted on ABC-TV in September 1993.

SHARI LEWIS LISTS THE 10 THINGS SHE ENJOYS DOING MOST

When you think of Shari Lewis, you probably think of her as Lambchop's mother. But did you know that this world-famous ventriloquist also sings, acts, dances, has written more than 25 books for children, and has conducted 40 of the leading symphonies in the United States? But when we asked Shari to list the things she likes to do best, she didn't mention any of those. Here's what she said.

1. Walking four or five miles to a place where I can get a really big breakfast, which I then feel that I have earned.

2. Playing with anybody's puppy.

3. Being where I can hear the ocean pounding on the beach.

4. A rainy day when I don't have to go out.

5. Watching anybody do anything perfectly (whether it's painting the house or performing in a ballet).

6. Completing a craft project.

7. Looking at a newborn baby's toes.

8. Living with a handmade piece of furniture or clothing, particularly if it's made by someone I know.

9. Trying to find my way back to the hotel when I'm in a country where the language is really foreign and nobody speaks English.

10. Talking to a brand-new puppet and having it talk back!

54 BAT-THINGS

1. Bat alarm
2. Batanalyzer
3. Batarang
4. Batarmor
5. Batawake
6. Batbeam
7. Batbeam Firing Button
8. Bat Blowtorch
9. Batboat
10. Batcamera's Polarized Batfilter
11. Batcave
12. Batcentrifuge
13. Batcharge Launcher
14. Batclaws
15. Batcommunicator
16. Batcopter
17. Batcostume
18. Batcuffs
19. Batcycle
20. Batcycle Go Cart
21. Batdrift Angle
22. Bat earplugs
23. Batgas
24. Batguage
25. Bathook
26. Batkey
27. Batknife
28. Batladder
29. Batlaser Gun
30. Batmagnet
31. Batmissile
32. Batmobile
33. Batmobile Antitheft Device
34. Batmobile Mobile Crime Computer
35. Batmobile's Superpower Afterburner
36. Batometer
37. Batostat Antifire Activator
38. Batphone
39. Batpole
40. Batram
41. Bat Ray Projector
42. Batresearch Shelf
43. Batrope
44. Batscanner Receiver
45. Batscope
46. Batshield
47. Batsleep
48. Batsignal
49. Bat Terror Control
50. Batzooka
51. Compressed Steam Batlift
52. Homing Battransmitter
53. Memory Batbank
54. Superblinding Batpellets

10 THINGS YOU PROBABLY DIDN'T KNOW ABOUT SHIRLEY TEMPLE

1. When Shirley Temple began making films, she was the youngest person ever to appear on the cover of *Time* magazine and the youngest actress to receive an Academy Award. It was an honorary award "for having achieved eminence among the greatest of screen actors." She was 7 years old.

2. Temple's insurance policy with Lloyd's of London stated that there would be no compensation if she were either injured or killed while intoxicated.

3. Temple did not begin formal schooling until she was 13.

4. Temple became a Republican at the age of 10 after the Democratic mayor of Boston accidentally slammed a car door on her hand.

5. Temple was made an honorary Ketucky colonel, an honorary captain of the Texas Rangers, a mascot of the Chilean Navy, and an honorary G-woman by J. Edgar Hoover of the F.B.I.

6. In a film entitled *Polly-tix in Washington,* Temple played the role of a prostitute.

7. Her movies earned between $1 and $2 million each in a time when the price of a movie ticket was 15 cents.

8. In 1938, Temple's income was the seventh highest in America; she was making more than $300,000 a year.

9. At the height of her fame, she was given a weekly allowance of $4.25.

10. For her eighth birthday, Temple received more than 135,000 gifts, including a baby kangaroo from a fan in Australia and a calf from a group of schoolchildren in Oregon.

KIDS WHO HAVE WON ACADEMY AWARDS

	Age	*Year*
Shirley Temple	6	1934
Margaret O'Brien	7	1944
Tatum O'Neal	10	1973
Anna Paquin	11	1994

80 BLACK AND WHITE MOVIES YOU SHOULD WATCH

Yes, they are old. And yes, they are in black and white. But they are all great. So if you come across one of these movies while you are channel surfing or see one in your local video rental store, check it out.

We've coded these movies in the following way:

C — Comedy
A — Adventure
D — Drama
W — Western
M — Musical
H — Horror

1. *Abbott and Costello Meet Frankenstein* (1948) C
2. *Abbott and Costello Meet the Invisible Man* (1951) C
3. *The Adventures of Mark Twain* (1944) A

4. *The Adventures of Robin Hood* (1938) A
5. *The Adventures of Robinson Crusoe* (1956) A
6. *The Adventures of Tom Sawyer* (1928) A
7. *Ali Baba and the Forty Thieves* (1944) A
8. *Androcles and the Lion* (1952) A,C
9. *Animal Crackers* (1930) C
10. *Anne of Green Gables* (1934) D
11. *Babes in Toyland* (1934) C
12. *The Bellboy* (1960) C
13. *Boys Town* (1938) D
14. *The Bride of Frankenstein* (1935) H
15. *Call of the Wild* (1935) A
16. *Captains Courageous* (1937) A
17. *The Champ* (1931) D
18. *The Count of Monte Cristo* (1934) A
19. *Curly Top* (1935) C,M
20. *David Copperfield* (1935) D
21. *The Day the Earth Stood Still* (1951) D
22. *Dracula* (1931) H
23. *Duck Soup* (1933) C
24. *Elephant Boy* (1937) A
25. *Frankenstein* (1931) H
26. *Frankenstein Meets the Wolf Man* (1943) H
27. *Ghost Catchers* (1944) C
28. *The Gold Rush* (1925) C
29. *Great Expectations* (1946) D
30. *The Great K&A Train Robbery* (1926) W
31. *Gunga Din* (1939) A
32. *Hard Day's Night* (1964) C,M
33. *Invasion of the Body Snatchers* (1956) H
34. *It's a Gift* (1934) C
35. *The Jackie Robinson Story* (1950) D
36. *Jailhouse Rock* (1957) D,M
37. *The Kid* (1921) A
38. *Kidnapped* (1938) A
39. *King Kong* (1933) A
40. *Last of the Mohicans* (1936) A
41. *Laurel and Hardy's Laughing 20's* (1956) C
42. *The Little Kidnappers* (1953) D
43. *Little Lord Fauntleroy* (1936)

44. *Little Miss Marker* (1934) C,M

45. *The Little Shop of Horrors* (1960) C

46. *The Mark of Zorro* (1940) A

47. *Mighty Joe Young* (1949) A

48. *Miracle on 34th Street* (1947) D

49. *The Miracle Worker* (1962) D

50. *Monkey Business* (1931) C

51. *The Mummy's Curse* (1944) H

52. *My Darling Clementine* (1946) W

53. *My Friend Flicka* (1943) A

54. *Night at the Opera* (1935) C

55. *No Time for Sargeants* (1958)

56. *Oliver Twist* (1948) D

57. *The Perils of Pauline* (1947) C

58. *Phantom of the Opera* (1943) H

59. *Pride of the Yankees* (1942) D

60. *The Scarlet Pimpernel* (1934) A

61. *The Sea Hawk* (1940) A

62. *Sargeant York* (1941) D,A

63. *Sons of the Desert* (1953) C

64. *Stagecoach* (1939) W

65. *Swiss Family Robinson* (1940) A

66. *Ten From Your Show of Shows* (1973) C

67. *Them* (1954) H

68. *The Thief of Baghdad* (1940) A

69. *The Three Musketeers* (1939) A

70. *Topper* (1937) C

71. *Treasure Island* (1934) A

72. *A Tree Grows in Brooklyn* (1945) D

73. *War of the Worlds* (1953) H

74. *Wee Willie Winkie* (1937) C

75. *When Comedy Was King* (1960) C

76. *The Wolf Man* (1942) H

77. *Yankee Doodle Dandy* (1942) M

78. *The Yearling* (1946) D

79. *You Can't Cheat an Honest Man* (1939) C

80. *Young Frankenstein* (1974) C

THE FIRST 100 DISNEY CHARACTERS

Between 1920 and 1950 Walt Disney revolutionized animated film by creating techniques and effects that the world had barely dreamed of. These accomplishments alone would have ensured him a place in film history, but Disney also went on to create some of the best-loved characters we've ever known. Mickey Mouse, for instance, was an immediate success when he was first presented to the world in 1928 in a film called *Steamboat Willie,* but Mickey was just one of the many who went on to become star of stage, screen, books, songs, toys, underwear, you name it.

The following list includes the first 100 Disney characters, the years in which they were introduced, and the movies in which they first appeared. These are not necessarily the most popular; some were selected because of historical facts. It is interesting, for instance, that Donald Duck did not start out as a star but as a character in a film called *The Little Wise Hen.* Others are on the list for their charming names. And did you know that Disney created characters based on such real personalities as Albert Einstein and Adolf Hitler?

1. Abner	1936	*Country Cousin*
2. Agnes	1942	*"Mickey Mouse" comic strip*
3. Apollo	1940	*Fantasia*
4. Ant Ena	1942	*Bambi*
5. Aunt Jemima	1935	*Broken Toys*
6. Baby Weems	1941	*The Reluctant Dragon*
7. Bambi	1942	*Bambi*
8. Bambi's Mother	1942	*Bambi*
9. Bashful	1937	*Snow White and the Seven Dwarfs*

10. Ben Ali Gator	1940	*Fantasia*
11. Ben Buzzard	1943	*Flying Jalopy*
12. Big Bad Wolf	1933	*Three Little Pigs*
13. Blynken	1938	*Wynken, Blynken and Nod*
14. Br'er Bear	1946	*Song of the South*
15. Br'er Fox	1946	*Song of the South*
16. Br'er Rabbit	1946	*Song of the South*
17. Captain Churchmouse	1932	*"Bucky Bug" comic strip*
18. Captain Doberman	1933	*"Mickey Mouse" comic strip*
19. Captain Katt	1936	*Three Blind Mouseketeers*
20. Casey	1946	*Make Mine Music*
21. Casey, Jr.	1941	*The Reluctant Dragon*
22. Chicken Little	1943	*Chicken Little*
23. Chip	1943	*Private Pluto*
24. Christopher Columbus	1949	*So Dear to My Heart*
25. Clarabelle Cow	1929	*The Plow Boy*
26. Clementine	1941	*The Reluctant Dragon*
27. Cock Robin	1935	*Who Killed Cock Robin?*
28. Daisy Duck	1937	*Don Donald*
29. Dale	1943	*Private Pluto*
30. Dewey	1938	*Donald's Nephews*
31. Doc	1937	*Snow White and the Seven Dwarfs*
32. Donald Duck	1934	*The Little Wise Hen*
33. Dopey	1937	*Snow White and the Seven Dwarfs*
34. Ducky Lucky	1943	*Chicken Litle*
35. Dumbo	1941	*Dumbo*
36. Eega Beeva	1948	*"Mickey Mouse" comic strip*
37. Einstein	1941	*The Reluctant Dragon*
38. Eli Squinch	1934	*"Mickey Mouse" comic strip*
39. Ezra Beetle	1947	*Bootle Beetle*

40. Ferdinand the Bull	1938	*Ferdinand the Bull*
41. Figaro	1940	*Pinnocchio*
42. Gepetto	1940	*Pinnocchio*
43. Goosie Gander	1933	*Old King Cole*
44. Grumpy	1937	*Snow White and the Seven Dwarfs*
45. Henny Penny	1943	*Chicken Little*
46. Hitler	1943	*Education for Death*
47. Hortense	1937	*Donald's Ostrich*
48. Huey	1938	*Donald's Nephews*
49. Humpty Dumpty	1931	*Mother Goose Melodies*
50. Ichabod Crane	1949	*The Adventures of Ichabod Crane*
51. Jack Horner	1931	*Mother Goose Melodies*
52. Jack Spratt	1933	*Old King Cole*
53. Jenny Wren	1935	*Who Killed Cock Robin?*
54. Jiminy Cricket	1940	*Pinocchio*
55. Johnny Appleseed	1948	*Melody Time*
56. King Neptune	1932	*Kin Neptune*
57. Little Hiawatha	1937	*Little Hiawatha*
58. Little Minnehaha	1940	*"Little Hiawatha" comic strip*
59. Little Toot	1948	*Melody Time*
60. Mademoiselle Upanova	1940	*Fantasia*
61. Mammy Two Shoes	1935	*Three Orphan Kittens*
62. Mary, Mary, Quite Contrary	1933	*Old King Cole*
63. Max Hare	1935	*Tortoise and the Hare*
64. Mickey Mouse	1928	*Steamboat Willie*
65. Minnie Mouse	1928	*Steamboat Willie*
66. Monstro	1940	*Pinocchio*
67. Montmorency Rodent	1941	*"Mickey Mouse" comic strip*
68. Mortimer Mouse	1936	*Mickey's Rival*
69. Mother Goose	1931	*Mother Goose Melodies*

70.	Mother Hubbard	1933	*Old King Cole*
71.	Mr. Bluebird	1946	*Song of the South*
72.	Noah	1933	*Father Noah's Ark*
73.	Nod	1938	*Wynken, Blynken and Nod*
74.	Pecos Bill	1948	*Melody Time*
75.	Pegleg Pete	1928	*Steamboat Willie*
76.	Phantom Blot	1939	*"Mickey Mouse" comic strip*
77.	Pied Piper	1933	*Old King Cole*
78.	Pinocchio	1940	*Pinocchio*
79.	Pluto	1930	*The Chain Gang*
80.	Reason	1943	*Reason and Emotion*
81.	Red Riding Hood	1934	*The Big Bad Wolf*
82.	Santa Claus	1932	*Santa's Workshop*
83.	Satan	1946	*Make Mine Music*
84.	Simple Simon	1931	*Mother Goose Melodies*
85.	Sleepy	1937	*Snow White and the Seven Dwarfs*
86.	Sluefoot Sue	1948	*Melody Time*
87.	Sneezy	1937	*Snow White and the Seven Dwarfs*
88.	Snow White	1937	*Snow White and the Seven Dwarfs*
89.	Stromboll	1940	*Pinocchio*
90.	Sylvester Shyster	1930	*"Mickey Mouse" comic strip*
91.	Tar Baby	1946	*Song of the South*
92.	Tetti Tatti	1946	*Make Mine Music*
93.	Three Blind Mouseketeers	1936	*Three Blind Mouseketeers*
94.	Thumper	1942	*Bambi*
95.	Thursday	1940	*"Mickey Mouse" comic strip*
96.	Turkey Lurkey	1943	*Chicken Little*
97.	Ugly Duckling	1931	*The Ugly Duckling*
98.	Widomaker	1948	*Melody Time*
99.	Wynken	1938	*Wynken, Blynken and Nod*
100.	Yensid	1940	*Fantasia*

10 OF THE WORST SCIENCE FICTION FILMS OF ALL TIME

These are the worst space films, as listed by TV historians Harry and Michael Medved in their wonderful book *The Golden Turkey Awards.*

1. *Cat Women of the Moon* (1953). A group of astronauts meets up with creatures on the moon—cat women, of course—in a story that has less depth than most TV commercials. The star, Sonny Tufts, is especially awful in this one, which was originally shown in 3-D.

2. *Frankenstein Meets the Space Monster* (1965). One of the worst plots ever: A robot astronaut gone berserk battles an outer space queen and an army of midgets. Not intended as a comedy but good for laughs anyway.

3. *The Green Slime* (1969). A Japanese rocket is attacked by tiny creatures that grow larger and slimier as they devour American and Italian astronauts. The title role is badly executed by a man in a slime suit. Very corny.

4. *Invasion of the Star Creatures* (1965). American soldiers are captured by female aliens who command an army of giant carrots (no kidding) who wear tights and potato sacks and have Ping-Pong balls for eyes.

5. *Message from Space* (1978). Japan's answer to *Star Wars,* and not nearly as much fun as Godzilla. Horrible special effects and one of the worst jobs of overdubbing ever.

6. *Plan Nine from Outer Space* (1959). Commonly considered one of the most awful movies ever made, mostly for having the most convoluted and ridiculous plot ever concocted. The special effects are so bad in this one that if you look closely, you can see that the flying saucers are actually paper plates. In the closing battle, they "blow up" a spaceship by setting fire to one of the plates.

7. *Queen of Outer Space* (1958). The trouble with this one is twofold: a ridiculous plot (Venutian slave girl betrays her people for the love of a human astronaut) and the actress who plays the girl from Venus—with a Hungarian accent! (That's Zsa Zsa Gabor.)

8. *Robot Monster* (1953). The robot monsters are actually men in gorilla suits with divers' helmets on their heads. Public reaction to this one was so bad that the director, Phil Tucker, tried to kill himself.

9. *Starship Invasions* (1977). Coneheads in flying saucers try to invade the earth, but Robert Vaughn saves the day with only his pocket calculator to guide him in his second most embarrassing film. (*Teenage Caveman* was his first.)

10. *Teenagers from Outer Space* (1959). Outer space teenagers plot to take over the earth, but romance gets in the way. (Boys will be boys!)

12 DINOSAUR MOVIES THAT PREDATE *JURASSIC PARK*

1. *Gertie the Dinosaur* (1914). The first animated movie ever made.

2. *The Lost World* (1925). A silent movie based on an adventure tale by Arthur Conan Doyle, the man who invented Sherlock Holmes. Great special effects for its time.

3. *One Million B.C.* (1940). The special effects in this film were considered so exceptional that they were used in many other movies, too.

4. *Godzilla, King of the Monsters* (1956). This Japanese movie features a fire-breathing lizard that threatens mankind. There were nine sequels to this movie, including *Godzilla vs. the Smog Monster.*

5. *Teenage Caveman* (1958). A teenager searches for adventure and finds dinosaurs instead.

6. *Journey to the Center of the Earth* (1959). Based on the famous novel by Jules Verne, this film features scenes with prehistoric monsters discovered miles below the earth's surface. A classic adventure movie—don't miss this one.

7. *Dinosaurs* (1960). Cavemen face danger. The effects are so silly you'll laugh, even though the movie is not meant to be a comedy.

8. *When Dinosaurs Ruled the Earth* (1970). Good acting, great effects, and beautiful scenery make this one worth watching.

9. *The Land That Time Forgot* (1975). Sailors on a submarine during World War I discover an unknown region of South America. Bad effects also make this one funny.

10. *Caveman* (1981). Starring Ringo Starr, of the Beatles, this is a comedy with some humorous effects and silly-looking dinosaurs.

11. *Baby... Secret of the Lost Legend* (1985). The baby dinosaur featured in this movie is adorable.

12. *The Land Before Time* (1988). An animated movie about an orphaned dinosaur trying to find a new home and family.

THE MONSTER HALL OF FAME

You probably wouldn't want to have a monster for a pet, and let's face it: You'd crawl out of your skin in a minute if one slithered up to your bed on Halloween night. Still, movie monsters have been entertaining us for years. Here are some of the most vile from the early days of the silver scream.

1. The Blob: In this 1958 film called *The Blob,* a meteor crashes to the earth. Amidst the smoke and rubble, a strange thing happens: The Blob is born. Made of jelly, though not the kind you'd want on your peanut butter sandwich, it starts out weighing just a few ounces and grows, as monsters often do, to tremendous proportions, until it is about the size of a house and weighs a few tons. Huge and pulsating, with an appetite you wouldn't believe, the Blob proceeds to devour everything in sight, including an entire diner and most of the other characters in the movie. But the hero, Steve McQueen, figures out the Blob's weakness: cold. Using carbon dioxide from a fire extinguisher, he and his buddy freeze the thing and ship it to Antarctica, where it remains until later that year, when Paramount releases *The Return of the Blob.*

2. Dracula: No monster hall of fame would be complete without our old friend Dracula, who got his first starring movie role in 1931 in the film called...what else? *Dracula.* Related to the bat, he is, of course, the Transylvanian vampire we've all come to know and love. Once he bites his victims, they, too, become sadistic vampires, living off the blood of others, ever hunting for their next meal. Extremely handsome and invulnerable to bullets and knives, Dracula is finally done in by sunlight and a wooden stake driven through his heart. (See "8 Ways to Kill or Repel Dracula" on page

313.) But not for long. Dracula returns in a long list of films, and even his relatives manage to follow in his evil footsteps in movies such as *Blacula* and the 1992 remake, *Bram Stoker's Dracula.* You just can't keep a good man down.

3. The Fly: You've got to feel sorry for the fly, who made his film debut in the movie called *The Fly.* This poor soul gets his start when a scientist, Andre Delambre, screws up an experiment and winds up trading heads with an innocent little fly. Delambre's huge fly head is determined to make him crazy, torturing him mentally until his wife finally kills him by squashing his head under a giant electric press. Of course, no one believes the wife's ordeal until a detective notices a small fly in their house with a screaming human head. He crushes the pathetic little creature with a rock, but the pesky insect somehow manages a few more appearances in *Return of the Fly, Curse of the Fly,* and the sequel, *The Fly II.*

4. Frankenstein: You've got to give Frankenstein credit—he did, after all, start the ball rolling as one of the first hideous movie creatures ever. Not only did he encourage other monsters to become actors, but he starred in a long list of his own films and even got his son, daughter, and bride into the act. Tall, superstrong, and completely horrifying, Frankenstein was known to break people in half and destroy anyone who tried to prevent him from performing his ghastly deeds. Well, you'd be cranky too if you were made up of parts of dead bodies that had been brought to life by electricity. In the end of the classic film *Frankenstein,* the monster is finally trapped in a windmill and burned to death.

5. Ghidrah: Talk about rude house guests. In *Ghidrah the 3-Headed Monster,* a Japanese film, we meet one of the strongest monsters in movie history. Visiting here from another planet, this fire-breathing dragonlike monstrosity manages to destroy Tokyo, mess up half of Japan, and even nearly finishes off three other monster favorites—Godzilla, Mothra, and Rodan. But as things turn out, three heads are not better than one, and Ghidrah is finally flung back into outer space by his earth-born monster enemies. Keep an eye out for Ghidrah—he was never actually killed.

6. Godzilla: Before Godzilla learned the error of his ways and fought to save mankind in movies such as *Childrah—The 3-Headed Monster, Godzilla's Revenge, Godzilla vs. the Smog Monster,* and others, he was as bad as the rest in his own film called *Godzilla.* Known as the King of the Monsters, he was created by radiation from atomic testing (a popular monster-movie theme), was about 200 feet tall, and weighed hundreds of tons. Godzilla managed to destroy ships, entire villages, and thousands of screaming Japanese before his creator, the peace-loving Dr. Serizawa, figured out that his superweapon, which would cut off all of Godzilla's oxygen, was the solution. Godzilla and the good doctor are both reduced to a pile of bones in the end of the film, with Tokyo left in ruins.

7. King Kong: What's 50 feet tall, has a chest that measures 60 feet around, a six-foot-wide mouth, and ears that are a foot long? A man-eating ape with a voracious appetite for humans as well as trains. Known as King Kong. The difference between Kong and most other movie monsters was that he had a heart. In the 1933 movie *King Kong*, he fell in love with lovely Ann Darrow. As if being shot by Cupid's arrow isn't bad enough, King Kong is finally felled by planes armed with machine guns that buzz all around him like flies on a hot summer's day. One of the most popular monsters of all time, King Kong actually had people rioting in the streets when his first film was released. Back for a number of encores, he also appeared in *King Kong Escapes, King Kong vs. Godzilla, King Kong vs. Frankenstein,* and in a 1977 remake of the original film.

8. Mighty Joe Young: In the film *Mighty Joe Young,* we meet the kindest monster of all time. Discovered in an African jungle by a bunch of movie producers, the 12-foot-tall ape is brought to the United States, where someone has the bright idea to make him a nightclub star. But Joe can't adjust to performing in front of an audience, and he breaks out of his cage in an uncontrollable rage and terrorizes all in his path. Unfortunately the authorities feel that anything that big has to be dangerous, and Joe is pursued by policemen who have been ordered to shoot him dead. But this movie has a happy ending. Joe manages to prove his good intentions by saving a little girl from the top floor of a burning orphanage. He is finally forgiven his past destruction and returned to the

African jungle, where he lives happily ever after.

9. Mothra: Picture a moth with wings the size of ocean liners and you've got a fair idea of one of the most popular film monsters of all time. In *Mothra,* the first of many Japanese films in which he starred, our old friend starts out as a giant caterpillar with silver eyes and goes on to become a virtually indestructible 200-ton moth whose wings can create tornadoes. Even a specially built atomic heat cannon does faze him, but this turns out to be for the good of all, as we learn that all Mothra wants out of life is to protect his homeland and live in peace. After he saves some little girls (destroying much of Tokyo in the process), he flies back home.

10. The Mummy: This is a present you definitely don't want to unwrap. When the Mummy is discovered in an ancient tomb by a group of archaeologists, he is actually dead. The trouble is, he doesn't know it, and he spends most of the movie chasing down and gruesomely killing his discoverers. The Mummy probably would have killed all of them, but he falls in love with the wife of one remaining archaeologist, and, in a moment of weakness, is shot by him. Nevertheless, he manages to return in subsequent films. If you ever come across the Mummy on some dark night, you won't have any trouble recognizing him. He'll be wrapped in gauze from head to toe, have one eye closed and one open, and will be dragging one foot behind him. He's not terribly fast, but if he corners you, watch out! Chances are he'll strangle you with one incredibly strong fist.

11. Nosferatu: "He bites, he sucks, he drains, he destroys." He's also one of the first vampires ever, having made his first film appearance in the film *Nosferatu* in 1922 in the starring role. In the 1979 film *Nosferateu the Vampyre,* the "chiller of the night" manages to take over an entire ship and its sailors, whose blood he uses to quench his evil thirst, Although Nosferatu seems indestructible with his superstrong snapping fangs and irresistible hypnotic powers, he is, after all, vulnerable to daylight. When he is detained into the morning by Lucy, with whom he is in love, the sun's rays strike him like flames, and he dissolves into a mess of awful flesh.

12. Phantom of the Opera: Eric, as he was called before a fire seriously destroyed his face in the film *Phantom of the Opera,* had been a music lover whose life centered around the Paris Opera House. Unfortunately, circumstances lead him to become a mean hermit living in a bizarre underground world, where he plays music, eats gourmet meals, and finds time to fall in love with one of the young opera stars, Christine. For most of the film he is hidden behind a mask, but when the kidnapped Christine finally pulls it off his face, we encounter the real Eric: "Extraordinarily thin, his dress coat hung on a skeleton frame," with "eyes so deep one could hardly see the fixed pupils."

Like many of his friends in the movies, the Phantom has a heart, and he spends many days teaching Christine to sing like an opera star. He is killed trying to save her from death in an accident that takes place in the midst of a performance.

13. Rodan: *Sesame Street*'s big bird must have learned a lot from the original Big Bird, Rodan, who thrilled movie audiences in the 1957 film in which he had the starring role. With a wingspan of over 500 feet and weighing more than 150 tons (the egg from which he hatched was a whopping 100,000 cubic feet in size), Rodan is the product of H-bomb tests that crack open the earth and hatch eggs that have been lying around for millions of years. For a bird, Rodan looks a lot like a lizard, with a long neck and a steel-hard beak, which he uses to eat planes and ships. Bullets, missiles, and artillery can't kill him, and Rodan has a monstrously good time blasting apart cities all over the world. After Peking and Singapore are gone, Rodan meets his match in the form of a volcano, whose hot lava eventually burns him to death. Gone but not forgotten.

8 MORE MOVIE MONSTERS AND THE WAYS IN WHICH THEY WERE FINALLY KILLED

1. *The Beast of Hollow Mountain*—drowned in quicksand

2. *The Beast from 20,000 Fathoms*—shot in the throat with a radioactive isotope

3. *The Creeping Unknown*— electrocuted by high-powered wires

4. *The Deadly Mantis*—gassed with cyanide bombs

5. *Invasion of the Saucermen*—the saucermen were dissolved by high-intensity auto headlight beams

6. *The Mole People*—killed in an earthquake

7. *The Tarantula*—burned to death by an aerial napalm bomb

8. *Them!*—burned to death by flamethrowers

8 WAYS TO KILL OR REPEL DRACULA

If things start going "bump" in the middle of the night and you think you've trapped him at last, use one of the following easy methods to rid the world once and for all of this terrible monster!

1. Exposure to sunlight will kill him.

2. Failure to return to his coffin before morning time will kill him.

3. He hates garlic and won't go near the stuff.

4. Holy water will destroy him.

5. Flashing a crucifix will burn him.

6. A shot with a silver bullet will be fatal.

7. A wooden stake hammered through his heart will nail him for good.

8. Turning off the TV usually works.

4 FILMS WITH MONSTER VEGETABLES

1. *Attack of the Killer Tomatoes** (1978). Much tomato juice is shed.

2. *Attack of the Mushroom People* (1963). A real fungus.

3. *Please Don't Eat My Mother* (1973). A giant vegetable gets its revenge.

4. *Invasion of the Star Creatures* (1965). An army of carrots terrorizes earthlings.

*Okay, so the tomato is really a fruit!

KING KONG'S DIMENSIONS

These are the big ape's statistics, according to RKO Pictures, who made the original movie.

Height: 50 feet
Face: 7 feet from forehead to chin
Nose: 2 feet long
Mouth: 6 feet from corner to corner
Eyes: 10 inches in diameter
Ears: 1 foot long
Chest: 60 feet around
Legs: 15 feet long
Arms: 23 feet long
Eye teeth: 10 inches long, 4 inches wide

E.T.'S VITAL STATISTICS

1. *Height:* 36 inches normally, but 40 inches when he gets excited and raises his neck

2. *Weight:* 62½ pounds

3. *Age:* 800 years old on June 11, 1982

SHARI LEWIS EXPLAINS WHY IT IS IMPORTANT TO PLAY A MUSICAL INSTRUMENT

Our favorite puppeteer starts every job interview by asking the applicant, "Have you ever studied a musical instrument?" According to Ms. Lewis, studies have been done showing that people who are taught to read and play music are deeply affected by it, no matter how well or poorly they played. As her mother used to tell her, "Wouldn't the woods be silent if only the best birds sang?"

1. Musical training teaches you that if you stick to what you're doing, you'll "get it."

2. People who have learned to play instruments know that you can start out knowing nothing and, with effort, accomplish whatever you set your mind to.

3. People who study music are better at solving math problems.

4. People who play an instrument have better posture.

5. People who play an instrument show up for work more regularly and on time.

In 1927, at the age of 10, American violinist Yehudi Menuhin became the youngest musician to play a solo at Carnegie Hall.

THE 6 WORST THINGS ABOUT MTV

1. The hype and advertising can get to be too much. The station is, after all, a 24-hour commercial for music, movies, fashion, and MTV itself. Ever get the feeling they're trying to tell you how to *think?*

2. MTV may have many videos on the air, but there are many you don't get to see because the people running the channel don't think they're appropriate for kids. They censor many rap groups and metal bands.

3. Sexism. Because young men comprise a large portion of MTV's audience, women are often treated unfairly. For instance, boys are made to believe that only girls who look like Cindy Crawford and Christie Brinkley are worth looking at.

4. The veejays. Have any of these people (besides Kurt Loder) ever read a book?

5. MTV often tells record companies that if they air a video they do not want it aired anywhere else, which means that if you don't get MTV, you're out of luck all together.

6. Beavis and Butthead.

9 GREAT THINGS ABOUT MTV

1. *Yo! MTV Raps* gives you the chance to see rap and hip-hop entertainment that you often don't see on any other channel. The multicultural angle is truly exciting.

2. MTV news tells you about what's going on in the world—and not just in the world of music. News reports are often more honest than those you'll find on other channels.

3. The MTV award shows give you a chance to see many of your fave stars perform. Plus they're funny.

4. MTV has aired specials on topics from racism and politics to environmental issues. President Clinton's appearances on MTV have given young people a chance to get involved in discussions that they might not otherwise be included in.

5. MTV urges people to vote. Very important!

6. The Top Ten Video Countdown lets you know what's hot in the world of rock videos.

7. The TV graphics are more creative and exciting than most commercials on TV.

8. *MTV Unplugged* gives you a chance to see artists bring a new and sometimes very different approach to their own music.

9. Beavis and Butthead.

STEVIE WONDER'S CHILDHOOD HOBBIES

Steveland Morris, better known as Stevie Wonder, is one of popular music's most successful and respected songwriters and musicians. He began his musical career at the age of 2, banging on pots and pans in time with the music, and had his first number-one hit single at the age of 12. Stevie Wonder was blind at birth but has never let his handicap stand in the way of his interests. These are some of the numerous activities he was involved in as a kid:

1. Bowling
2. Piano lessons
3. Skating
4. String bass lessons
5. Swimming
6. Tree climbing
7. Violin lessons
8. Wrestling

15 ROCK SONGS ABOUT GROWING UP

(*and the Artists Who Recorded Them*)

1. "The Circle Game," Joni Mitchell
2. "Growin' Up," Bruce Springsteen
3. "Hey Little Tomboy," The Beach Boys
4. "I'm Just a Kid," Hall and Oates
5. "Janey's Blues," Janis Ian
6. "Kodachrome," Paul Simon
7. "She's Leaving Home," The Beatles
8. "Society's Child," Janis Ian
9. "Someday Never Comes," Creedence Clearwater Revival
10. "Stay Free," The Clash
11. "Teach Your Children," Crosby, Stills, Nash & Young
12. "When I Grow Up," The Beach Boys
13. "Young Man's Blues," The Who
14. "You're a Big Boy Now," John Sebastian
15. "You're a Big Girl Now," The Stylistics

14 ROCK SONGS ABOUT SCHOOL

1. "Adult Education," Hall and Oates
2. "Be True to Your School," The Beach Boys
3. "Charlie Brown," The Coasters
4. "Harper Valley P.T.A.," Jeannie C. Riley
5. "Hot for Teacher," Van Halen
6. "Rock and Roll High School," The Ramones
7. "School Days," Chuck

Berry
8. "School Days," The Kinks
9. "School Is Out," Gary U.S. Bonds
10. "School's Out," Alice Cooper
11. "School's Out for the Summer," Crokus
12. "To Sir With Love," Lulu
13. "We Don't Need No Education," Pink Floyd
14. "Welcome Back," John Sebastian

YOUNGEST ARTISTS TO HAVE NUMBER-ONE SINGLES IN THE U.S.

	ARTIST	SONG	YEAR	ARTIST'S AGE
1.	Michael Jackson	"Ben"	1972	11
2.	Jimmy Boyd	"I Saw Mommy Kissing Santa Claus"	1952	12
3.	Stevie Wonder	"Fingertips, Part 2"	1963	13
4.	Donny Osmond	"Go Away Little Girl"	1971	13
5.	Laurie London	"He's Got the Whole World (In His Hands)"	1958	14
6.	Peggy March	"I Will Follow Him"	1963	15
7.	Brenda Lee	"I'm Sorry"	1960	15
8.	Paul Anka	"Diana"	1957	16
9.	Tiffany	"I Think We're Alone Now"	1987	16
10.	Little Eva	"The Loco-Motion"	1962	17
11.	Lesley Gore	"It's My Party"	1963	17

11 ROCK SONGS ABOUT FATHERS

1. "Cat's in the Cradle," Harry Chapin
2. "Daddy's Baby," James Taylor
3. "Daddy's Tune," Jackson Browne
4. "Don't Cry Daddy," Elvis Presley
5. "Father and Son," Cat Stevens
6. "My Daddy Knows Best," The Marvelettes
7. "My Father," Judy Collins
8. "My Old Man," Steve Goodman
9. "Papa, Don't Preach," Madonna
10. "Papa Was a Rolling Stone," The Temptations
11. "This Old Man," Steve Goodman

12 ROCK SONGS ABOUT MOTHERS

1. "Coat of Many Colors," Dolly Parton
2. "Ma," The Temptations
3. "Mama Said," The Shirelles
4. "Mama's Song," Jackie DeShannon
5. "Mama, Weer All Crazee Now," Quiet Riot
6. "Momma," Bob Seger
7. "Mother and Child Reunion," Paul Simon
8. "Mother," Danzig
9. "Mother," John Lennon
10. "My Mama," Jessi Colter
11. "When I See Mommy I Feel Like a Mummy," Captain Beefheart
12. "Your Mother Should Know," The Beatles

TOP 10 KARAOKE SONGS IN THE U.S.

1. "New York, New York," Frank Sinatra
2. "My Way," Frank Sinatra
3. "Love Shack," B-52s
4. "Mack the Knife," Bobby Darin
5. "The Rose," Bette Midler
6. "Takin' Care of Business," Bachman-Turner Overdrive
7. "Hello Dolly," Louis Armstrong
8. "Friends in Low Places," Garth Brooks
9. "Greatest Love of All," George Benson
10. "Crazy," Patsy Cline

OUR TOP 20 WEIRD AL YANKOVIC SONG TITLES

1. "Stop Draggin' My Car Around"
2. "My Bologna"
3. "Another One Rides the Bus"
4. "Mr. Frump in the Iron Lung"
5. "I Lost on Jeopardy"
6. "Like a Surgeon"
7. "Dare to Be Stupid"
8. "I Just Want a New Duck"
9. "Slime Creatures from Out of Space"
10. "Girls Just Want to Have Lunch"
11. "Toothless People"
12. "Stuck in a Closet with Vanna White"
13. "(This Song's Just) Six Words Long"
14. "The Biggest Ball of Twine in Minnesota"
15. "Attack of the Radio-active Hamsters from a Planet Near Mars"
16. "Let Me Be Your Hog"
17. "Spatula City"
18. "Spam"
19. "Smells Like Nirvana"
20. "Fat"

FREDDY KRUEGER'S PERSONAL JUKEBOX

1. "Addams Family Theme," Vic Mitzy
2. "The Creature From The Black Lagoon," Dave Edmunds
3. "Dead Man's Party," Oingo Boingo
4. "Haunted House," Jumping Jean Simmons
5. "I Put a Spell on You," Screamin' Jay Hawkins
6. "The Monster Mash," Bobby Pickett
7. "The Purple People Eater," Sheb Wooley

50 FUNNY (BUT REAL) NAMES FOR BANDS

If you're looking for a name for your rock band, don't use any of the following—they're taken!

1. ? and the Mysterians
2. Balloon Farm
3. Bananarama
4. The Banana Splits
5. B. Bumble and the Stingers
6. The Bee Gees
7. Blind Melon
8. Boffalongo
9. Bread

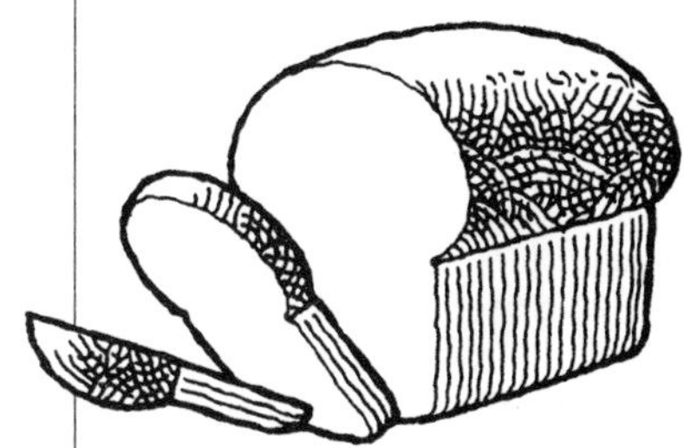

10. Chocolate Milk
11. Cracker
12. Digable Planets
13. Dog Eat Dog
14. Dr. Feelgood and the Interns
15. Dr. West's Medicine Show and Junk Band
16. The Electric Prunes
17. Everything Is Everything
20. Funkdoobiest
21. Fuzz
22. Green Day
23. Guess Who
24. Hedgehoppers Anonymous
25. Human Beinz
26. Iron Butterfly
27. It's a Beautiful Day
28. Kasenetz-Katz Singing Orchestral Circus
29. The Knack
30. Lynyrd Skynyrd (pronounced Linard Skinard)
31. New Kids on the Block
32. Nine Inch Nails
33. Oingo Boingo
34. Parliament Funkadelic
35. The Peanut Butter Conspiracy
36. Psychafunkapus
37. Red Hot Chili Peppers
38. The Rock & Roll Dubble Bubble Trading Card

Company of Philadelphia
39. Strawberry Alarm Clock
40. 10,000 Maniacs
41. The The
42. Them
43. Toad the Wet Sprocket
44. Ultimate Spinach
45. Uncle Dog
46. Vanilla Fudge
47. Was (Not Was)
48. The Who
49. Wiggy Bits
50. Yes

THAT'S EASY FOR YOU TO SING

Rock Songs with Sound Effects for Titles

1. "Bang-Shang-a-Lang," The Archies
2. "Be-Bop-A-Lula," Gene Vincent
3. "Bon-Doo-Wah," The Orlons
4. "Boo, Boo, Don't 'Cha Be Blue," Tommy James
5. "Boom-A-Dip-Dip," Stan Robinson
6. "Cha-Hua-Hua," Bobby Rydell
7. "Chee Chee-Oo-Chee," Perry Como
8. "Da Doo Ron Ron," The Crystals
9. "De Do Do Do, De Da Da Da," The Police
10. "Do Wah Diddy Diddy," Manfred Mann
11. "Dum Dum Dee Dum," Johnny Cymba
12. "In-a-Gadda-da-Vida," Iron Butterfly
13. "I.O.I.O.," The Bee Gees
14. "Ka-Ding-Dong," The Diamonds
15. "La La La La La La La Means I love You," The Delfonics
16. "Ooby Dooby," Roy Orbison
17. "The Oogum Boogum Song," Brenton Wood
18. "Ooh PooPah Doo, Part II," Jessie Hill
19. "Papa Oom Mow Mow," The Rivingtons
20. "Sh-Boom," The Chords

6 OPERAS THAT KIDS ENJOY

1. *Aida,* by Giuseppe Verdi. Most people might not think *Aida* is an opera for kids, but this masterpiece has many elements that kids will enjoy. The tunes are thrilling, the story is direct, and the "spectacle" of the piece is better than any circus (in fact, some big theaters even use horses and elephants when the hero returns in a triumphal march from winning a battle). The story is about an enslaved Ethiopian princess, Aida, who loves an Egyptian general, Radames, the enemy of her people. She persuades him to share military secrets that help her people escape, and Radames is found guilty of treason. When he is sentenced, Aida stays to die with him instead of fleeing to Ethiopia. The opera is more than an ordinary love story, and the music is unforgettable.

2. *Amahl and the Night Visitors,* by GianCarlo Menotti. Amahl is a crippled boy who lives with his impoverished mother. They are ready to become beggars when the three Wise Men stop at their house on their way to visit the Christ child. While the kings are asleep, Amahl's mother tries to steal some of the gold they are bringing to present to Jesus. She is caught and the guard makes a huge scene. After the kings describe who this Christ is, Amahl decides he wants to send the baby a present, too. All he has is his homemade crutch-and when he presents it, he is miraculously cured and can walk on his own. He decides to ride off with the kings to offer the gift in person.

3. *Carmen,* by Georges Bizet. The most popular question among kids when it comes to opera is, "Why are they always love stories?" But Carmen's flashy, daring personality makes the opera very exciting. Carmen lives with a group of gypsies who dance and steal and tell fortunes. She falls in love with both a soldier and a bullfighter.

The different settings that arise make a most colorful opera. The character of Carmen has always been popular because she remains a heroine even though she is not particularly good. She is brave and strong, and it is those virtues that make us admire her. Many of the tunes in this opera will be familiar, and the music always maintains the excitement of the story.

4. *Die Zauberflote* (*The Magic Flute*), by Wolfgang Amadeus Mozart. This is, and will always be, a special fave. It contains everything a kid could want in an opera: magic bells and flute, a dragon, enchanted animals, a wicked queen, a Prince Charming, and great music. It follows Prince Tamino's effort to rescue Pamina, who is being held captive by her father, Sarastro. Tamino is often misled, but all of his adventures only prove his love and devotion. This opera gets a bit long for kids who aren't used to sitting in a theater, but there are perfect moments in Sarastro's temple when you can catch a quick nap or go to the bathroom.

5. *Gianni Schicchi,* by Giacomo Puccini. One thing kids always enjoy is watching adults make fools of themselves. The Donati family does exactly that in *Gianni Schicchi.* They meet to mourn the death of their rich uncle, but after they read the will and realize that they've all been left out, they really start to cry. They hire Gianni to impersonate their uncle so he can change the will and then conveniently "die." Gianni is more clever than any of them realize, however, for when he changes the will, he bequeaths the money to himself and teaches them a lesson. This short opera contains some of Puccini's most beautiful melodies.

6. *L'Enfant et les Sortilèges* (*The Child and the Magic Spells*), by Maurice Ravel. This beautiful, magical tale based on a story by the French writer Colette is a favorite for any age. The hero of the story is a boy who is sent off without his supper. Locked away in his room, he throws a tantrum and almost destroys the nursery.

Then the magic starts. The boy's mistreated toys come to life and begin to complain—and the shards of a Chinese teacup chase the boy into a garden. There the magic turns to nightmare as all the animals outside threaten the boy. But when the toys realize that he is afraid and truly sorry for misbehaving, they all rally to his side and lead him home to plead his defense to his mother.

11 CLASSICAL MUSICIANS AND THE AGES AT WHICH THEY BEGAN TO PLAY MUSICAL INSTRUMENTS

1. Johann Sebastian Bach first played the violin at the age of 4.

2. Ludwig van Beethoven was taking piano lessons at the age of 3.

3. At 5, Johannes Brahms was playing the viola, the violin, and the piano and was already beginning to compose music.

4. Frederic Chopin played melodies on the piano at 5—before anyone had shown him how.

Johann Sebastian Bach

5. By the time he was 2, Stephen Foster was playing the guitar and the organ and was singing songs.

6. George Gershwin was able to play a song on the piano the first time he ever tried to play at all. He was 10 years old.

7. Jerome Kern taught himself to play the piano at the age of 4.

8. Wolfgang Amadeus Mozart could play melodies on the harpsichord at age 3.

9. Franz Schubert started taking music lessons at the age of 7 but studied piano on his own before that.

10. Peter Ilich Tchaikovsky was able to play the piano at age 4, but it was not until he was 23 years old that he began studying music seriously for the first time in his life.

11. Giuseppe Verdi started playing the piano at age 7.

Gioacchino Rossini, one of the most famous Italian composers, got his start in 1804 at the age of 12, when he began to sing professionally and write sonatas.

CHAPTER SEVEN

IT'S A FACT

THE 10 BASIC RIGHTS OF ALL CHILDREN

In 1959 the United Nations declared that all children all over the world have the following rights. These were listed as the Declaration of the Rights of the Child.

1. To enjoy the rights listed regardless of race, color, religion, or nationality.

2. To be able to grow in a healthy, normal way, free and dignified. Children should be specially protected and should be given special opportunities to grow.

3. To a name and nationality.

4. To social security. This includes a decent place to live, good food, health care, and opportunities to play.

5. To special treatment, schooling, and care if handicapped.

6. To love and understanding. Children should be raised so that they feel secure and loved, and they should live with their parents if possible.

In 1990, a group of 75 students from 10 countries rode their bicycles 3,000 miles across the United States. The students rode to make people aware of the fact that 40,000 kids around the world die of hunger and disease every day. This group, called Youth Ending Hunger, received newspaper and TV coverage in each town that they stopped in. By the end of their journey, 100 million people were made aware of the seriousness of this problem and the ways in which they could help.

7. To free schooling and an equal opportunity to become everything they can be.

8. To prompt protection and relief in times of disaster.

9. To protection against all kinds of neglect, cruelty, and abuse from others.

10. To protection from any kind of unfair treatment because of race or religion.

YOUR LEGAL RIGHTS

Being young doesn't mean you aren't a citizen with rights. The following are not all written laws, but based on the judges' decisions in cases that have involved kids, this is pretty much what you can expect from our judicial system. However, keep in mind that legal tendencies do change from state to state.

1. Within limits, you have the right to dress and wear your hair any way you and your parents wish when you go to school. If school authorities want to challenge you, they must show that your clothing or hairstyle interferes with the educational process or that it is disruptive.

2. You have the constitutional right to demonstrate in an orderly fashion within the school as long as the demonstration is not disruptive or violent.

3. If you have a job, you are entitled to the same minimum wage as adults earn, but your salary can be limited based on your lack of experience.

4. Girls must receive the same salary as boys for doing the same work.

5. As a minor, no contract you sign is valid unless your parent or guardian signs it, too.

HOW THE WORLD IS LIKELY TO CHANGE BY THE TIME YOU GROW UP

And Other Predictions for the Future

According to the *Omni Future Almanac,* here's a rundown of what your life will be like beyond the year 2000. On the other hand, you've got to be careful about predictions; in 1948, a pioneer in the field of radio development claimed that TV would never last, and in 1899 the director of the U.S. Patent Office claimed that there was nothing new left for anyone to invent. You'll find the list "10 Predictions That Didn't Come True (and Which Aren't Likely To)" on page 343.

1. For one thing, you might become one of more than 2,000 people who live and work on the moon, although your chances are greater if you're male, since women will make up only a small percentage of those who get to go. Back on earth, things won't look so rosy. According to the United Nations, more than 600 million people will be living in poverty.

2. You won't have to worry about carrying books to school, since reference books and those with lots of pictures will be too expensive to reproduce. Instead, when you need information, you'll get it from your computer or videodisc system.

3. You'll still be able to dance to rock 'n' roll music, but most of it will be generated by synthesizers and other computerized methods.

4. By 2020 the first "test tube dog" will be created by genetic engineering techniques.

5. Lifespans will increase; an American born in the year 2000 will expect to live for 120 years.

6. The typical family room in the American household will be replaced by a "video environment." At the touch of a button on your computerized entertainment system, you'll be able to surround yourself with a tropical rain forest or a Saturnian landscape. Of course, you'll still be able to tune in your favorite movie—on your 360-degree movie screen.

7. By 2020, genetic engineering will have made possible the picking and choosing of traits that people want their babies to have. You'll be able to order such traits as blue eyes, good singing voices, and blond hair. However, it is likely that such practices will also be the center of legal and moral disputes.

8. Scientists may begin a process called terraforming, in which outer space environments are made fit for human occupation. This may well lead to a colony of humans living on Mars. It is expected that terraforming will become a reality sometime between 2010 and 2020.

9. The clothing you wear will probably be made from thin fabric that provides great durability. More important, the warmth that the clothing provides will be controlled by pushing a button on a special power belt. That is, you'll wear the same clothing in summer as you do in winter; you'll just "program" your clothing differently depending on the weather.

10. By 2050 the population of outer space will exceed 7,500.

11. The state of California, it is believed, will have been all but wiped out by a devastating earthquake. In fairness, it should be pointed out that many have predicted this earthquake for at least the past decade.

12. There will be 50 percent more cars on the road than there are now, but air pollution will have dropped because these automobiles will be smaller and more efficient than those we drive now.

RULES OF CONDUCT FOR TEACHERS, 1915

The following rules of conduct applied to teachers in a town in West Virginia in 1915, but they are much like the rules all teachers in the United States were required to follow at the time. Can you believe it?

1. A female teacher was not allowed to date men.

2. A teacher was not allowed to get married during the school term.

3. Unless they were at a school function, all teachers had to be home between the hours of 8:00 P.M. and 6:00 A.M.

4. Teachers were not allowed to loiter at downtown ice cream parlors.

5. They were not allowed to travel outside the city limits unless they had special permission from the school board.

6. A female teacher could not ride in a carriage or automobile with a man other than her brother or father.

7. Smoking was not allowed.

8. Teachers could not wear brightly colored clothing.

9. Teachers were not allowed to dye their hair.

10. A female teacher had to wear at least two petticoats.

11. Dresses could be worn no shorter than three inches above the ankle.

12. Teachers had to keep the schoolroom neat and clean. Each day the floor had to be swept and scrubbed with hot, soapy water and the blackboards had to be cleaned. The teacher also had to start a hearth fire by 7:00 A.M. each morning in winter so the room would be warm by 8:00 A.M., when the students showed up for school.

9 FAMOUS PEOPLE WHO WERE MISJUDGED

1. Isaac Newton got lousy grades in elementary school. He went on to become one of the greatest scientists and thinkers of all time.

2. A newspaper publisher once fired Walt Disney because he "had no good ideas."

3. An editor once told Louisa May Alcott that she would never write anything that people would buy. He was wrong. She wrote *Little Women* in 1868.

4. Beethoven's music teacher told him that he was "hopeless" as a composer.

5. Winston Churchill failed the sixth grade and finished last in his class when he graduated from college. He later became the prime minister of England.

6. Charles Darwin, who wrote *Origin of the Species,* never made it through medical school.

7. Elvis Presley flunked the audition for an amateur TV show called *Talent Scouts,* which was popular in the 1950s.

8. When Bruce Springsteen was in elementary school, one of the nuns at the parochial school he attended stuffed him in a garbage can under her desk because, she said, he belonged there.

9. When Marlon Brando was in kindergarten, no one thought he would amount to much. He played hooky so often that his sister Jocylyn finally took him to school on a leash!

10 FAMOUS PEOPLE WHO NEVER GRADUATED FROM GRADE SCHOOL

1. Andrew Carnegie, U.S. industrialist
2. Charlie Chaplin, British actor
3. Charles Dickens, British writer
4. Isadora Duncan, American dancer
5. Thomas Edison, American inventor (deaf from the time he was 12, Edison spent just three months in public schools)
6. Claude Monet, French painter
7. Sean O'Casey, Irish playwright
8. Alfred E. Smith, American politician
9. John Philip Sousa, American composer
10. Mark Twain, American writer

KIDS WHO HAVE INVENTED THINGS

1. Louis Braille, a blind boy from France, invented a "language" of raised dots that could be "read" by blind people.

2. Chester Greenwood loved ice skating but hated the fact that his ears got cold. So when he was 15 years old, he invented earmuffs.

3. Robert Patch is the youngest inventor ever. In 1962, when he was only 5, he designed a toy truck that could be taken apart and put back together.

4. Eric Van Paris, from Belgium, was 14 when he invented a "cooling fork." It blew air onto hot food so that kids could eat more easily.

4 FAMOUS DYSLEXICS

1. Hans Christian Andersen
2. Tom Cruise
3. Thomas Edison
4. Henry Winkler

100 FAMOUS LEFTIES

1. Dan Aykroyd
2. Alexander the Great
3. Harry Anderson
4. Dave Barry
5. Peter Benchley
6. Yogi Berra
7. Larry Bird
8. Napolean Bonaparte
9. William Bonney (Billy the Kid)
10. Bruce Boxleitner
11. George Bush
12. Rod Carew
13. Lewis Carroll
14. Bill Clinton
15. Kurt Cobain
16. Ty Cobb
17. Natalie Cole
18. Jimmy Connors
19. Tom Cruise
20. Quinn Cummings
21. Leonardo da Vinci
22. Matt Dillon
23. Lefty Dreisell
24. Richard Dreyfuss
25. Len Dykstra
26. Bob Dylan
27. Albert Einstein
28. W. C. Fields
29. Peter Fonda
30. Whitey Ford
31. Ben Franklin
32. James Garfield
33. Judy Garland
34. Lou Gehrig
35. Cary Grant
36. Ron Guidry
37. Marvin Hagler
38. Mark Hamill
39. Tess Harper
40. Rex Harrison
41. Goldie Hawn

42. Jimi Hendrix
43. Keith Hernandez
44. Carl Hubbell
45. Kathy Ireland
46. Reggie Jackson
47. Caroline Kennedy
48. Ted Koppel
49. Sandy Koufax
50. Cloris Leachman

Queen Victoria

51. Dawnn Lewis
52. Cleavon Little
53. Andrew McCarthy
54. John McEnroe
55. Kristy McNichol
56. Howie Mandel
57. Marcel Marceau
58. Dave Marsh
59. Harpo Marx
60. Mary Stuart Masterson
61. Don Mattingly
62. Michelangelo
63. James Michener
64. George Michael
65. Paul McCartney
66. Marilyn Monroe
67. Stan Musial
68. Martina Navratilova
69. Oliver North
70. Sarah Jessica Parker
71. Ross Perot
72. Luke Perry
73. Bronson Pinchot
74. Richard Pryor
75. Robert Redford
76. Shanna Reed
77. Keanu Reeves
78. Julia Roberts
79. Nelson Rockefeller
80. Bill Russell
81. Babe Ruth
82. Gayle Sayers
83. Wally Schirra
84. Norman Schwarzkopf
85. Jerry Seinfeld
86. Monica Seles
87. Paul Simon
88. Ringo Starr
89. Darryl Strawberry
90. Casey Stengel
91. Cree Summer
92. Harry Truman
93. Mark Twain
94. Bill Veeck
95. Queen Victoria
96. Bill Walton
97. Treat Williams
98. Bruce Willis
99. Oprah Winfrey
100. Mare Winningham

PROBLEMS LEFTIES HAVE

We're all different. And often we don't think about problems some people have, just because we don't have that problem. Read this list even if you're right-handed. We bet you didn't know that your left-handed pal has to deal with these problems day in and day out. If you are right-handed, try performing these tasks "switching hands" and see what happens.

1. In school, penmanship lessons are taught as though everybody is right-handed. Lefties are often made to feel like there's something wrong with them because they're not able to write if they follow the same posture guidelines as the others. *If you're a lefty (or you think you are), make sure you let your parents and teachers know.*

2. Chairs that come with writing desks attached are almost always designed for righties, so that lefties have to twist their bodies awkwardly in order to lean on the desk.

3. When a left-handed person tries to use ordinary scissors, the blades wind up in the wrong position. There *are* scissors made for lefties, but they are expensive.

4. If a lefty tries to draw a straight line using a ruler, he holds the ruler down with his right hand and then has to cross his left hand *over* the right to draw the line, which he would start at the left. Whew! To make matters worse, teachers show students how to use rulers assuming that everyone is right-handed.

5. Left-handed kids have

trouble learning to set the table, which is "properly" set up for righties.

6. A left-handed person sitting next to a right-handed person at the dinner table is going to bump elbows with her neighbor if she cuts her food with the knife in her right hand. A lefty is better off sitting at the corner of a table, so that her left hand can remain free.

7. Left-handed people have to remember that the proper way to shake hands with someone is with your *right* hand.

8. Some left-handed people have to change the order of strings on a guitar in order to play it.

9. Public telephones are designed for righties.

10. Barbers, gardeners, doctors, dentists, cooks, and knitters all must use "standard" equipment designed for right-handed people.

GO TO THE HEAD OF THE CLASS

I.Q. Classifications

Intelligence Quotients—or I.Q.'s, as they're commonly called—meant a whole lot more when your parents went to school. These days, many educators regard them as irrelevant, saying that the tests on which I.Q.'s were based were never fair to begin with and that a student's potential, rather than performance, is what counts. In any case, Terman's Classification (one system for labeling I.Q. ranges) assigned the following labels for I.Q.'s:

Genius above	*140*
Very Superior	*120–140*
Superior	*110–120*
Normal	*90–110*
Dull	*25–90*

16 WEIRD LAWS YOU SHOULD KNOW ABOUT

If you like putting pennies in your ears, don't go to Hawaii—it's illegal there. And did you know that it's illegal to fish while sitting on a horse in Washington, D.C.? There are actually hundreds of laws that made sense when they were passed but that now sound ridiculous. Still, they're real laws, so you should obey them, right?

1. No one in Hanford, California, can stop a child from jumping over a puddle.

2. It is illegal to give a child a cup of coffee in Lynn, Massachusetts.

3. Restaurants serving ice cream on a piece of cherry pie in Kansas are breaking the law.

4. You are not allowed to rollerskate on the streets of Quincy, Massachusetts.

5. It is illegal for a baby-sitter in Altoona, Pennsylvania, to eat the entire contents of their employer's refrigerator.

6. A person living in Saco, Missouri, is not allowed to wear a hat that might frighten a child.

7. Sheep are not allowed to run wild in schoolyards in Vermont.

8. It is against the law to pretend your parents are rich in the state of Washington.

9. It's illegal for youngsters in Mesquite, Texas, to have unusual haircuts.

10. In Indiana, it is against the law for a parent to drink beer if his or her child is present.

11. In Gary, Indiana, you may not attend the theater within four hours of eating garlic.

12. In Dyersburg, Tennessee, it is illegal for a girl to telephone a boy and ask for a date. And, girls, whatever you do, don't propose marriage to your boyfriend in Whitesville, Delaware. You might be arrested for breaking the law!

13. In Halethorpe, Maryland, a kiss may not last for more than a second.

14. In Muskogee, Oklahoma, it is against the law for any member of a ball team to hit a ball over a fence or out of a park. (This could be one reason Muskogee has no baseball team!)

15. Kite-flying is illegal in Washington, D.C.

16. You cannot play hopscotch on the sidewalk in the state of Missouri.

8 ITEMS OF CLOTHING THAT HAVE BEEN BANNED IN SCHOOLS

In 1992, beepers were a small problem in a Washington, D.C., high school. They banned the beepers, and now they have a *big* problem: Half the students are carrying them. Authorities are cracking down on crime in the schools. Will prohibitions on the following help solve the problem?

1. Baggy jeans—banned in California because of the large pockets, which make good hiding places

2. Bandannas—outlawed in some schools because they are considered gang garb

3. Gold jewelry—considered to start fights and is therefore against the law in Baltimore schools

4. Net blouses—cause problems in the summer, when some girls wear them with nothing underneath

5. Leggings—At the Bates Academy in Detroit, girls are forbidden to wear anything "form-fitting, suggestive, or cut out too much."

6. Underwear sticking out of the top of your pants, like Marky Mark wore—a no-no at Eastern High School in Washington, D.C.

7. Baseball caps—Many Boston public schools have outlawed these, as they can hide small handguns and knives.

8. T-shirts that promote drugs—violate the drug-free policy of some Atlanta schools

10 PREDICTIONS THAT DIDN'T COME TRUE

(*and Which Aren't Likely To*)

A playwright named Eugene Ionesco once said, "You can predict things only after they've happened." The following list of some of the worst predictions ever made proves he was right.

1. "Man won't fly for a thousand years," said Wilbur Wright to his brother Orville in 1901.

2. Edward Welsh, former executive secretary of NASA, predicted that by 1982 there would be one or more permanent bases on the moon.

3. *Life* magazine predicted in 1970 that instead of having family cars, the average family would soon own helicopters.

4. *U.S. News and World Report* disagreed; in 1969 the publication predicted that families would still own cars but that each family would own about four or five of them.

5. That same year, the professors Harold and June Shane predicted that kids would soon start public school at the age of 2.

6. "Three-dimensional color television, with smell, touch, and taste added, may be available by the 1990s," predicted scientist and mathematician Desmond King-Hele. (We predict he will be proven wrong!)

7. In 1904, Lord Kelvin, an engineer and physicist, said, "Radio has no future."

8. Waldemar Kaempffert wasn't too optimistic about the future of robots. In 1927 he said that there would never be such things because "even the most ingenious technologist cannot make a collection of wheels, shafts, magnets, and wires think."

9. "The Beatles are just a passing phase," said the Reverend Billy Graham in 1964.

10. In 1990, John Elfreth Watkins Jr. predicted that by the year 2001, the letters C, X, and Q would be dropped from the alphabet.

HOW KIDS GET MONEY

According to a study at Texas A & M University, kids between 4 and 12 receive more than $14.4 billion a year. Where do they get all that money?

Fifty-four percent comes from allowances.

Twenty percent is earned by doing chores around the house.

Ten percent is earned outside the home.

Sixteen percent is received as gifts.

HOW KIDS SPEND THEIR MONEY

The following statistics come from that same study at Texas A & M University:

$6 billion winds up in savings.

$2 billion is spent on junk food.

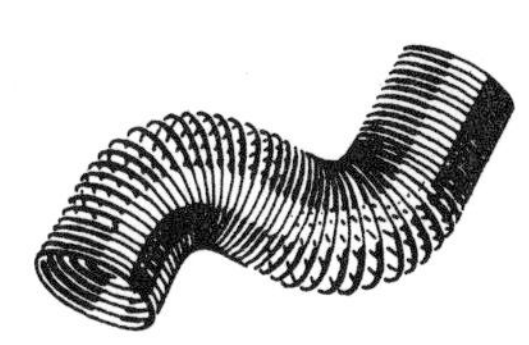

$1.9 billion goes for toys and games.

$600 million is spent on movies, shows, concerts, and sports events.

$700 million is spent on clothing.

$486 million is spent on arcade video games.

$264 million is spent on miscellaneous items, which means everything from stereos and compact discs to cosmetics, jewelry, telephones, and other living expenses.

KIDS' AVERAGE WEEKLY ALLOWANCES IN 1994

According to Youth Monitor, a service that checks up on what kids are up to:

AGE	AMOUNT
6–8	$1.99
9–11	$4.17
12–13	$5.82
14–15	$9.68
16–17	$10.80

10 REASONS WHY GIRLS ARE BETTER THAN BOYS

You boys out there may not like these facts, but they're true, according to Jacqueline Shannon's book of surprising facts, *Why It's Great to Be a Girl* (Warner, 1994).

1. Girls see better in the dark.

2. Girls start talking earlier than boys.

3. Girls make better astronauts (they're smaller, weigh less, require less food and oxygen).

4. Girls handle pain better than boys.

5. Girls have better hearing.

6. Girls get fewer viral and bacterial illnesses than boys.

7. Girls don't get as many zits as boys.

8. Girls don't get hiccups as often as boys do.

9. Girls handle extreme weather conditions—hot and cold—better than boys.

10. Girls have longer attention spans than boys.

WHAT YOU'RE PROBABLY GETTING FOR CHRISTMAS NEXT YEAR

A 1992 Harris poll showed that the following are your parents' most popular choices for Christmas presents for kids.

1. Clothing—77 percent
2. Nonelectronic games—70 percent
3. Books—69 percent
4. Cash or gift certificate—46 percent
5. Stuffed animals—41 percent
6. Sports equipment—40 percent

19 LANGUAGES MOST COMMONLY SPOKEN AT HOME IN THE U.S.

Almost 32 million Americans speak a language other than English at home. In fact, more than 300 languages are spoken in America. In order of the most common:

1. Spanish
2. French
3. German
4. Italian
5. Chinese
6. Tagalog
7. Polish
8. Korean
9. Vietnamese
10. Portuguese
11. Greek
12. Arabic
13. Hindi
14. Russian
15. Yiddish
16. Thai/Lao
17. Persian
18. Creole
19. Armenian

STATES IN WHICH MEN MAY MARRY UNDER THE AGE OF 18 WITH A PARENT'S CONSENT

Without the consent of a parent or guardian, most states require that men be at least 21 years old when they marry. If a parent or guardian signs, the requirements change to 18 in all states except for the following:

STATE	AGE	STATE	AGE
Alabama	17	California	16
Colorado	16	Pennsylvania	16
Connecticut	16	South Carolina	16
Mississippi	17	Tennessee	16
Missouri	15	Texas	16
New Hampshire	14	Utah	16
New York	16	Washington	17

STATES IN WHICH WOMEN MAY MARRY UNDER THE AGE OF 16 WITH A PARENT'S CONSENT

Without the consent of a parent or guardian, most states require that women be at least 18 years old if they're going to get married (and some demand that you're 21). If you have a parent's consent, you can get married in Washington at age 17 and in Kansas at age 18. Women may marry at the ages listed below in the following states without the consent of a parent or guardian.

STATE	AGE
Alabama	14
Massachusetts	15
Missouri	15
New Hampshire	13
New York	14
North Dakota	15
Oklahoma	15
South Carolina	14
Texas	14
Utah	14
Vermont	14

23 SPORTS REPRESENTED IN THE SPECIAL OLYMPICS

We all have much to learn from the people who run and participate in the Special Olympics, which holds competitions in different categories for children and adults who are mentally retarded. Their motto is especially notable: "Let me win, but if I cannot win, let me be brave in the attempt." If you want to participate in any way at all, contact: Special Olympics International Headquarters, 1350 New York Avenue NW, Suite 500, Washington, D.C. 20005; (202) 628-3630.

1. Alpine skiing
2. aquatics
3. athletes
4. badminton
5. basketball
6. bowling
7. bowling
8. cycling
9. equestrian
10. figure skating
11. floor hockey
12. football (soccer)
13. golf
14. gymnastics
15. hockey
16. powerlifting
17. roller skating
18. softball
19. speed skating
20. table tennis
21. team handball
22. tennis
23. volleyball

8 KIDNAPPINGS WITH HAPPY ENDINGS

In 1874, 4-year-old Charles Brewster "Charley" Ross became the first victim of a sensational kidnapping in American history. Little Charley was told that he could have firecrackers and balloons if he went along with the two men who made the offer. Although the kidnappers were captured months later, little Charley was never heard from again.

Throughout the years there have been horrible stories of kidnappings that have ended in tragedy. A lucky few, however, were able to live through the ordeal. Here are eight of them.

1. Edward A. Cudahy Jr., the son of a rich meatpacker, was 15 when he was approached by two men on the street who said they were detectives and that they needed Edward to come with them. Eddie was held for two days, until his father paid a $25,000 ransom. The kidnapper, Pat Crowe, must have had second thoughts about what he'd done, even though Edward had not been harmed. He sent Christmas presents to his little victim years after the kidnapping, and finally, in 1906, six years after the crime, he returned the money and confessed. Crowe was acquitted.

2. Eight-year-old Willie Whitla, the son of a rich lawyer, was kidnapped from his boarding school in 1909 when a man and a woman told him that they were taking him to visit his parents. They demanded a ransom of $10,000 and got it, and Willie was released. However, a while later, as the kidnappers were celebrating their victory in a Cleveland bar, they were picked up by the police. The ransom money was recovered, and the criminals, Helen and James Bogle, were given long jail sentences.

3. When 9-year-old George Weyerhaeuser was abducted from the home of his wealthy family in Tacoma, Washington, in 1935, his $200,000 ransom was paid with bills that the police had specially marked. George was returned safely home after a week, but when a department store clerk recognized the bills, which the kidnapper was using to make a purchase, he called the police. William Mahon, the kidnapper, was given 60 years in prison.

4. Lee Crary was 8 when he was kidnapped in 1957 from his home in Everett, Washington. George E. Collins Jr., the kidnapper, demanded $10,000 for the child's return, but before it could be paid, little Lee escaped and led police to Collins's hideout. Collins was given a life sentence in prison.

5. In 1960, Eric Peugeot, the son of the famous car manufacturer, was kidnapped from a playground at a golf course in Paris by a group of kidnappers. The $300,000 ransom was paid, and Eric was released a few days later. Only two of the kidnappers were found, and they were sent to prison.

6. Eleven-year-old Kenneth King was kidnapped in 1967 from his home in California. His kidnapper demanded and was given $250,000 for the boy's safe return, three days after the kidnapping. The kidnapper was never found.

7. The kidnapping of John Paul Getty III in June of 1973 was one of the most publicized ever, since he was the grandson of J. Paul Getty, who was, at the time, the richest man in the world. The young Getty was 16 when four men seized him and drove off with him. But Getty's grandfather refused for many months to pay the ransom, thinking that it was just a trick that had been set up by his grandson to get money. Finally, in October, the brutal kidnappers sent one of the boy's ears (and a photo of his head) to Getty, threatening to do worse if the $2.9 million ransom was not paid. Getty paid the ransom and the young Getty was released, but the kidnappers were never found.

8. In July of 1976, one of the most horrible kidnappings ever occurred. Three kidnappers captured a schoolbus carrying 26 children and a driver; they forced the bus into a large hole that they had dug. The bus and its riders were buried in the hole with just enough air to allow them to breathe. The kidnappers, James and Richard Schoenfeld and Fred Woods, demanded $5 million in ransom, but they were apprehended before the sum was paid. All the children and the driver were rescued after having been buried for 30 hours. The kidnappers were sent to prison for life.

7 FACTS ABOUT KIDS AND GUNS

For information about handgun control and safety, write to: Center to Prevent Handgun Violence, 1225 Eye Street NW, Suite 1100, Washington, D.C. 20005. Here are some things you should know:

1. Every day, 12 children under the age of 20 are shot and killed.

2. One out of six pediatricians nationwide has treated a child who was shot.

3. Gunshot wounds are the leading cause of death for both black and white teenage boys in America.

4. Every six hours, a youth between the ages of 10 and 19 commits suicide with a gun.

5. Roughly 100,000 students take guns to school every day.

6. A gun in the home is more likely to kill a family member or friend than a criminal.

7. One-third of all high school students say they can get a gun whenever they want to.

THE SEVEN DWARFS

You can remember their names by remembering that two names start with D, two start with S, and three of them are named after emotions.

1. Doc
2. Dopey
3. Sleepy
4. Sneezy
5. Bashful
6. Grumpy
7. Happy

1 REAL MONSTER THAT WAS REPORTED KILLED

(*And 10 That Are Still Believed to Be Alive Today!*)

1. The Abominable Snowman. For more than 100 years, this monster, reported to be a large, hairy humanoid creature that lurks in the icy Himalayan region, has been sighted and sometimes even photographed. It is still believed to be alive today.

2. Alma. The Russian version of the Abominable Snowman was described in 1957 by one witness as having "hairy arms longer than the ordinary man" and being covered all over with reddish-gray hair.

3. The Beast of 'Busco. Each year the people of Churubusco, Indiana, hold a festival known as Turtle Days, during which they honor their local monster, a 200-pound snapping turtle called the Beast of 'Busco. The monster is said to have nearly been captured in 1948 by hunters, but Oscar, as he is sometimes known, finally slipped back into the murky waters of the local pond, where many claim he hides today, waiting to surface again.

4. The Beast of Le Gevaudan. A strange-looking wolf-like creature with short ears and hooflike feet was killed in France in 1767 after murdering numerous young children. He was finally shot by a hunter with silver bullets, and the carcass of the monster was displayed as proof of his death.

5. The Berkeley Square Horror. If you travel to 50 Berkeley Square in England, you'll find only a bookstore there. But legend has it that long ago the house that stood there was occupied by a gruesome, slimy, slithering thing that had crawled up from the sewers and came to occupy the top floor of the building. Anyone who tried to spend a night in the room —as a few unfortunate souls reportedly did—was found dead by morning, a frozen look of horror upon his or her face.

6. The Giant Sloth. A gigantic armadillo seen in Patagonia, Argentina, seemed to be resistant to the bullets and arrows that were shot at him. It is believed that he has become extinct since his last sighting in the nineteenth century.

7. Goatman. Known as the Monster of Lover's Lane, Goatman roams Prince George's County in Virginia. He is popularly believed to have once have been a scientist whose experiments with goats went awry.

8. Hairy Hands. A surprising number of gruesome accidents have been reported on a stretch of road between the villages of Postbridge and Two Bridges in the Dartmoor region of England. Those who have lived through the ordeal (some never made it) swear that a pair of large, hairy hands reached out from the darkness to claim their victims. The last account of an attack dates back to 1921, but some residents claim that the creature—whatever it is—still dwells there.

9. Mngwa. Mngwa is described by witnesses as a catlike animal that will mutilate any human who confronts it in the central African jungle where it dwells. Attempts have been made to capture the beast, but none have been successful.

10. Mo-Mo. As recently as 1972, residents of Louisiana

panicked at repeated reports of an apelike monster with long, dangling, hairy arms.

11. Slimy Slim. In 1941 a man named Thomas L. Rogers, of Boise, Idaho, reported seeing a "serpent about fifty feet long" with a head that resembled "a snub-nosed crocodile." But Rogers wasn't the only one to see it. After a number of other residents also reported seeing the monster, all agreeing on its description, they nicknamed the creature Slimy Slim. It has not been seen since 1941, nor has anyone reported its death.

7 WHITE HOUSE GHOSTS

According to "official government records," the following ghosts have all been detected in the White House.

1. The ghost of Abigail Adams, wife of John Adams, who was the second president, has been seen in the East Room, where she used to hang laundry.

2. Andrew Jackson has occasionally haunted the White House.

3. Thomas Jefferson has been heard playing his violin.

4. Abraham Lincoln is the most famous White House ghost, and Eleanor Roosevelt's maid claims to have seen him. Rumor has it that just before something awful happens in the country, Lincoln shows up and paces the floors of the mansion.

5. The ghost of Dolly Madison, wife of the fourth president, James Madison, shows up each year at the White House to see the roses she planted in the garden long ago.

6. The ghost of an old janitor has been seen roaming the halls, dusting.

7. The ghost of the original owner of the land on which the White House is built is occasionally heard (but never seen) greeting White House guests.

THE OLDEST AMERICAN AMUSEMENT PARKS

	Year Opened
1. Lake Compounce Amusement Park, Bristol, CT	1846
2. Rocky Point Park, Warwick, R.I.	1847
3. Cedar Point, Sandusky, OH	1870
4. Idlewild Park, Ligonier, PA	1878
5. Sea Breeze Park, Rochester, N.Y.	1879
6. Dorney Park, Allentown, PA	1884
7. Beech Bend Park, Bowling Green, KY*	1888
8. Geauga Lake, Aurora, OH	1888
9. Elitch Gardens, Denver, CO	1890
10. Carousel Gardens, New Orleans, LA*	1891
11. Columbian Park, Lafayette, IN*	1892
12. Conneaut Lake Park, Conneaut Lake Park, CT	1892
13. Trimper's Rides and Amusements, Ocean City, MD	1893
14. Whalom Park, Fitchburg, MA	1896
15. Lakemont Park, Altoona, PA	1894
16. Waldameer Park, Erie, PA	1896
17. Lagoon Park, Farmington, UT	1896
18. Village Park, Old Orchard Beach, ME	1898
19. Midway Park, Maple Springs, N.Y.	1898
20. Kennywood Park, West Mifflin, PA	1898
21. Toledo Zoo, Toledo, OH*	1899
22. Pullen Park, Raleigh, N.C.*	1901
23. Caobie Lake Park, Salem, OH	1902
24. Camden Park, Huntington, W.V.	1902

* These parks have only a few rides still running today.

THE TOP 10 AMUSEMENT PARKS IN THE U.S.

Paul Ruben, who writes for the magazine *Park World* and who is known as one of the world's leading authorities on roller coasters, prepared this list just for us. He judged these amusement parks on the basis of their scenic settings and the excitement level of the attractions.

1. Walt Disney World, Lake Buena Vista, FL. There are three separate attractions here: the Magic Kingdom, EPCOT Center, and the Disney-MGM Studios. The Magic Kingdom, a larger and more elaborate version of Disneyland, is where you will find the best rides. Its collection of eight dark rides, including the ominous Haunted Mansion, is the best in the world. Space Mountain, an indoor coaster, and the Pirates of the Caribbean, a rollicking dark boat ride, should not be missed.

2. Disneyland, Anaheim, CA. More compact than the Magic Kingdom and with many of the same attractions, this is the park that started the theme park revolution. Attention to architectural detail throughout the park is notable. Be sure

to ride the Matterhorn Bobsleds, an on-the-edge adventure.

3. Cedar Point, Sandusky, OH. No theme, just rides. Fifty-six of them, more than any other park in the world. There are 11 coasters (also the most in the world) including three of world-class caliber. These are Magnum XL-200, a 205-foot-high steel thriller, Mean Streak, the world's tallest woodie, and Raptor, where passengers dangle from an overhead track and experience inversions. Three carousels, a water park, shows, and just about every spin-and-barf ride you can imagine complete the offering.

4. Kennywood, West Mifflin, PA. Outside Pittsburgh, this is the finest traditional park in the country. You will find four coasters, each with its own distinct personality, including the 80-mile-per-hour Steel Phantom, the world's fastest. Noah's Ark is one of four funky dark rides. The new Lost Kennywood section commemorates the park's Victorian beginnings with a classic collection of rides.

5. Six Flags California, Valencia, CA. You've seen many of their eight roller coasters in motion pictures and on television; now ride them for yourself. Surrounding the mountain in the middle of the park are a handful of theme water rides, spinners, shows, and an elaborate area of kiddie attractions.

6. Busch Gardens, Williamsburg, VA. America's most beautiful park is themed on four countries: England, France, Germany, and Italy. The rides, including the Big Bad Wolf suspended coaster and Escape from Pompeii, and theme shoot-the-chutes are great fun, while the unique shows, such as Haunts of the Olde Country, Questar, and Enchanted Laboratory provide cutting-edge entertainment.

7. Paramount's King Island, Kings Mills, OH. Thrill to Days of Thunder, the park's new NASCAR racing ride simulator, or ride The Beast, the world's longest wooden roller coaster. Located north of Cincinnati, the park features many rides and shows that are themed on Paramount's motion pictures.

8. Six Flags Over Georgia, Atlanta, GA. Climb aboard the Georgia Cyclone coaster, meander through the deserted Monster Plantation dark ride, or hold on for the Great Gasp parachute drop. Nine theme areas contain nearly three dozen rides.

9. Paramount's Ming's Dominion, Doswell, VA. Four wooden roller coasters, including the Hurler in the new Wayne's World theme area, are the most to be found in any park. Float the Haunted River, loop head over heels on the Berserker, and splash in the Hurricane Reef water park.

10. Knott's Berry Farm, Buena Park, CA. There is a unique and wonderful atmosphere in four theme areas: the Old West Ghost Town, Fiesta Village, Roaring Twenties, and Camp Snoopy. Visit the unusual Mystery Lodge, Kingdom of the Dinosaurs dark ride, and the Calico Mountain Mine Ride. Don't leave without sampling Mrs. Knott's chicken dinner.

THE BEST ROLLER COASTERS

In 1920 there were more than 1,500 roller coasters in the U.S.; today there are less than 400. But look at the bright side—back in 1920, you couldn't ride at the speed of 80 miles per hour. You can now!

1. The Steel Phantom in West Mifflin, Pennsylvania, is presently the fastest roller coaster, traveling at a speed of 80 miles an hour.

2. The Riverside Cyclone in Agawam, Massachusetts, has the roughest ride of them all. The first drop takes you from 0 to 60 miles per hour in just three seconds.

3. The Yankee Cannonball in Salem, New Hampshire, has the smoothest ride, which takes two minutes and covers 2,000 feet.

4. The Twister in Denver, Colorado, is the scariest. It has a 65-mile-an-hour plunge into a tunnel that has a high-banked curve.

5. The Dragon Coaster at Rye Playland in Rye, New York, is perhaps the oddest of all the coasters. It's two-minute ride travels through the mouth of a dragon.

6. The Beast in King Island, Ohio, has the longest ride, which is slightly over four minutes.

7. The Tidal Wave in Santa Clara, California, has the shortest ride—it's just 36 seconds. This may seem like a waste of time, but consider that you get hurled from 0 to 55 miles per hour in just 4.2 seconds.

THE 10 BEST KIDS' ATTRACTIONS IN EUROPE

1. Hamleys, London, England. Hamleys Toy Store in London, founded in 1760, is the biggest in the world, and around Christmastime, it must be the most crowded place in the world as well. Spread over six floors in the heart of London, it sells every kind of toy you could imagine, from tiny tin soldiers to super-huge stuffed animals. There are books, models, puppets, computer and video games, some really terrific train sets, dolls and dollhouses, and lots more. You'll be familiar with a lot of the stuff—Fisher-Price and Mattel toys, for instance, are as popular in Europe as they are in America—but there are also tens of thousands of toys from Britain and the rest of the world that you won't find gathered together anywhere else, such as a life-size model of Darth

Vader and a four-foot-long motorized replica of a Rolls-Royce, which you can drive yourself, providing you can talk your mom and dad into parting with $2,000. Hamleys is on Regent Street in London, about two blocks south of Oxford Circus.

2. Potter's Museum of Curiosity, Arundel, West Sussex, England. Potter's Museum of Curiosity is quite simply one of the most amazing places you could ever hope to spend a rainy afternoon at. Walter Potter, who opened the museum in 1862, was a taxidermist with a very weird approach to his work. While most taxidermists would stuff owls or squirrels and put them under glass domes for people to look at, Potter dressed up his stuffed creations and put them in elaborate scenes. There is, for instance, a kitten's tea party in which 37 cats are dressed up for a croquet match as others have tea on the lawn of a country house. The Rabbits School has 20 young rabbits sitting at school desks doing their arithmetic and learning to read. There is a two-headed lamb and a great goat with six legs. The effect is like wandering though the attic of some demented old man—terrific! Potter's Museum is at 6 High Street in Arundel, West Sussex, England. It is open only between April 1 and September 30.

3. De Efteling Amusement Park, Kaatsheuvel, the Netherlands. This is the place for you if scary rides are your thing. This amusement park boasts Europe's largest roller coaster as well as a slew of other stupefying attractions, including the Piranha (a swirling water ride) and the Half Moon (a lurching, swinging pirate ship), both of which have you hanging on for dear life. There is a truly enchanting fairy tale forest with animated models of Sleeping Beauty and Arabs on flying carpets, plus a steam railway, a puppet theater, and a playground. There is a haunted house that you shouldn't miss and many other interesting points, like a trash can that says "Thank you" when you throw something into it, a swimming pool, a paddling pool, and a life-size model of an elephant that shoots water from its trunk. The park is open from March 31 through October 2 from 10:00 A.M. to 6:00 P.M.

4. Madurodam, the Miniature Village, The Hague, the Netherlands. Europe is filled with dozens of miniature villages where you'll feel like a giant no matter how short you are, and the best of these is Madurodam, which was built by a Dutch couple as a memorial after their son was killed at war. It's a complete Dutch town, built 1/25th the size of a real one, with castles, churches, shops, windmills, houses, and even canals. A two-mile model railway runs through the farms and factories, and many parts of the transportation system really move: Ships glide on the tiny waterways, small airplanes taxi on a runway, and a miniature band plays music at a county fair. The scene is especially exciting at night, when 50,000 tiny lights come on at the windows and along the little streets. All together the place is wonderful, and the whole family is bound to enjoy it. Madurodam is at 175 Harkingkade in The Hague and is open from April 1 to the first Sunday in October from 9:30 A.M. to 11:00 P.M.

5. The Torture Museum, The Hague, the Netherlands. Here is one of Europe's spookier attractions: It's a museum of torture that displays almost everything that was used to get confessions out of people—and inflict pain—from the fifteenth century to the nineteenth century. The museum is spread over four awesome floors and all the devices are appropriately displayed, as the building was an actual prison until 1828. The museum is at 33 Buitenfhof in The Hague and is open Monday through Friday from 10:00 A.M. to 5:00 P.M. from April through September.

6. The German Museum of Masterworks of Natural Science and Technology, The Deutches Museum, Munich, Germany. Here is truly one of the most amazing museums in the world, for it brings education to life. It is the largest technological museum in the world, covering six floors and consisting of 300 rooms filled with 45,000 exhibits along ten miles of corridor! Aside from the size, the exhibits themselves are wonderful. Here you'll find model coal mines, salt mines, iron mines, cars, airplanes, rocket ships, an Alpine chalet, musical instruments, ocean-going ships, and the first diesel engine. Many of the displays have buttons you can push or handles you can crank to make the models move. Learning has never been this much fun.

7. Phantasialand, Bruhl, Germany. You'll definitely want to spend a whole day at Phantasialand, the largest amusement park in Europe. Here you'll find Viking ships and pirate ships that you can really ride on, an exciting water flume ride, and a monorail that circles the entire park. You'll also visit a full-size Polynesian village, a Chinatown, a fairy tale park, a Wild West town called Silverstone City, and an area called Old Berlin that replicates what that city was like in 1900. When you get fatigued touring the park, you can sit and watch the performing dolphins and seals or the chimpanzee jazz band, the only one of its kind in Europe. Phantasialand is located just outside of Bruhl, between Bonn and Cologne, and is open every day between April 1 and November 1 from 10:00 A.M. to 5:00 P.M.

8. The Historical-Archaeological Experimental Center, Lejre, Denmark. The name may be a mouthful, but this is an exciting place. If you've ever wondered what life was truly like in the Stone Age, you can find out here. There are farms, workshops, and dwellings inhabited by volunteers who live, work, dress, and even eat as people did from prehistoric times up to the nineteenth century. You can find out how roads were built, crops were cultivated, animals tamed, and food cooked. In a stone field, you can watch experiments designed to discover how primitive tools could be used to build the vast European monuments like Stonehenge, and you can participate in fire experiments in Fire Valley—under supervision, of course. If you visit during the summer months, you will be treated to weaving, pottery, and flint-working demonstrations. Open May 1 through September 26 and October 16 through October 24 from 10:00 A.M. to 5:00 P.M.

9. Legoland, near Billund, Denmark. If you've ever built anything with Legos, or even if you haven't, you'll be fascinated by Legoland, one of the most unusual attractions in all of Europe. It's built entirely of Legos! It began as a model village in which the world's most famous structures—the Taj Mahal, Mount Rushmore, the Acropolis—were reproduced with Legos. The park grew to include rides, a marionette theater, a western town called Legoredo, a wonderful collection of antique dolls, and many educational exhibits. An interesting attraction is Titania's Palace, the most expensive dollhouse ever built. It contains miniature paintings by master artists of the nineteenth century, musical instruments that really work, and other tiny treasures—all of which were made for a very lucky British girl. Legoland is open from May 1 until the last Sunday in September from 10:00 A.M. to 5:30 P.M.; in July and August the park is open until 7:30 P.M.

10. Maihaugen Museum, Lillehammer, Norway. All over Scandinavia there are dozens of open air museums where ancient buildings have been gathered to give spectators an idea of what life was like in olden times. Maihaugen is one of the best of these. It was started by a nineteenth-century dentist named Anders Sandvig. Since Sandvig's patients were sometimes too poor to pay him the money they owed him, they gave him whatever objects they could spare, such as a spoon or a small piece of furniture, instead. These objects, and some old buildings, are assembled here to illustrate what life was like for the Norwegians from the eleventh through the nineteenth centuries. Grouped around a large, shady park, there are cottages that make up a complete manor farm, and these are furnished with more than 30,000 period pieces. There are also modern gunsmiths and other craftspeople at work. Maihaugen is open from 10:00 A.M. to 5:00 P.M. from the beginning of June until the end of August.

8 STUPENDOUS, SHOWSTOPPING STATISTICS ABOUT "THE GREATEST SHOW ON EARTH"

In 1870, P. T. Barnum's Museum, Menagerie, Caravan, and Hippodrome was founded. That same year, the seven Ringling brothers presented their "backyard circus" for the first time. It wasn't until 1919 that both circuses were combined to what is now known as the Ringling Brothers and Barnum & Bailey Circus. Here are some amazing facts about "The Greatest Show on Earth."

1. There are actually two different circus units that tour each year.

2. These circuses entertain 25 million people in 97 counties each year.

3. The circus has more than 1,000 costumes.

4. It takes about eight hours to set up all the rigging before a performance.

5. The animals are fed 364 tons of hay, 46,800 pounds of meat, 62,400 pounds of carrots, 39,000 pounds of apples, and 15,288 loaves of bread each year.

6. The circus owns 42 elephants, 10 lions, 14 tigers, 6 bears, 33 horses, 2 camels, 2 llamas, and 4 zebras.

7. Approximately 1,075 performances are given each year.

8. When the circus train of 53 cars is fully loaded, it weighs one and a half billion pounds.

36 AMERICAN CITIES WITH THE WEIRDEST NAMES

1. Bummerville, California
2. Cabbage Patch, Illinois
3. Constant Friendship, Maryland
4. Disco, Illinois
5. Do Stop, Kentucky
6. Dreamworld, Florida
7. Frog Jump, Tennessee
8. Frostproof, Florida
9. Fugit, Indiana
10. Fussville, Wisconsin
11. Good Luck, Tennessee
12. Goofy Ridge, Illinois
13. Goose Pimple Junction, Virginia
14. Hoo Hoo, West Virginia
15. Jolly Dump, South Dakota
16. Mosquitoville, Vermont
17. Muck City, Alabama
18. Nameless, Tennessee
19. Oddville, Kentucky
20. Only, Tennessee
21. Oz, Kentucky
22. Puddle Town, Connecticut
23. Roaches, Illinois
24. Shortly, Delaware
25. Snowball, Alaska
26. Sweet Lips, Tennessee
27. Tight Squeeze, Virginia
28. Two Egg, Florida
29. Wham, Louisiana
30. What Cheer, Iowa
31. Who'd a Thought It, Alabama
32. Why, Arizona
33. Whynot, Mississippi
34. Wigwam, California
35. Zip City, Alabama
36. Zzyzx, California

10 CITIES OF LOVE

1. Lovejoy, Illinois
2. Lovelady, Texas
3. Loveland, Colorado
4. Loveland, Iowa
5. Loveland, Ohio
6. Loveland, Oklahoma
7. Lovelock, Nevada
8. Love, Mississippi
9. Love Point, Maryland
10. Love, Saskatchewan, Canada

HOW TO BE POLITE IN 6 LANGUAGES

Here's how to say "hello," "goodbye," "please," and "thank you" in six languages.

1. Esperanto
Hello: bonan matenon
(*BOH-nahn mah-TEH-nohn*)
Goodbye: adiau
(*ah-DEE-ow*)
Please: bonvole
(*bohn-VOH-leh*)
Thank you: dankon
(*DAHN-kohn*)

2. French
Hello: bonjour
(*bohn-ZHOOR*)
Goodbye: au revoir
(*OH uh-VWAHR*)
Please: s'il vous plait
(*seel voo PLEH*)
Thank you: merci
(*merh-SEE*)

3. Italian
Hello: buon giorno
(*BWAN JOHR-noh*)
Goodbye: arrivederci
(*ah-ree-vay-DAYR-chee*)
Please: per favore
(*payr fah-VOH-ray*)
Thank you: grazie
(*GRAH-tsyay*)

4. Japanese
Hello: ohayo
(*Oh-hah-YOH*)
Goodbye: sayonara
(*sah-yoh-nah-ra*)
Please: kudasai
(*koo-dah-sahee*)
Thank you: arigato
(*ah-rih-gah-TOH*)

5. Russian
Hello: zdravstvuite
(*ZDRAH-st'eh*)
Goodbye: do svidanya
(*duh sv'i-DAH-n'uh*)
Please: pozhaluista
(*puh-SHAL-stuh*)
Thank you: blagodaryu
(*bluh-guh duh-R'OO*)

6. Spanish
Hello: buenos dias
(*BWEN-nohs DEE-ahs*)
Goodbye: adios
(*ah-dee-OHS*)
Please: por favor
(*POHR fa-VOHR*)
Thank you: gracias
(*GRAH see-uhs*)

WHEN YOU GOTTA GO, YOU GOTTA GO

14 Words for "Bathroom"

1. Can
2. Commode
3. Hopper
4. Jane
5. John
6. Loo
7. Potty
8. Powder room
9. The little girls' (or little boys') room
10. The smallest room in the house
11. Throne room
12. Toidy
13. Toilet
14. W.C. (for "water closet," which is what toilets were once called and are still called in England)

45 PHOBIAS

Everyone is afraid of *something.* Here are some fancy names for fears of some ordinary things.

1. Acrophobia: fear of heights
2. Amychophobia: fear of being scratched
3. Arachiutyrophobia: fear of peanut butter sticking to the roof of your mouth
4. Astrapophobia: fear of lightning
5. Automysophobia: fear of being dirty
6. Batrachophobia: fear of reptiles
7. Bibliophobia: fear of books
8. Blennophobia: fear of slime
9. Chionophobia: fear of snow
10. Clinophobia: fear of going to bed
11. Cynophobia: fear of dogs

12. Eisoptrophobia: fear of mirrors
13. Ereuthophobia: fear of blushing
14. Ergasiophobia: fear of work
15. Gephydrophobia: fear of crossing a bridge
16. Gymnophobia: fear of being naked
17. Helminthophobia: fear of worms
18. Hydrophobia: fear of water
19. Hypnophobia: fear of going to sleep
20. Musophobia: fear of mice
21. Mysophobia: fear of dirt
22. Nyctophobia: fear of night
23. Ombrophobia: fear of rain
24. Pantophobia: fear of everything
25. Paraskavedekatriaphobia: fear of Friday the 13th
26. Pediophobia: fear of dolls
27. Phasmophobia: fear of ghosts
28. Phonophobia: fear of speaking aloud
29. Pnigerphobia: fear of smothering
30. Pogonoophobia: fear of beards
31. Poinephobia: fear of punishment
32. Pyrophobia: fear of fire
33. Scholionophobia: fear of school
34. Sciophoiba: fear of shadows
35. Scopophobia: fear of being stared at
36. Shamhainophobia: fear of Halloween
37. Sitophobia: fear of food
38. Teratophobia: fear of monsters
39. Tonitrophobia: fear of thunder
40. Topophobia: stagefright
41. Triskaidekaphobia: fear of the number thirteen
42. Trypanophobia: fear of injections
43. Wicaphobia: fear of witches
44. Xenophobia: fear of strangers
45. Zoophobia: fear of animals

69 TWO-LETTER WORDS

Two-letter words may not seem important to know, but the next time you do a crossword puzzle or play a game of Scrabble, they'll probably come in very handy. These are all legitimate words; they appear in *Funk & Wagnalls Standard College Dictionary.*

1. aa
2. ad
3. ae
4. ah
5. ai
6. am
7. an
8. ar
9. as
10. at
11. ax
12. ay
13. ba
14. be
15. by
16. de
17. do
18. eh
19. el
20. em
21. en
22. ex
23. fa
24. go
25. ha
26. he
27. hi
28. ho
29. id
30. if
31. in
32. is
33. it
34. ja
35. jo
36. ka
37. la
38. li
39. lo
40. ma
41. mi
42. mu
43. mu
44. my
45. na
46. no
47. nu
48. od
49. of
50. oh
51. on
52. or
53. os
54. ox
55. pa
56. pe
57. pi
58. re
59. si
60. so
61. ti
62. to
63. up
64. us
65. ut
66. we
67. wo
68. xi
69. ye

CHAPTER EIGHT

JUST FOR FUN

14 QUESTIONS YOU WOULD BE ASKED IF YOU WENT TO CLOWN COLLEGE

If running away and joining a circus is more than just a fantasy for you, there's hope! Every winter, the Ringling Brothers and Barnum & Bailey Circus holds a clown college, where applicants are trained to look like clowns, dress like them, juggle, walk on stilts, and do all the other things you've seen circus clowns do. Anyone over 17 can apply, and tuition is free. You can get an application for clown college by writing to: Ringling Brothers and Barnum & Bailey Clown College, 8607 Westwood Center Drive, Vienna, VA 22182.

Here are some of the questions you will be asked when you apply.

1. What was your very first job for money?
2. What has given you the most pleasure during the past year?
3. Describe your first accomplishment.
4. If you could be someone else, who would you be and why?
5. What character trait in yourself would you most like to change?
6. What is your worst hang-up?
7. What is the most important lesson you have learned?
8. Describe memorable turning points in your life.
9. Rate your anger "boiling point" from one to ten.
10. Name three favorite musical groups and several of their recordings that you consider outstanding.
11. Name your favorite foods.

12. List your all-time favorite movies.
13. When was the last time you cried?
14. What does being a clown mean to you?

CIRCUS SLANG

1. Antipodist: a man or woman who juggles with his or her feet
2. Auguste: the clown who always gets it in the face when a pie is thrown or water is sprayed
3. Bender: the circus contortionist
4. Bull: an elephant
5. Cats: the wild animals, including tigers, lions, leopards, etc.
6. Cherry pie: extra work done by employees for extra pay
7. Denari: money
8. Diddy: a gypsy
9. Dona: a woman
10. Ducat: a ticket to the circus
11. Flattie: a circus spectator
12. Jackpots: tall tales about the circus
13. Joey: a clown
14. Jonah's bad luck: when a circus wagon gets stuck in the mud
15. Josser: anyone who isn't in the circus business
16. Kicking sawdust: following the circus, or being part of it
17. Kid show: the freak show
18. Letty: lodgings for circus performers
19. Little people: dwarfs or midgets

20. Lunge: the safety device used to keep performers from injuring themselves while doing difficult tricks
21. Missing a tip: missing a trick
22. Omney: a man
23. Run-in clown: the clown who runs out in between acts to perform while the next act is being set up
24. Shandy-man: the electrician
25. Star-backs: the most expensive seats in the audience

1 WAY YOU CAN HELP THE TOOTH FAIRY

Well, it's not really the tooth fairy—but it's close! The University of Bergen in Norway studies baby teeth to find out more about the effects of pollution. When your baby (first) teeth fall out, you can help researchers by sending them to:

Gisle Fosse, Professor of Anatomy
Bergen University
Arstadveien, 5009
Bergen, Norway

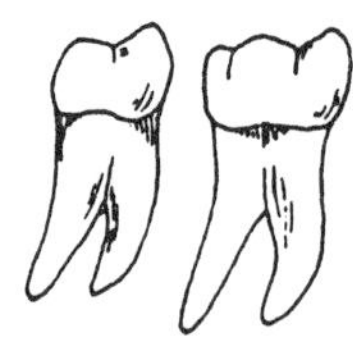

P.S. Make sure you include proper airmail postage; Norway is a different country. And wash 'em before you send 'em!

6 HORRIBLE NAMES TO CALL KIDS WHO WEAR BRACES

1. Fence Face
2. Foil Face
3. Hi-Ho Silver
4. Metal Mouth
5. Shiny Smile
6. Tinsel Teeth

5 SONGS TO PLAY ON YOUR PUSH-BUTTON TELEPHONE

Before you begin your career as a "telephonist," you'll need to remember that if you just sit down to play these songs, pushing buttons right and left, you're liable to find yourself connected to someone in Hawaii or even Europe. To avoid the whopping phone bill that you'd get as a result, just call someone who lives close by and play the songs for them. You won't disconnect the call in the course of playing the songs, and the two of you can enjoy the concert.

1. "Here We Go Round the Mulberry Bush"

Here we go round the mul-ber-ry bush,

4 4 4 2 2 6 6 2 4

The mul-ber-ry bush, the mul-ber-ry bush,

4 8 8 8 8 6 2 4 4 4

Here we go round the mul-ber-ry bush

4 4 4 2 4 4 8 8 4

So ear-ly in the mor-ning.

4 8 8 6 8 4 4

2. "Mary Had a Little Lamb"

Ma-ry had a lit-tle lamb, lit-tle lamb, lit-tle lamb

6 0 4 0 6 6 6 2 2 2 6 6 6

Ma-ry had a lit-tle lamb

6 0 4 0 6 6 6

It's fleece was white as snow.

6 8 8 6 8 4

3. "Jingle Bells"

Jin-gle bells, jin-gle bells

6 6 6 6 6 6

Jin-gle all the way,

6 # 7 8 6

Oh what fun it is to ride

9 9 9 9 9 5 5

In a one-horse o-pen sleigh

5 5 5 7 4 5 6

4. "Old MacDonald Had a Farm"

Old Mac-Don-ald had a farm, EE-I-EE-I-O!

6 6 6 7 8 8 7 9 9 0 0 4

And on this farm he had some chicks, EE-I-EE-I-O!

4 6 6 6 7 8 8 7 9 9 0 0 4

Here a chick, there a chick, ev-ery-where a chick chick,

4 4 4 4 4 4 4 4 4 4 4 4

Old Mac-Don-ald had a farm, EE-I-EE-I-O!

6 6 6 7 8 8 7 9 9 0 0 4

5. "Happy Birthday"

Hap-py Birth-day to you,

1 1 2 1 # 6

Hap-py Birth-day to you,

1 1 2 1 # 3

Hap-py Birth-day dear __________,

1 1 # # 8 4 1

Hap-py Birth-day to you

6 4 2 1

12 THINGS THAT ARE IMPOSSIBLE TO DO

1. Be in two places at once
2. Breathe water
3. Build castles in the air
4. Catch the wind in a sieve
5. Fall up
6. Find the secret of perpetual motion
7. Fix mercury so it won't move
8. Grow another foot
9. Live forever
10. Make parallel lines meet
11. Weave a rope of sand
12. Write on water

9 TONGUE TWISTERS

Tongue twisters were originally used in schools to teach children how to speak correctly. See if you can say each of the following three times fast. (The first one, by the way, is considered the hardest of all by the *Guinness Book of World Records.*)

1. The sixth sick sheik's sixth sheep's sick.
2. The swan swam out to sea. Swim, swan, swim!
3. A big black bug bit a big black bear and the big black bear bled blood.
4. The skunk sat on a stump; the skunk thunk the stump stunk, but the stump thunk the skunk stunk.
5. She's so selfish she could sell shellfish shells but shells of shellfish seldom sell.
6. Three gay geese sat on the green grass grazing.
7. Some shun sunshine; do you shun sunshine?
8. How much wood would a woodchuck chuck if a woodchuck could chuck wood?
9. Peter Piper picked a pack of pickled peppers.

KERMIT THE FROG LISTS 7 GOOD THINGS ABOUT BEING A FROG

Born on a lilypad in a Mississippi swamp, Kermit the Frog was one of several thousand children. The most traumatic moment of Kermit's brief youth came during his transformation from a pollywog to a frog; he literally lost his tail in the process. Displaying an early gift for music, Kermit learned to sing and play the banjo. With only his talent and his banjo, Kermit, green but hopeful, left home in 1955 and headed for New York. On the way he stopped off in Washington, D.C., where he performed on television live for five minutes every night for eight years. Dressed up as a green lizard who denied he was a frog, Kermit became a celebrity and won an Emmy for outstanding television entertainment. In 1963, he made his debut on network television on *The Tonight Show* with Steve Allen. One of his biggest breaks came in 1969 with his invitation to be a featured player on *Sesame Street.* In 1976, he became the international star of *The Muppet Show* — and the rest is history. The crowning experience for Kermit during *The Muppet Show* years was being presented to Queen Elizabeth II at a jubilee performance in London.

1. Being green
2. Getting kissed by princesses hoping to turn you into a handsome prince
3. Going to the hop
4. Having bears and pigs and dogs and chickens as your friends
5. Having thousands of brothers and sisters
6. Playing leapfrog
7. Sitting in the sun on a lilypad

5 MAGIC POTIONS

Well, you can't really call them magic potions, since most people agree that there are no such things. We can't swear that these potions will work, but people in past centuries believed they did. Perhaps believing is the key ingredient.

1. American Indian Love Tonic. *If love just isn't working the way you'd like it to, try this:*

Bring to a boil 2 tablespoons of unrefined oatmeal and ½ cup of raisins in 1 quart of water. Reduce heat. Now add 2 tablespoons (or more or less, depending on your taste) of honey to the liquid. Cool, then add the juice of 2 lemons. Refrigerate the tonic until you're ready to use it.

2. Apple-Ade Potion to Cure Shyness. *Those who've used this say that if served to a shy friend, it is bound to bring on lively conversation.*

Mix 1 glass each of chilled apple juice and seltzer. Pour into 2 glasses and add a sprig of mint to each.

3. Apricot Love Potion. *Share this with someone you like and see what happens!*

Combine 1 cup of apricot juice, 1 cup of seltzer, 1 tablespoon of honey, and ½ teaspoon of vanilla. Drink this while it's still fizzing.

4. Celery Soother to Forget a Misfortune. *Try this one if you just can't get your mind off some bad luck.*

Cook 1 cup of celery slices in ½ cup of water until the celery is soft. Now pour into a blender with 1 teaspoon of honey and 1 tablespoon of lemon juice. Blend for one minute. Serve over crushed ice and sip it though a straw.

5. Exam Potion. *Take this the morning before a test to sharpen your senses.*

Mix 1 glass of strawberry juice with 1 glass of seltzer. Shake and add crushed ice. Makes two servings.

WHEN TO MAKE A WISH

1. If a ladybug lands on you, make a wish just as it is leaving and then don't talk for three minutes.

2. If you see a duck, make a wish and then say "Quack!" If the duck quacks back, your wish will come true.

3. If you see three birds on a telephone wire, make a wish before they fly away.

4. Catch a firefly in your hand and start counting to ten. If the firefly flashes five times before you're finished counting, make a wish and let it go.

5. Wish on a new pair of shoes. By the time you have outgrown the shoes, your wish will come true.

6. If you find a turtle on its back, pick it up and turn it over. You will get four wishes.

7. If you find a dandelion, make a wish and then blow off all the seeds. If all the seeds blow away in one breath, your wish will come true.

8. Stick a watermelon seed on your forehead and make a wish. If the seed sticks until you've made your wish, the wish will come true.

9. Make a wish every time you eat a green M & M.

10. If you see a black cat with green eyes, pet it ten times and make a wish.

11. When you see a mail truck, cross your fingers and make a wish. Keep your fingers crossed until you see a dog.

12. If you can peel the silver foil from the wax paper on a gum wrapper without tearing it, make a wish and the wish will come true.

13. If the clasp on a necklace works its way to the front of your neck, make a wish while you move the clasp back to the back of your neck.

20 SIGNS OF BAD LUCK

1. If you sing while you walk upstairs and don't finish the song by the time you get to the top
2. If while riding over the railroad tracks in a car you don't pick up your feet
3. If the initials of your name spell a word
4. If your name has thirteen letters
5. If you play cards near a church
6. If you cross the path of a black cat
7. If you walk across a grave
8. If you find a penny tails up
9. If you spend a coin that you have found
10. If you walk with one shoe on and one shoe off
11. If you leave a house through a different door than the one you used to enter
12. If you talk while riding over a bridge
13. If you watch a friend who has been visiting you when they drive away
14. If you hit something with your left foot while taking a walk
15. If someone pinches your fourth finger and you scream
16. If you cut your fingernails on Friday
17. If a mouse leaves your house
18. If you cut the part of the birthday cake with your name on it
19. If you cry on your birthday
20. If you walk under a ladder

20 SIGNS OF GOOD LUCK

1. If your name has seven letters

2. If you see three nuns riding in a car

3. If you find a horseshoe

4. If you sleep with a silver dollar under your mattress

5. If you say "rabbit, rabbit," on the first day of a month as soon as you wake up

6. If on the first day of a month you fill your mouth with water, turn around, walk down a flight of stairs backwards with your eyes closed, then, upon reaching the bottom of the stairs, you swallow the water, open your eyes, turn around, and kiss the first person you see

7. If you cross your fingers when you see a mail truck and don't uncross them until you see another

8. If you hold your breath and cross your fingers when you pass a graveyard

9. If you point your thumbs up when passing a graveyard

10. If you put on a piece of clothing inside out

11. If you find a penny heads up

12. If you find a stone with a hole in it

13. If you eat an apple dipped in honey on New Year's Day

14. If you tie a red bow on a new car

15. If you pinch the person sitting next to you in a car just after you have seen an out-of-state license plate

16. If you hit something with your right foot while taking a walk

17. If in the morning you put your right shoe on first

18. If June the 13th falls on a Friday

19. If you eat figs for breakfast on your birthday

20. If you tie your shoe with three loops for the bow instead of two

7 VOODOO CHARMS TO BRING YOU LUCK

Throughout history, people have practiced the art of voodoo — or black magic — and for just as long, other people have been coming up with ways to counteract voodoo hexes. All of the following are intended for that purpose.

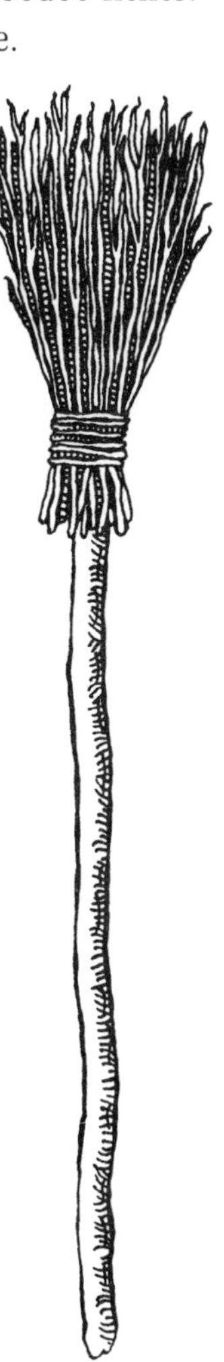

1. To break a hex that has been placed on you, get a friend to read a Bible verse to you backwards, then fold the page, place a silver fork in it, and close the book. Before you go to sleep at night, put the Bible under your pillow and recite the Lord's Prayer backwards before lying down.

2. To protect yourself from evil spirits, cross your fingers tightly when passing a cemetery.

3. To prevent evil spirits from doing harm in your home, carry black pepper in your pockets.

4. You can change bad luck to good by tossing the hair of a black cat over your left shoulder.

5. An old broom hung over a door will supposedly keep disease away from the home.

6. If you pour champagne on all four corners of your property on a moonless night, you will have the help of good spirits when you need them.

7. Plant mustard seed at your front and back doors and you will have success and luck in everything you do.

GUMPS, GAZOOKS, AND GOOPS

If you've ever been told to stop calling your little brother Stupid, try any one of the following names instead, all of which have become part of the English language. If you haven't heard of all of these, there's no need for you to feel like a yap. Most of these haven't been used in years.

1. Addlebrain
2. Beetlebrain
3. Cabbagehead
4. Calabash
5. Chowderhead
6. Chucklehead
7. Dunderhead
8. Flibbertigibbet
9. Hockey puck
10. Jellybean
11. Jingle brain
12. Muff
13. Mushhead
14. Rattlehead
15. Sao
16. Yahoo
17. Yap
18. Yo-yo

HOW TO SIGN YOUR FRIEND'S AUTOGRAPH BOOK

1. Take the local,
   Take the express,
   Don't get off
   Till you reach success.

2. Remember me,
   When this you see,
   And what good friends
   We used to be.

3. 2 nice
   + 2 be
   4 gotten

4. You asked me to write,
   So what shall it be?
   Two little words:
   "Remember me."

5. The more you study,
   The more you know.
   The more you know,
   The more you forget.
   The more you forget,
   The less you know.
   So why study!?

6. I love you bip
I love you bop
I love you more
Than a pig loves slop.

7. I have a picture of you,
I think its very nice.
I hang it in the cellar
To scare away the mice.

10 WAYS TO SIGN YOUR NAME

Yours till...

1. Butter flies
2. Ginger snaps
3. Soda pops
4. The banana peels
5. The bed spreads
6. The bed springs
7. The board walks
8. The kitchen sinks
9. The pillowcase is solved
10. Sugar bowls

YOU FEEL LIKE ZIGGY WHEN...

Poor Ziggy! As one of America's best-loved cartoon characters, he's been making people laugh for years. We all have bad days, but Ziggy seems to get more than his share. You feel just like him when...

1. All the mail you get is addressed to "Occupant."

2. Your alphabet soup makes snide remarks.

3. Your clock radio goes off in the morning and asks you what time it is.

4. You have to pay an overdue fine at the library for a book entitled *How to Improve Your Memory.*

5. Opportunity knocks at the front door while you're in back taking out the garbage.

6. You know how to spell "banana" but you don't know when to stop.

7. You're an underachiever and your teacher is an over-expecter.

8. Your TV set breaks down on the same day your warranty expires.

9. Your palmist can't find your lifeline.

10. You drop your open-faced peanut butter and jelly sandwich and it lands jelly side down.

25 REASONS TO SKIP SCHOOL

Holidays Your Teacher Probably Never Heard Of

1. January 3: Sip-a-Drink-Through-a-Straw Day
2. January 11: Banana Boat Day
3. January 16: National Nothing Day
4. January 20: Hat Day
5. January 30: Swap-the-Brown-Bag-Lunch Day
6. March 1: National Pig Day
7. March 22: National Goof-off Day
8. April 15: National Gripers Day
9. May 8: Children-Should-Be-Seen-and-Not-Heard Day
10. June 15: Smile Power Day
11. June 18: International Picnic Day
12. June 22: National Fink Day
13. July 11: National Cheer-Up-the-Lonely Day
14. July 15: National Ice Cream Day
15. August 6: Summer-Is-Half-Over Day
16. August 13: International Left-Handers Day
17. August 15: National Failures Day
18. September 5: National Be-Late-for-Something Day
19. September 12: Snack-a-Pickle Day
20. September 30: Ask-a-Stupid-Question Day
21. October 15: National Grouch Day
22. November 17: Homemade Bread Day
23. November 23: Horror Movie Day
24. December 12: National Ding-a-Ling Day
25. December 21: Look-at-the-Bright-Side Day

6 FANCY WORDS FOR GROSS SOUNDS THAT EVERYBODY MAKES

Don't make a big deal out of these, whether they're yours or someone else's.

1. Borborgymus: When your stomach "growls." The sound your stomach muscles make when your stomach is empty. Your stomach also growls as you digest food.

2. Eructation: Burping. It happens when your stomach releases air that you swallowed while you were eating. If you eat slowly, it happens less.

3. Flatulence: The dreaded F word: fart. If you swallowed air and didn't burp, it'll come out the other end. Lots of fun at bath time!

4. Pandiculation: Yawning—the body's way of trying to get more oxygen as you get tired, although the exact cause is not completely understood.

5. Singulthus: Caused when your diaphragm has a spasm, throwing off the rhythm of the air going into your lungs. In the meantime, as you breathe more air, it gets stuck in the back of your throat, resulting in a hiccup.

6. Stenutation: A big word for a sneeze. Your nose automatically cleans out dust, mucus, or certain smells.

THE DISNEY CHANNEL'S "ADVENTURES IN WONDERLAND" KNOCK-YOUR-SOCKS-OFF, SPREAD-THE-WORD, STRAIGHT-FROM-THE-HORSE'S-MOUTH LIST OF 35 IDIOMS YOU'RE LIKELY TO COME ACROSS

Adventures in Wonderland is a Disney Channel TV series that teaches language and vocabulary skills. An idiom is an expression that cannot be understood from the individual meanings of its words; it doesn't mean what it sounds like. "Lend us your ears" means *listen.* A friend who "looks down his nose at you" is *acting like a snob.* Here are 35 more idioms you're likely to come across in your travels.

1. Be in hot water: get into really big trouble
2. Bite off more than you can chew: take on too big of a project
3. Cat got your tongue: not speaking
4. Change your tune: change your mind
5. Clotheshorse: someone who loves buying clothes
6. Covered his tracks: didn't leave evidence of what he did

7. Doggy bag: leftovers from a restaurant meal
8. Down in the dumps: depressed
9. Face the music: do something that's hard to do
10. Fishing for compliments: hinting for someone to say something nice about you
11. Fit as a fiddle: in perfect health
12. Fruits of labor: the results of work
13. Go fly a kite: Get out of here!
14. Have the last laugh: Be the winner in a prank
15. Heart of gold: genuinely kind
16. His bark is worse than his bite: He doesn't behave as badly as he talks
17. Hit the deck: get down
18. Hold your horses: Be patient!
19. Hot under the collar: angry
20. In the doghouse: in trouble
21. Keep it under your hat: keep a secret
22. A lemon: something of poor quality
23. Make tracks: hurry
24. Needle in a haystack: impossible to find
25. Nothing to sneeze at: something that should be taken seriously
26. Playing with a full deck: your brain is working well
27. Pulling my leg: teasing
28. Rose-colored glasses: sees only the good
29. See red: enraged
30. Spill the beans: tell a secret
31. Took the words right out of my mouth: You said what I planned to say
32. Until the cows come home: forever
33. Walls have ears: Someone might hear you, even if you think they can't
34. Wet behind the ears: inexperienced
35. White elephant: a thing of little value

10 LOUSY EXCUSES

All of these excuses were actually handed in to teachers in Illinois. We suspect they were forged.

1. Dear School: Please eckuse John for been absent January 28, 29, 30, 32, and 33.

2. Chris has a acre on his side.

3. John has been absent because he had two teeth taked out of his face.

4. Please excuse Gloria. She has been sick and under the doctor.

5. My son is under the doctor's care and should not take PE. Please execute him.

6. Lily was absent from school yesterday as she had a going over.

7. Please excuse Joey Friday. He had loose vowels.

8. Please excuse Blanche from PE for a few days. Yesterday she fell out of a tree and misplaced her hip.

9. Carlos was absent yesterday because he was playing football, he was hut in the growing part.

10. Please excuse Jimmy for being. It was his father's fault.

CAROLE KING'S "THINGS YOU SEE OUTSIDE YOUR WINDOW"

Carole King was one of the most popular songwriters of the 1960s, with such hits as "Will You Still Love Me Tomorrow?" and "Up on the Roof." Today she is one of the best-loved kids' performers, and she is well known for *Really Rosie,* which she composed and performed. Ms. King's special talent for helping us appreciate life through her imaginative lyrics is as evident in her recording of that program as it is in this poem, which she wrote especially for this book.

Things You See Outside Your Window

Frost-covered trees like cotton balls;
Animal tracks that zigzag
Teardrops on telephone lines;
Vegetable looking like flowers;
Venus looking at Mars;
The past, the present, and the future;
Weaving among the stars;
City streets teeming with people;
Mountains covered in snow;
Other people at windows;
A whole world for you to know.

7 REASONS TO WRITE TO THE AUTHORS OF THIS BOOK

Our address is: P.O. Box 142, Haworth, N.J. 07641. Tell us what you think. Tell us if you hated some part of this book or if something in it made your day or if...

1. You have ideas for other lists that you'd like us to consider using in a future edition of this book.

2. You found something in the book that you think is wrong or stupid.

3. You have to use up the weird stationery that your Aunt Ida gave you for your birthday last year. (Don't waste paper!)

4. You didn't understand something.

5. You like to write letters.

6. You like to lick stamps.

7. You'd like a reply. (In which case, please enclose a stamped, self-addressed envelope.)

INDEX

A

Abuse
  child, 23
  of drugs, 24-25
  what to do about, 22-23
Academy Awards, to children, 297
Acne, 39
Acronyms, on-line, 248, 249
Action, problem solving and, 72
Activities, impossible, 379
Addiction, reasons for, 24
Addresses
  of contests you can enter, 124-126
  E-mail, 249-250
  for fighting hunger, 79-81
  for fighting racism, 78
  for girls' rights, 76
  of government offices, 73-74
  for hosting foreign exchange student, 93
  National Association for the Deaf, 104
  organizations helping children, 87-92
  for pen pals, 86-87
  of television and movie characters, 289-291
  television networks, 269-270
Adventure, Richard Byrd and, 36
Advertising, to make you buy toys, 133-134
African-Americans
  culture, 211-212
  school integration by Carol Brown, 41
Africare, 80-81
AIDS, ways you *can't* get, 94
Airsickness, 36
Alanon/Alateen, 32
Alcohol, 24
  people to talk to about, 32
Allowances, handling, 66-67
Alphabet, manual, 104
Amusement parks
  best roller coasters, 361-362
  oldest American, 358
  top U.S., 359-361
Animals, Peter Billingsley and, 353
Appearance
  freckles, 38-39
  in school picture, 40
  zits, 39
Arguments, fighting fairly and, 101-102
Artwork, collages, 150-151. *See also* Hobbies
Asian culture, 214
Asner, Edward, books everyone should read (list), 201
Astronauts, John Glenn, 44-45
Athletes. *See* Sports stars
Authors. *See also* Writers
  John Irving, 51-52
  James Michener, 49-51
  Ellen Rosenberg, 110
Autograph book, signing friends', 386-387
Autograph collecting, 146-147

B

Babilonia, Tai, on falling in skating without getting hurt, 164
Babysitting, 19-20
Backpack, buying tips, 63-64
Bad luck, signs of, 383
Bands, names of, 323
Banks, using, 64
Barbie dolls, history of, 139-141
Bathroom, words for, 370
Bat-things, 295
Baum, L. Frank, *Wizard of Oz* books by, 208
Bedroom, sharing, 111-112
Ben & Jerry's ice cream, 181
Bialik, Mayim, on kids' misconceptions, 14-15
Bicycling, 161-163
Billingsley, Peter, animals he's met, 353
Bill of rights, for girls, 76
Binders, buying, 62-63
Blossom (television show), Mayim Bialik as, 14
Board games
  from books, TV shows, and movies, 143

about money, 145-146
Scrabble, 143
Body. *See* Appearance
Books
advice on, 194-195
about African-American culture, 211-212
about Asian culture, 214
Edward Asner's favorite, 201
banned or challenged in public schools, 202-204
best-selling children's, 195
Amy Carter's favorites, 202
celebrity favorites, 198-200
fighting censorship, 204-205
about Jewish culture, 213
about Latin culture, 212
Spike Lee's favorites, 201
about legendary places, 206-207
about Native American culture, 214-215
Newbery Medal winners, 196-198
reference, 50, 51
sequels to *The Wizard of Oz*, 208-210
Boys. *See* Girls; Fathers
Braces, names for kids with, 376
Brain. *See* Thinking
Brandis, Jonathan, 277
Brother, worst things about younger, 119
Brown, Carol, school integration by, 41
Bugs Bunny, friends of, 291-292
Bullies, handling, 102-103
Business, starting your own, 68-69
Byrd, Richard, 36

C

Cancer, family member with, 105-106
Candy
best-selling brands, 184
calories and fat content of, 183
favorites, 183
Carnivals, game ripoffs at, 128-129
Carter, Amy, favorite books of, 202
Cartoons, Bugs Bunny, 291-292
Celebrities. *See also* Authors; Famous people; Movie stars; Sports stars; Television stars
autographs from, 146-147
books liked by, 198-200
getting answers from, 147-148
teen hangouts, 277
who have appeared on *Simpsons*, 267
Censorship, fighting, 204-205
Change, causing, 71-72
Checking accounts, 64
Child abuse, what to do, 22-23
Childhood
Michael Jordan's memories of, 27
Bruce Springsteen's memories of, 26
Children
fighting hunger and, 78-81
helping foreign, 80
organizations for, 87-92
publishing works of, 215-222
rights of, 330
special-interest magazines for, 222-224
Children's books, best-selling, 195
Chocolate chip cookies
baking tips, 186-187
extra ingredients for, 187-188
Chocolates, insides of, 188
Christmas, popular gifts for, 347
Circus
facts about, 367
slang in, 375-376
Cities, weirdest names of, 368
Classical music
musicians, 325-327
opera, 325-327
Clothing, banned in schools, 342-343
Clown colleges, 374-375
Cocktails, nonalcoholic, 189-190
Collage, materials for, 150-151
Collecting. *See also* Hobbies
autographs, 146-147
comic books, 149
items for, 144
lunch box values, 174
trading cards, 148-149
Comic book characters

Justice Society of America and, 234
Olive Oyl, 234
Popeye, 234
superheroes, 232-233
Superman, 292-293
Comic books, storing, 149
Communicating, with parents, 110-111
Computers
CD-ROM problems, 253-256
Cybermania awards, 252-253
DOS, Windows games, 257, 258
E-mail addresses, 249-250
game ratings, 240-241
jargon and, 246-247
lame games, 253
Macintosh games, 258
on-line acronyms, 248, 249
on-line courtesy for, 242-245
on-line homework help, 251-252
smileys on, 250
Conduct, for teachers (1915), 334-335
Construction toys, 142
Consumers
environmental protection by, 81-82
protection of, 60-61
toy buying and, 133-134
Contests, 124-126
for creative kids, 229-232
Cookies, chocolate chip, 186-188
Cosmos (television series), 10
Courtesy, on-line, 242-245
Cowboys, on television, 283-287
Crayons
new colors, 136
old colors, 136
Creativity, contests for, 229-232
Credit cards, 64
Crime, keeping safe and, 17
Crop walk, 80
Culkin, Macauley, 274
Cultural experiences, 13
Culture(s)
African-American, 211-212
Asian, 214
fighting racism, 77-78
Jewish, 213
Latin, 212
Native American, 214-215
Customers, treatment of, 69. *See also* Consumers
Cybermania, awards for, 252-253
Cyberspace, 242-245

D

Daniels, Bill, Young Americans Bank and, 64
D.A.R.E. (Drug Abuse Resistance Education), 24
dealing with someone offering drugs, 25
Dark, fear of, 27-28
Deafness, manual alphabet and, 104
Death
of friend, 108-110
of pet, 29-30
Dictionary, spelling and, 51
Dinosaur movies, 305-306
Disabled friend, comfort with, 106-108
Discs
catching, 160-161
throwing, 159-160
Disease. *See* Sickness
Disney, Walt, 300
Disney Channel, idioms list of, 390-392
Disney characters, 300-303
Divorce, kids' reactions to, 114-115
Doctors, nosebleeds and, 35. *See also* Medicine; Sickness
Double Dare, 271
Dracula, repelling, 313-314
Drinks, nonalcoholic cocktails, 189-190
Drugs, reasons kids take, 24-25
Dying children, organizations granting wishes of, 94
Dyslexics, famous, 337

E

Ecology. *See* Environment
Education. *See also* School
in drug resistance, 24
importance of, 44-45

vocabulary improvement, 47-48
E-mail, 245
addresses for, 249-250
Embarrassing moments, 97-99
handling, 99
Entertainment. *See* Books; Computers; Hobbies; Movies; Music; Sports; Television; Toys
Environment, protecting, 81-82
E.T., 315
Europe, best kids' attractions in, 362-366
Excuses, lousy, 392
Explorers, Richard Byrd, 36

F

Facts. *See* Rights
Families
being an only child in, 120
difficulty in large, 118
11 different kinds of, 115-116
good things in large, 118-119
stepfamilies, 116-117
twins in, 121
younger brother or sister in, 119
Famous, becoming, 56
Famous people
child inventors, 336
dyslexics, 337
lefties, 337-338
misjudged, 335
who didn't graduate from grade school, 336
Farting, 192
Fast foods, calories of, 182
Fathers, rock music about, 32
Fear
of the dark, 27-28
phobias as, 370-371
Fighting
handling bullies, 102-103
between parents, 113
Fighting fairly, 101-102
Flatulence, food causes of, 192
Food(s)
biggest, 176-177
calories of fast foods, 182
candy, 183, 184
chocolate chip cookies, 186-188
chocolates, 188
to eat before tests, 175
flatulence of, 192
gum, 185
ice cream, 179-181
Jell-O, 191
junk foods, 178
M&Ms, 185
movie snacks, 181-182
nonalcoholic cocktails, 189-190
origins of popular, 175-176
pizza, 178
popcorn, 191
potato chips, 184
regional delicacies, 172
table manners and, 170-171
vegetables, 191
Food drives, 80
Foods
Foreign exchange students, hosting, 93
Foster children, in foreign countries, 80
Fraud, handling, 60-61
Freckles, reducing, 38-39
Friedman, Harvey, school studies of, 45
Friends
death of, 108-110
disabled, 106-108
ending friendships, 101
letting people know you like them, 100
peer pressure from, 95-96
signing autograph book of, 386-387
Fun, clown colleges, 374-375
Furlong, Eddie, 276
Future, predictions for, 332-333

G

Gak, 136-137
Games. *See also* Hobbies; Toys
board, 143
computer, 240-241, 257-259
flying discs, 159-161
Nintendo, 259
pinball, 238-240
ripoffs at carnivals, 128-129

Sega CD, 262
Sega Genesis, 261
Super Nintendo, 260
video, 235-237, 240-241
Gangs, keeping safe and, 16
Gender. *See* Girls
Genesis. *See* Sega Genesis
Ghosts, in White House, 357
Gifts
free, 153-155
under $10, 152-153
G.I. Joe, 139
Girls. *See also* Mothers; Women
bill of rights for, 76
superiority of, 346
Girls Incorporated, 76
Glenn, John, on importance of school, 44-45
Good deeds, 84-85
Good luck, signs of, 384
Gootman, Marilyn E., *When a Friend Dies*, 108
Gosselaar, Mark-Paul, 273
Government offices, addresses of, 73-74
Grades, on tests, 53-55
Growing up
rock songs about, 318
warning signs of, 14-15
Gum, best-selling brands of, 185
Guns, kids and, 352

H

Häagen-Dazs ice cream, 180
Helping others. *See also* Environment
ending hunger, 78-81
good deeds, 84-85
Heroes. *See* Superheroes
Hiccups, stopping, 37
Hitchhiking, danger in, 17
Hobbies. *See also* Games; Sports; Toys
autograph collecting, 146-147
collages, 150-151
collecting, 144
comic book collecting, 149
kite flying, 158-159
lunch box collecting, 174
trading card collecting, 148-149
of Stevie Wonder, 317
Home
being alone at, 18
runaways from, 25-26
Homework
excuses for not doing, 55-56
on-line help for, 251-252
Hotlines
for alcohol help, 32
for runaway children, 25-26
Hunger, ending, 78-81

I

Ice cream
best-selling Ben & Jerry's, 181
best-selling Häagen-Dazs, 180
favorite flavors, 180
unusual flavors, 179
Ice skating
Tai Babilonia's rules for, 164
buying skates, 165-166
Idioms, list of, 390-391
Information. *See also* Addresses; Telephone numbers
on consumer protection agencies, 60-61
government offices, 73-74
toy trivia, 130
Interests, Carl Sagan on, 10-11
International Paper Company, vocabulary development book of, 47
Internet, 242
Inventors
kids as, 336
Robert Patch, 125
I.Q. classifications, 340
Irving, John, spelling tips from, 51-52

J

Jargon
restaurant lingo, 173-174
technological, 246-247
Jell-O, flavor flops, 191
Jewish culture, 213
Job, keeping, 70
Jordan, Michael, worst childhood

memories, 27
Junk foods, 178
Justice Society of America, 234

K

Karaoke songs, 321
Kermit the Frog, 380
Kidnappings, 350-352
Kid's Guide to Social Action, The (Lewis), 72
King, Carole, lyrics of, 392-393
King Kong, 314
Kite flying, 158-159
Krueger, Freddy, music and, 322

L

Language(s)
circus slang, 375-376
polite phrases in, 369
spoken at home in USA, 347
two-letter words, 372
Latin culture, 212
Laws, weird, 341-342
Leach, Robin, on becoming rich and famous, 56
Learning, Carl Sagan on, 10-12
Lee, Spike, favorite books, 201
Lefties, 337-338
problems of, 339-340
Legal rights, 331
Legendary places, reading about, 206-207
Lewis, Barbara, *Kid's Guide to Social Action, The*, 72
Lewis, Shari
favorite activities of, 294
on playing a musical instrument, 315
Library, how to use, 49-51. *See also* Books
Lies, parental, 33-34
Listening, Carl Sagan on, 11-12
Looks. *See* Appearance
Love, cities of, 368
Luck
signs of, 383, 384
voodoo charms for, 385
Lunch boxes, as collectibles, 174

M

Magazines
publishing works by kids, 215-221
special-interest, 222-224
submitting work to, 227-228
Magic potions, 381
M&Ms, colors in, 185
Manners
eating fancy meals, 170-171
on-line courtesy, 242-245
polite phrases in various, 369
Marbles, twenty kinds of, 135
Marijuana, 24
Marriage, state age regulations, 348
Martial arts, selecting school for, 163-164
Maturity, warning signs of, 14-15
Meals, table manners for, 170-171
Media
contacting, 72, 75-76
publicity to fight hunger, 78
Medicine
acne, 39
avoiding motion sickness, 35
nosebleeds and, 35
Memory, improving, 42-43
Men, states allowing marriage under 18, 348-349. *See also* Fathers
Menuhin, Yehudi, 315
Michener, James, how to use a library, 49-51
Money
allowances, 66-67, 346
board games about, 145-146
controlling, 64
kids' spending of, 345
making it grow, 65-66
raising, 72
sources of kids', 345
starting your own business, 68-69
Monopoly, most landed-on squares in, 145
Monsters, 307-312
fear of, 27-28
killing of, 313

King Kong, 314
reportedly real, 355-357
vegetables as, 314
Morris, William Richard, 69
Mortal Kombat II, 263-264
Mothers, rock music about, 32
Motion sickness, avoiding, 35
Movies. *See also* Videos
black and white, 297-299
dinosaur, 305-306
Disney characters, 300-303
Dracula, 313-314
E.T., 315
King Kong, 314
monsters in, 307-312, 313
most popular kids', 287-288
vegetable monsters in, 314
worst science fiction films, 304-305
writing to characters in, 289-291
Movie snacks, 181-182
Movie stars
child Academy Award winners, 297
Macauley Culkin, 274
Eddie Furlong, 276
Spike Lee, 201
Tony Randall, 47-48
Shirley Temple, 296
Elijah Wood, 274
Mr. Potato Head, 141
MTV, worst and best things about, 316-317
Music. *See also* Rock music
band names, 323
classical musicians, 327-328
karaoke songs, 321
Carole King lyrics, 392-393
operas, 325-327
songs for push-button phones, 377-378
Weird Al Yankovic, 322
Musical instrument, importance of playing, 315
Music stars
with number-one singles, 319
Bruce Springsteen, 26
Stevie Wonder, 317

N

Name, signing, 387
Name-calling
of kids who wear braces, 376
strange names, 386
National Council on Child Abuse and Family Violence, 23
Native American culture, 214-215
Newbery Medal winners, 196-198
911, for phoning police, 17. *See also* Police; Protecting yourself
Nintendo entertainment system (NES) games, 259
Nosebleed, stopping, 35
Notebooks, buying, 62

O

Olive Oyl, 234
Olsen twins, differences between, 122
Onassis, Jaqueline Kennedy, advice to readers, 194-195
On-line. *See* Computers
Only child
best things about being, 120
worst things about being, 120
Operas, 325-327
Organizations
for children, 87-92
and contests you can enter, 124-126
for granting wishes of dying children, 94

P,Q

Parents. *See also* Families; Fathers; Mothers
lies told by, 33-34
people to talk with instead of, 32
rude things done by, 30-31
talking with, 110-111
what to do when they fight, 113
Patch, Robert, 125
Peace, Samantha Smith's letter about, 11
Peer pressure, causes of, 95-96
Pen pals, 86-87
Perry, Luke, 276
Pet, death of, 29-30

Phobias, 370-371
Pictures, looking good in, 40
Pimples, 39
Pinball games, historic dates in, 238-240
Pizza, facts about, 178
Play-Doh, history of, 137-138
Police. *See also* Protecting yourself
  reporting crimes to, 17
  reporting strangers to, 20
Politics, involvement in, 13
Popcorn, flavors of, 191
Popeye, 234
Potato chips, best-selling brands, 184
Potato Head, Mr. *See* Mr. Potato Head
"Power of the Printed Word," copies of, 47
Practice, importance of, 58
Predictions, that didn't come true, 343-344
Pressure, from peers, 95-96
Prices, of toys (1897), 134-135
Prizes. *See* Contests
Problems
  discussing with parents, 110-111
  in sharing a room, 111-112
Problem solving, causing social change and, 71-72
Protecting yourself. *See also* Babysitting; Safety
  phoning police, 17, 18
  in public places, 16-17
  runaway hotlines, 25-26
  staying home alone, 18
Public places, protecting yourself in, 16-17
Publishing
  of children's works, 215-221
  submitting work for, 227-228
  tips for young writers, 225-227
Punishments, non-abusive, 23

R

Racism, fighting, 77-78
Randall, Tony, on vocabulary improvement, 47-48
Readers, advice to, 194-195
Reading, about legendary places, 206-207
Reference books. *See* Books; Dictionary; Library
Reporters, contacting, 75-76
Responsibility, babysitting and, 19-20
Restaurants, lingo for, 173-174
Rich, becoming, 56
Rights
  children's, 330
  legal, 331
Ringling Brothers and Barnum & Bailey Circus, 367
Rock music
  about fathers, 320
  about growing up, 318
  about mothers, 32
  about school, 318-319
  sound effects titles for, 324
Rock stars, Bruce Springsteen, 26. *See also* Music stars
Rogers, Fred, on starting at a new school, 41
Rollerblading, safety tips for, 167
Roller coasters, best, 361-362
Roller-skating, falling while, 166
Roseanne, list of what she doesn't do anymore, 33
Rosenberg, Ellen, 110
Rossini, Gioacchino, 328
Rudeness, by parents, 30-31
Russia, Samantha Smith's letter to, 11

S

Safety. *See also* Protecting yourself
  in door-to-door selling, 21-22
  in ice skating, 164-165
  in rollerblading, 167
  in roller-skating, 166
  of skateboard, 168
Sagan, Carl, 12 things he wishes they taught at school, 10-13
Salespeople, getting good treatment from, 59
Santa Claus
  hometown of, 354

names for, 354
reindeer of, 354
Savage, Fred, acting advice from, 70
Savings. *See* Money
School
backpack for, 63-64
books banned or challenged in, 202-204
clothing banned in, 342-343
foods to eat before tests, 175
homework and, 55-56
importance of, 44-45
integrating, 41
martial arts, 163-164
reasons for skipping, 388
rock songs about, 318-319
skipping a grade, 46
starting new, 41
supplies for, 62-63
teacher doesn't like you, 43-44
test grades, 53-55
School picture, looking good in, 40
Science and technology, learning about, 12
Science fiction films, worst, 304-305
Scientists, Carl Sagan, 10-11
Scrabble, highest-scoring words in, 143
Seasickness, 36
Sega, CD games, 262
Sega Genesis, games, 261
Selfishness, 13
Self-protection. *See also* Protecting yourself; Safety; Telephone numbers
in public places, 16-17
staying home alone, 18
Selling, safety for door-to-door, 21-22
Separation, of parents, 114-115
Seven Dwarfs, 355
Shannon, Jaqueline, *Why It's Great to Be a Girl*, 346
Sharing, of room, 111-112
Shatner, William, 275
Shopping
good treatment during, 59
for ice skates, 165-166
for toys, 132-133
Siblings, worst things about younger, 119
Sick children, organizations granting wishes of, 94
Sickness
AIDS and, 94
cancer, 105-106
hiccups, 37
motion, 35
nosebleeds, 35
Sidis, William James, as brilliant student, 46
Signing your name, 387
Sign language, 104
Sinclair, Upton, 228
Singers. *See* Music; Music stars; Rock stars
Sister, worst things about younger, 119
Skateboard, safety of, 168
Skating. *See* Ice skating; Roller-skating
Skills, Carl Sagan on, 10-11
Skipping, of grade in school, 46
Slang, circus, 375-376
Slenczynska, Ruth, 58
Smartness, skipping grade in school and, 46
Smileys, on-line, 250
Smith, Samantha, meeting with Yuri Andropov, 11
Snacks, at movies, 181-182
Social action, 71-72
ending hunger, 78-81
government offices listing, 73-74
Special Olympics, sports in, 349
Spelling, tips for, 51-52
Sports. *See also* Games
bicycling, 161-163
flying discs, 160-161
ice skating, 164-166
martial arts, 163-164
rollerblading, 167
roller-skating, 166
skateboarding, 168
in Special Olympics, 349
Sports stars

Tai Babilonia, 164-165
Michael Jordan, 27
youngest, 155-158
Springsteen, Bruce, memories of growing up, 26
Star Trek, 275
States, marriage age in, 348
Stepfamilies, living in, 116-117
Strangers, 16-17
reporting to police, 20
Stuttering, statistics about, 34
Sugar, names for, 185
Superheroes, 232-233
Superman, 292-293
Super Nintendo games, 260
Supplies, for school, 62-63

T

Table manners, 170-171
Talking, with people other than parents, 32
Teachers
rules of conduct in 1915, 334-335
who don't like you, 43-44
Techno-jargon, 246-247
Teeth, 376
Telephone, songs for push-button, 377-378
Telephone numbers. *See also* Addresses
for alcohol help, 32
Amnesty International, 78
for child abuse, 23
for consumer protection agencies, 60-61
for fighting hunger, 79-81
for hosting foreign exchange students, 93
for media, 75-76
for police emergency, 17
runaway hotlines, 25-26
Television. *See also* Comic book characters
best moms on, 267-268
cowboys on, 283-287
Double Dare, 271
kids' shows, 271-272
MTV, 316-317
network addresses, 269
Saturday morning programs, 278-283
Simpsons, 267
using brain and, 266
watching too much, 12-13
worst moms on, 268-269
writing to characters on, 289-291
Television stars
Edward Asner, 201
Mayim Bialik, 14-15
Jonathan Brandis, 277
Mark-Paul Gosselaar, 273
Robin Leach, 56
Shari Lewis, 294, 315
Olsen twins, 122
Luke Perry, 276
Fred Rogers, 41
Roseanne, 33
Fred Savage, 70
William Shatner, 275
Jenna Von Oy, 276
Jaleel White, 273
Temple, Shirley, facts about, 296
Tests
foods to eat before, 175
getting good grades on, 53-55
Thinking, exercises for, 56-57
Tobacco, 24
Tongue twisters, 379
Toys. *See also* Games; Hobbies
advertising about, 133-134
assembling tips, 127
Barbie dolls, 139-141
construction, 142
crayons and, 136
Gak and, 136-137
G.I. Joe, 139
judging, 131-132
Mr. Potato Head, 141
Play-Doh, 137-138
prices of (1897), 134-135
shopping for, 132-133
still popular from 1950s, 142
trivia information about, 130
Trading cards, tips for collectors, 148-149
Trick-or-treaters, 22

Truth
Carl Sagan on, 10
parental lies and, 33-34
Twelve things Carl Sagan wishes they taught at school, 10-13
Twins
differences between Olsen twins, 122
problems of, 121
Two-letter words, 372

U

Unfair practices, handling, 60-61
United States
languages spoken at home in, 347
weirdest city names, 368
Urkel, Steve, 273

V

VCRs, countries with most, 266
Vegetables, 191
as monsters, 314
Video games. *See also* Games
landmark dates for, 235-237
ratings of, 240-241
Videos, most popular animated, 288-289
Vocabulary, improving, 47-48
Von Oy, Jenna, 276
Voodoo charms, for luck, 385

W

Waiters/waitresses, lingo of, 173-174
Webster-Doyle, Terrence, *Why Is Everybody Always Picking on Me?*, 102-103
When a Friend Dies (Gootman), 108
White, Jaleel, 273
White House, ghosts in, 357
Why Is Everybody Always Picking on Me? (Webster-Doyle), 102-103
Why It's Great to Be a Girl (Shannon), 346
Wish, when to make, 382
Wish grants, to sick or dying children, 94
Wizard of Oz, The, sequels to, 208-210
Women, states allowing marriage under 16, 348-349. *See also* Girls; Mothers
Wonder, Stevie, hobbies of, 317
Wood, Elijah, 274
Words
for gross sounds, 389
two-letter, 372
World, changing, 71-72
World Food Day, 79
Writers, tips for, 225-227. *See* Authors
Writings, of children, 215-221

X,Y,Z

Yankovic, Weird Al, 322
Young Americans Bank, 64
Youth Ending Hunger, 330
Ziggy, feeling like, 387-388
Zits, fighting, 39

BIBLIOGRAPHY

Ash, Russell. *The Top 10 of Everything*. Boston: Dorling Kindersley, 1994.

Barkin, Carol, and Elizabeth James. *Jobs for Kids*. New York: Lothrop, 1990.

Berg, Adriane, and Arthur Bochner. *The Totally Awesome Money Book for Kids*. New York: Newmarket Press, 1993.

Bergstrom, Joan, and Craig Bergstrom. *All the Best Contests for Kids.* Berkeley: Ten Speed Press, 1993.

Berkeley Pop Culture Project. *The Whole Pop Catalog*. New York: Avon, 1991.

Bodner, Janet. *Kiplinger's Money-Smart Kids*. Washington, D.C.: Kiplinger, 1993.

Brainard, Beth, and Sheila Behr. *Soup Should Be Seen and Not Heard!* New York: Dell, 1990.

Caney, Stephen. *Stephen Caney's Kids' America*. New York: Workman, 1978.

Carrel, Annette. *It's the Law!* Volcano, Calif.: Volcano Press, 1994.

Chafetz, Michael. *Smart for Life.* New York: Penguin, 1992.

Child magazine, various issues.

Childress, Casey, and Linda McKenzie. *A Kids' Guide to Collecting Baseball Cards*. Tucson, Ariz.: Harbinger House, 1994.

Coffey, Wayne. *303 of the World's Worst Predictions*. Tribeca, 1983.

Dacyczyn, Amy. *The Tightwad Gazette.* New York: Villard, 1992.

Dickson, Paul. *Slang!* New York: Dell, 1990.

Dossey, Donald. *Holiday Folklore, Phobias and Fun*. Asheville, N.C.: Outcomes Unlimited, 1992.

Drew, Bonnie, and Noel Drew. *Kid Biz.* Austin, Tex.: Eakin, 1990.

Dunn, Jerry, ed. *Tricks of the Trade.* Boston: Houghton Mifflin, 1991.

Earthworks Group, *Fifty Simple Things Kids Can Do to Save the Earth.* Kansas City, Mo.: Andrews and McMeel, 1990.

Earthworks Group, *Fifty Simple Things Kids Can Do to Recycle.* Schenevus, N.Y.: Greenleaf Publishers, 1991.

Editors of *Prevention* magazine health books. *The Doctors' Book of Home Remedies.* Emmaus, Penn.: Rodale, 1990.

Elwood, Ann, Carol Orsag, and Sidney Solomon. *Macmillan*

Illustrated Almanac for Kids. New York: Macmillan, 1981.

Elwood, Ann, and Carol Orsag Madigan. *Life's Big Instruction Book*. New York: Warner Books, 1995.

Erickson, Judith B. *Directory of American Youth Organizations*. Minneapolis: Free Spirit, 1994.

Essoe, Gabe. *The TV Book of Lists*. New York: Carol Publishing Group.

Fiffer, Steve, and Sharon Sloan. *50 Ways to Help Your Community*. New York: Doubleday, 1994.

Ford, Clyde. *We Can All Get Along*. New York: Dell, 1994.

Galbraith, Judy. *The Gifted Kid's Survival Guide*. Minneapolis: Free Spirit, 1983.

Gootman, Marilyn. *When a Friend Dies*. Minneapolis: Free Spirit, 1994.

Howard, Tracy Apple, with Sage Howard. *Kids Ending Hunger: What Can We Do?* Kansas City, Mo.: Andrews and McMeel, 1992.

Johnson, Stancil. *Frisbee*. New York: Workman, 1981.

Kadrey, Richard. *Covert Culture Sourcebook*. New York: St. Martin's Press, 1993.

Kinchner, Jonni. *Psychology for Kids*. Minneapolis: Free Spirit, 1990.

Krantz, Les. *America by the Numbers*. Boston: Houghton Mifflin, 1993.

Kroloff, Charles A. *Fifty-four Ways You Can Help the Homeless*. Southport, Conn.: H. L. Levin, 1993.

Levine, Michael. *The Kids' Address Book*. New York: Perigee, 1994.

Lewis, Barbara. *The Kids' Guide to Social Action*. Minneapolis: Free Spirit, 1991.

Lindsell-Roberts, Sheryl. *Loony Laws and Silly Statutes*. New York: Sterling, 1994.

Logan, Suzanne. *The Kids Can Help Book*. New York: Perigee, 1992.

Lucaire, Ed. *Celebrity Setbacks*. Englewood Cliffs, N.J.: Prentice Hall, 1993.

McLoone-Basta, Margo, Alice Siegel, and the editors of World Almanac. *The Second Kids' World Almanac of Records and*

Facts. Mahwah, N.J.: World Almanac, 1987.

McLoone-Basta, Margo, and Alice Siegel. *The Kids' Book of Lists.* Austin, Tex.: Holt, Rinehart and Winston, 1980.

Marsh, Dave, and James Bernard. *The New Book of Rock Lists.* St. Louis, Mo.: Fireside, 1994.

Moore, Lawrence. *Lightning Never Strikes Twice and Other False Facts.* New York: Avon, 1994.

Neary, Kevin, and Dave Smith. *The Ultimate Disney Trivia Book.* New York: Hyperion, 1992.

Reiser, Howard. *Skateboarding.* New York: Ventura, 1989.

Rosenberg, Ellen. *Growing Up Feeling Good.* Beaufort, S.C.: Beaufort, 1982.

Shannon, Jaqueline. *Why It's Great to Be a Girl.* New York: Warner Books, 1994.

Siegel, Alice, and Margo Basta. *The Information Please Kids' Almanac.* Boston: Houghton Mifflin, 1992.

Stang, Ivan. *High Weirdness by Mail: A Directory of the Fringe.* Taft, Tex.: S&S, 1988.

Terrell, Ruth Harris. *A Kid's Guide to How to Stop the Violence.* New York: Avon, 1992.

Thompson, C. E. *101 Wacky Facts About Kids.* New York: Scholastic, 1992.

Wallace, Amy, David Wallechinsky, and Irving Wallace. *The Book of Lists 3.* New York: Morrow, 1983.

Weston, Carol. *Girltalk.* New York: HarperCollins, 1992.

Windeler, Robert. *The Films of Shirley Temple.* New York: Citadel Press, 1978.

ILLUSTRATION CREDITS

Illustrations by Lynn Jeffery: pp. 15, 19, 21, 28, 31, 35, 37, 42, 55, 65, 79, 84, 95, 97, 107, 117, 121, 171, 239, 308, 309, 321, 339, 361, 371, 375, 389.

Illustrations by Sara Mintz Zwicker: pp. 129, 137, 143, 152, 167, 168, 177, 178, 179, 181, 184, 225, 268, 285, 323, 341, 345, 385.

Page 207: Illustration from *Alice's Adventures in Wonderland* by Lewis Carroll.

Page 270: Illustration © MTV Networks.